Accounting, Finance, Sustain
& Fraud: Theory and Applic

Series Editor

Kıymet Tunca Çalıyurt, Iktisadi ve Idari Bilimler Fakultes, Trakya University
Balkan Yerleskesi, Edirne, Turkey

This Scopus indexed series acts as a forum for book publications on current research arising from debates about key topics that have emerged from global economic crises during the past several years. The importance of governance and the will to deal with corruption, fraud, and bad practice, are themes featured in volumes published in the series. These topics are not only of concern to businesses and their investors, but also to governments and supranational organizations, such as the United Nations and the European Union. Accounting, Finance, Sustainability, Governance & Fraud: Theory and Application takes on a distinctive perspective to explore crucial issues that currently have little or no coverage. Thus the series integrates both theoretical developments and practical experiences to feature themes that are topical, or are deemed to become topical within a short time. The series welcomes interdisciplinary research covering the topics of accounting, auditing, governance, and fraud.

More information about this series at http://www.springer.com/series/13615

Kıymet Tunca Çalıyurt
Editor

New Approaches to CSR, Sustainability and Accountability, Volume II

 Springer

Editor
Kıymet Tunca Çalıyurt
Trakya University
Edirne, Turkey

ISSN 2509-7873 ISSN 2509-7881 (electronic)
Accounting, Finance, Sustainability, Governance & Fraud: Theory and Application
ISBN 978-981-33-6809-5 ISBN 978-981-33-6808-8 (eBook)
https://doi.org/10.1007/978-981-33-6808-8

This Springer imprint is published by the registered company Springer Nature Singapore Pte Ltd.
The registered company address is: 152 Beach Road, #21-01/04 Gateway East, Singapore 189721,
Singapore

Acknowledgements

As founding president of *International Group on Governance Fraud Ethics and CSR* (IGonGFESR), I would like to dedicate this book to the distinguished academician, Prof. Dr. in Law Ranbir Singh. Prof of Eminent Singh was our keynote speaker in **10th IConGFESR** and **International Sustainable Cooperative and Social Enterprise Conference** which were organised in April 25–27, 2019 in Trakya University, Turkey. However, before this conference, we held two conferences with Vice Chancellor Prof Ranbir at National Law University under his honorary presidency. I would like to introduce distinquished academician and rector, Prof. Ranbir.

Prof. (Dr.) Ranbir Singh, B.Sc., LL.B., LL.M., Ph.D.

Professor (Dr.) Ranbir Singh is the former and founder Vice-Chancellor of National Law University, Delhi established by the Delhi Government in 2008. In just a short span of 12 years he has steered NLU, Delhi which has been ranked as the 2nd best law school of India in the NIRF—2018 rankings. It's the acknowledgement of his administrative and leadership abilities that NLU, Delhi is now recognized not only in India but also at the international level. With over two decades of experience in heading the law school he carries the aura of a visionary who as an outstanding statesmen and academician shown immense commitment and contribution towards changing the legal education landscape of the country. Prior to his stint in NLU, Delhi, he was the founder Vice-Chancellor of NALSAR, University of Law, established by the Andhra Pradesh Government and had been at its helm since its inception in 1998. Professor Singh's acumen took NALSAR to great heights as a well-known premier institution for legal education and research in the country. He has been a Vice-Chancellor for over 20 years now.

Professor Singh had a long association with Kurukshetra University, first as a student, a Ph.D. scholar and as faculty member in its Department of Law. In 1978, he moved to Maharshi Dayanand University at Rohtak as part of the founding Faculty and continued there till 1996 in various capacities as Professor, Head, Dean and Proctor. On invitation from the National Law School of India University, Bangalore, he served as Professor of Law at NLSIU during 1996–1997. Professor Singh's contribution in redesigning legal education in the country has been significant being a member of the Legal Education Committee of the Bar Council of India. His legal writings span the areas of Jurisprudence, Human Rights, Legal Education, Legal Aid, Personal Laws and Justice Education and has more than 50 research publications to his credit. He has edited two publications one on "Human Rights Education, Law and Society" and the other on "Cyber Space and the Law—Issues and Challenges". He has also authored along with Prof. A. Lakshminath two scholarly publications, one on 'Fiscal Federalism—Constitutional Conspectus' and the other on 'Constitutional Law'. Under his guidance several scholars have been awarded Ph.D. Degrees and his rich teaching/research experience enabled him to visit and participate in several International Conferences and Seminars and present papers in several countries like Australia, Brazil, Bhutan, China, Taiwan, South Africa Cyprus, Canada, France, Hong Kong, Israel, Italy, Pakistan, Switzerland, Sri Lanka, Singapore, Thailand, Russia, Germany, South Korea, UK and USA. He has visited best of law schools in UK and USA and interacted with leading legal academics and functionaries of higher judiciary in these countries.

He has association with several national and international organisations in advisory capacities—more important among them being Executive Committee of the National Legal Services Authority, Indian Law Institute, National Police Academy, National Committee in IPR (Confederation of Indian Industries), Indian Society of International Law, Committee of Experts on Law, National Commission for Women, National Institute of Criminology and Forensic Science, DNA Profiling Advisory Committee (D-PAC), SAARCLAW India Chapter, Commonwealth Legal Education Association. Under his Chairmanship a Committee with the assistance of ILO, Regional Office prepared a draft bill for the "Abolition of the Child Labour" and submitted to the State Government. He served as a member of the DNA Profiling Advisory Committee constituted by the Department of Bio-technology, Government of India to recommend a draft legislation for enactment by the Parliament. Related to this he also served as Chairperson of the Sub-Committee on Legal Issues and prepared the DNA Profiling Bill. He was also a member of the Shri Soli Sorabjee Committee appointed by the Ministry of Home Affairs, to draft the New Police Act which was submitted to the Ministry. He is also interested in issues like Corporate Law and Governance and Corporate Social Responsibility.

He has also been a part of the high level delegation which presented India's National Report on Human Rights in the third Universal Periodic Review at United Nations Human Rights Council, Geneva, Switzerland held in May, 2017. Professor (Dr.) Ranbir Singh prepared the India's National Report for the First UPR, while he was the Vice-Chancellor of NALSAR University of Law, Hyderabad and the Second and Third UPR has also been prepared by Prof. (Dr.) Ranbir Singh at NLUD on behalf of MEA and Government of India. He is a Member of the Board of Governors of Indian Institute of Corporate Affairs. He is a Member of the Advisory Board and Executive Council of Maharashtra National Law University. He was also a Member of Sectoral Innovation Council on IPR, constituted by DIPP, Min. of Commerce, GOI. He was a Member of National Committee to administer the "Rajiv Gandhi Advocate's Training Scheme" constituted by Ministry of Law and Justice, Government of India. He was a Member (part-time) of The 19th Law Commission of India. He was a member of Committee for Consultations on the situation in Andhra Pradesh. He is the Visitor's nominee in the Academic Council of the Indian Law Institute, New Delhi. He has been the Vice-President and President of Shastri Indo-Canadian Institute, Delhi.

Professor Singh has been the recipient of many awards in recognition of accomplishments, both, as an administrator and teacher/researcher and some of them are:

1. Symbiosis-IALS (International Association of Law Schools, USA) Lifetime Achievement Award: For excellence in legal and justice education during the 2017 Global Law Dean's Forum.
2. Life Time Achievement Award: In recognition of the exemplary contribution towards Legal Education by Dr. N. M. Veeraiyan, Chancellor, Saveetha University.
3. Karmayogi Samman: Haryana Institute of Fine Arts, by Shri Kuldeep Sharma, Speaker, Haryana Legislative Assembly.
4. "Professor N. R. Madhava Menon Best Law Teacher Award 2011" by Hon'ble Mr. Justice Altamas Kabir, Judge, Supreme Court of India.
5. Lex Witness recognized him in the "Hall of fame: Top 50", as an individual who have helped shape the legal landscape of modern India.
6. "Alumnus of Distinction" at the Golden Jubilee Commemorative Special Convocation of Kurukshetra University, 2007, by His Excellency, Dr. A. P. J. Abdul Kalam, former President of India.

7.   "Excellence Award 1998": Maharshi Dayanand University, Rohtak, by Governor of Haryana.
8.   Educationist of the Year—Metro-Vision, 3rd Annual Media Awards—2005.

The British Council had portrayed him as one of the 12 talented, creative and generous spirits who are making an effort personally and through their institution to ensure their engagement with the UK, works to mutual benefit. His services to Legal Education has been acknowledged and commemorated by many institutions and educational bodies.

Professor of Eminent Ranbir Singh was our honorary president for "9th International Women and Business Conference" which was organised in National Law University in New Delhi with a theme 'Business Empowerment of Women & Sustainability' on October 24–26, 2018. During the conferences, as vice-chancellor of National Law University, Prof. Ranbir have also signed MOU with Trakya University.

(from the left) Prof. (Dr.) G.S. Bajpai, Professor of Criminology & Criminal Justice, Prof. (Dr.) Ranbir Singh, Vice-Chancellor, National Law University Delhi, Prof. (Dr). Kıymet Tunca Çalıyurt CPA, CFE, Prof. (Dr.) Harpreet Kaur.

9th International Conference on Governance Fraud Ethics & Social Responsibility
https://nludelhi.ac.in/news2.aspx?id=22164

The summary captures the 9th International Conference on Governance, Fraud, Ethics and Social Responsibility organised by National Law University Delhi in collaboration with the Institute of Company Secretaries of India and Trakya University and (24–26 October, 2018). The event brought together around 40 paper presenters from different parts of India and the world including Turkey, South Africa, Nigeria and Israel etc. The conference began with the opening remark of Hon'ble Justice Ravi R. Tripathi (Retd. Judge High Court of Gujarat), who was the chief guest for the function, Prof. Ranbir Singh (Vice-Chancellor, NLU Delhi), Prof. Dr. Kıymet Çalıyurt (Trakya University) and Prof. Harpreet Kaur (President of the conference and Professor NLU Delhi).

9th International Women and Business Conference
https://nludelhi.ac.in/news2.aspx?id=22165

The conference was inaugurated on the evening of October 24, 2018. The deliberations began form October 25, 2018. Two plenary sessions and Four parallel sessions on 'Law and Accountable Business' were conducted on Day one. Day one continued with the presentations from legal professors, scholars and experts of the field. The presenters deliberated on the credit risk governance framework, role of institutional investors in corporate governance, the powers of independent directors in corporate governance, corporate fraud, risk management, corporate digital responsibility, corporate social responsibility and various other issues.

In our conferences, Springer India office opened book corner to promote books published in our book series *Accounting, Finance, Sustainability, Governance & Fraud: Theory and Application* indexed in Scopus. We would like to thank you for excellent opportunity for Nupoor Singh, Springer Editor, India.

Prof. Dr. Kıymet Tunca Çalıyurt
Founding President—IGonGFESR

Introduction: New Conference Series from International Group on Governance Fraud Ethics and CSR

As the founder of the International Group on Governance Fraud Ethics and CSR, I would like to give some information about our 2019 conference (10th IConGFESR) and **new conference series** started in 2019 on cooperative management and social entrepreneurship, both organised by Trakya University, Turkey. With this conference series, we will find opportunity to meet with academicians, practioners who study and conduct research on cooperative management and social entrepreneurship. We plan to organise next conference in 2021. In our first conference, we found opportunity to meet speakers from *Turkey, India, Bulgaria, Greece, South Africa, United Kingdom.* Papers presented in the conference will be published in our book series. Some of papers presented in our new conference series.

1ˢᵗ International Sustainable Cooperative and Social Entrepreneurship Conference

International Sustainable Cooperative and Social Enterprise Conference (April 25–27, 2019)
https://iscsec.trakya.edu.tr/

- Prof. Dr. Rory Ridley, Cooperative Social Entrepreneurship, Sheffield Business School, UK
- Cliff Southcombe, Founder of Social Enterprise International, UK
- Prof. Dr. Ranbir Singh, National Law University, India
- Ünal Örnek, Agriculture Engineer, Researcher and Consultant, Turkey
- Prof. Dr. Diana Kopeva, UNWE, Sofia, Bulgaria
- Prof. Dr. Harpreet Kaur, National Law University, India
- Yasemin Başçavuşoğlu, Founder, Perseus, Turkey

Parallel Sessions

- *Remuneration to the Plastic Bag in Turkey, the Declaration and Audit of the Recovery Participation Shares*, Havva Arabacı, Fatih Çavdar, Trakya University, Turkey
- *The Role of Cooperatives in Achieving Sustainable Development Goals, Gamze Yakar, Namik Kemal University*, Kıymet Çalıyurt, Trakya University, Turkey
- *Technology Usage Levels Of Cooperatives And E-Commerce Model In Cooperatives Proposal*, Yasin Akkuş, Dindar Şino, Trakya University, Turkey
- *Social Entrepreneurship Activities by Banking Sector: How to Reach Women Entrepreneurs to Finance?*, Tayfun Sert, Expert on Entrepreneurship, Kıymet Çalıyurt, İlke Oruç, Busines Administration Department, Trakya University, Turkey
- *Corporate Sustainability Report Assurance and Control: A Research on Turkish Companies in GRI Index*, Esra Atabay, Karadeniz Technical University, Trabzon, Turkey
- *Sustainability Reports in Universities: Content Analysis*, Serap Kurt, Seda Karagoz Zeren, Cagatay Akdogan, Kiymet Caliyurt, Trakya University, Turkey
- *Startup—Modern Concept of Innovative Entrepreneurship*, Stoyan Tranev, Velichka Traneva, Prof. Dr. A. Zlatarov University, Bourgas, Bulgaria
- *Content and Research Method Analysis in Published Articles in AAA Journals on Audit Quality*, Hazal Tukuc, Master Student, Accounting and Auditing Master Programme, Ozgur Tasdemir, Assist. Prof. Dr., Department of Business Administration, Trakya University, Turkey
- *Environmental Accounting and Sustainability in the Hospitality Industry*, Seda Karagöz Zeren, Kıymet Çalıyurt, Business Administration Department, Trakya university, Turkey
- *Waste Management in Turkey and Opportunities to be Created by Sustainable Development*, Emel Yıldız, İbrahim Keklicek, Business Administration Department, Trakya University, Turkey
- *The Future of Independent Audit: Opinions of Accounting Academics for New Auditor's Report*, Özkan Sarısoy, Nazlı Kepçe, Namık Kemal University, Turkey
- *Sustainable Tourism and Cooperatification*, Emel Gonenc Guler, Trakya University, Turkey
- *A General Evaluation of Prepared Graduate Thesis for Ethical Leadership*, Sezer Bolur, Prof. Dr. Agah Sinan Ünsar, Business Administration Department, Trakya University, Turkey
- *An Ethical Problem In The Personnel Selection Process And Terminal: Nepotism*, Ali İhsan Durgut, Uğur Can Tan, Agah Sinan ÜNSAR, Business Administration Department, Trakya University, Turkey
- *Development of Women Entrepreneurship: A Study on "Rural Natural Market" Edirne Province*, İlknur Kumkale Assoc. Prof., Master Student Büşra Akyıldız, Master Student Çilem Elmas, Master Student Nuran Caldu, Master Student Tülay Yelken, Trakya University, Turkey

- *The Mediating Role of Affective Commitment in the Effect of Psychological Resilience on Life Satisfaction: A Research on Auditors*, Sadiye Oktay, Serdar Bozkurt, Halil Emre Akbaş, Tolga Atasoy, Yıldız Technical University, Turkey
- *An Examination of Assurance Practices on Turkish Companies' Greenhouse Gas Emissions Disclosures*, Halil Emre Akbaş, Seda Canikli, Semih Yılmazer, Bertaç Şakir Şahin, Yıldız Technical University, Turkey
- *Climate Change Related Risk and Opportunity Drivers and Their Potential Impacts: An Investigation on Turkish Firms*, Serap Aktogan, Sanem Kaptanoğlu, Arzu Karaman Akgül, Halil Emre Akbaş, Yıldız Technical University, Turkey
- *Sectoral Basis Changes and Development of Carbon Performance in European Countries*, Hasan Ağan Karaduman, Mehmet Çağlar, Halil Emre Akbaş, Gamze Varank, Yıldız Technical University, Turkey
- *From A Climate Changing Perspective Monitoring of Sustainable Development: On the Way To A Renewable Energy Solution to the European Union*, Erhan Atay, Assoc. Prof. Economy Department, Business Sciences and Economics, Trakya University, Turkey
- *Green Energy Fraud in the European Union Versus Green Paradox*, Erhan Atay, Assoc. Prof. Economy Department, Business Sciences and Economics Trakya University, Turkey
- *Enhancing Risk Management Procedures in Audit Firms: Acceptance & Continuance, Tzvetelina Andreeva, Stoyan Deevski*, Assist. Dr. CPA, Department "Industrial Business", Business Faculty, UNWE, Bulgaria
- *Internal and External Aspects of Corporate Governance: A Cluster Analysis in Logistics Business*, İsmail İyigün, Dr. Lecturer, Social Science Vocational College, Trakya University, Turkey
- *Value Relevance of Intangibles: A Literature Review*, Ömer Faruk Güleç, Business Administration Department, Kırklareli University, Turkey
- *Corporate Social Responsibility in South Africa: Regulation by Hard Law, should it be considered?*, Senior Lecturer Marie Preston, MJ Preston, Faculty of Economics and Management Sciences, School of Accounting, North West University, South Africa
- *The use of Renewable Energy with Blockchain Technology: Zero Carbon Project and Blockchain Carbon Emission Trade*, Seda Karagöz Zeren, Engin Demirel, Deparment of Business Administration Department, Trakya University, Turkey
- *Risk Management in the Insurance Company*, Chief Assistant Tzvetelina Andreeva, Ph.D., UNWE, Bulgaria
- *A Qualitative Perspective to Green Business*, İlke Oruç, Assist. Prof. Dr., Business Administration Department, Trakya University, Turkey
- *Corporate Social Responsibility Reporting: Investigation Of Glass Manufacturing Companies Listed in Istanbul Industrial Association 500*, Ilknur Eskin, Dr. Assist. Prof., Trakya University, Uzunköprü Applied Science High School, Turkey

- *Corporate Governance and Ethics, The Role that GRI Plays for the Business of the Banks in Greece*, Kolokytha Eleftheria, Chatzianastasiou Anastasia, Mandilas Athanasios, Valsamidis Stavros, EmaTTech Institute of Eastern Macedonia and Thrace, Turkey

Contents

Editor and Contributors

About the Editor

Prof. Dr. Kıymet Tunca Çalıyurt CPA, CFE, graduated from the Faculty of Business Administration at Marmara University, Istanbul, Turkey. Her Masters and Ph.D. degrees are in Accounting and Finance Programme from the Social Graduate School, Marmara University. She has worked as auditor in Horwath Auditing Company, manager in McDonalds and finance staff in Singapore Airlines. After vast experience in private sector, he has started to work in academia. She is holding CFE and CPE titles. Her research interests are in accounting, auditing, fraud, social responsibility, corporate governance, finance and business ethics, with a special interest in aviation management, NGOs, women rights in business. She has been as visiting researcher in Concordia University, Canada and Amherst Business School, Massachussetts University, USA. She is the founder of the International Group on Governance, Fraud, Ethics and Social Responsibility (IGonGFE&SR) which was founded in 2009. In 2009, she also founded the International Women and Business Group, which organizes a global, annual conferences. Kiymet has published papers, book chapters and books both nationally and internationally on fraud, social responsibility, ethics in accounting/finance/aviation disciplines in Springer and Routledge. She is book series editor in Springer with the title *Accounting, Finance, Sustainability, Governance & Fraud: Theory and Application*, and book series editor in Routledge with the title *Women and Sustainable Business*. Some book titles: *Emerging Fraud, Corporate Governance: An International Perspective, Women and Sustainability in Business: A Global Perspective, Sustainability and Management: An International Perspective, Globalization and Social Responsibility, Regulations and Applications of Ethics in Business Practice, Ethics and Sustainability in Accounting and Finance, Volume I*. She is acting as member in editorial board Journal of *Financial Crime, International Journal on Law and Management, Journal of Money Laundering Control*. She is regular speaker at International Economic Crime Symposium in Jesus College, Cambridge University. She is partner of Herme Consulting in Trakya University Technopark.

Contributors

Stavros Apostolakis holds a Ph.D. in Political Economy, Political Sociology and Comparative Policy Analysis from the Department of Political Science and History of the Panteion University of Athens. He is currently working as Head of the Asylum Unit of Fast Track International Protection applications of the Hellenic Asylum Service and simultaneously teaching entrepreneurship, innovation and crisis management at the Tourist Enterprises Department of the Higher Technological Educational Institution of Western Greece, in Patras.

Nurdan Ateş graduated from Trakya University 2001 Business Administration, 2012 Postgraduate Degree in Economics. She has worked 10 years in the Türkiye İş Bank. Before that, she worked as an Accounting Specialist for 7 years in foreign trade, textile and packaging sectors.

Anne Goujon Belghit is Assistant Professor in Management and Human Resources Management at the University of Bordeaux, France. She is in co-editor in chief of the review VSE (*Vie & Sciences de l'Entreprise*), a journal that publishes articles in French and in English. Her research deals with human capital and human resources management. She has written many scientific articles and has coordinated a book dedicated on the subject of Human Capital.

Pervin Bilir (Assoc. Prof. Pervin Güler) working as an Associate Professor at Çukurova University, Faculty of Sport Sciences, Department of Sports Management, as a faculty member in the Department of Sports Management Sciences. Dr. Bilir is also the Head of the Department of Sports Management and Vice Dean of the Faculty of Sport Sciences. She has completed her undergraduate study and graduate study at Gazi University and her doctorate at Çukurova University. In 2015, she received the title of Associate Professor in Management and Strategy field. Bilir has national and international publications in sports management and training field. She particularly works on subjects such as organizational climate and culture, leadership, entrepreneurship, communication and violence in sports. By undertaking volunteer duties in sports organizations and institutions, as well as the sports club management, sports federations and non-governmental organizations, she gained considerably important experiences on this matter.
e-mail: pbilir@cu.edu.tr

Assistant Professor Fatma Cesur teaches at the Department of Economics, Faculty of Business Sciences and Economics. Her bachelor's degree is from the Economics Department of Anadolu University, master's degree is from Economics Department, Social Graduate School at Istanbul University. Her thesis title is "Relation Between Money Supply and Inflation: Case of Turkey". Her research fields are Macroeconomics, Monetary Theory, Monetary Policy, Applied econometrics, Business Cycles, and Sustainable Economy. She has also worked at the family company for several years. She is an active member of the International Group on Governance

Fraud Ethics and CSR. She published many articles and book chapters in national and international journals and books.
e-mail: fatmacesur@trakya.edu.tr

Evangelos Drimpetas is university professor at Democritus University of Thrace. He has a B.A. in Economics for Aristotle Universtity of Thessaloniki and M.Sc. and Ph.D. for Sorbonne University. He has worked as researcher at Sorbonne University for 4 years and he was a visiting lecturer at Paul Valery University of Montpellier for 1993–1996. His work has appeared in academic journals such as: *Corporate Governance: The International Journal of Business in Society, Eurasian Economic Review* and *International Journal of Law and Management* and in various conferences.

Drago Dubrovski took his doctorate degree in Economics, from the Business Faculty in Maribor (Slovenia), field International Business. He is a part-time Associate Professor at Faculty of Management Koper and International School for Social and Business Studies Celje and managing director in a private management consulting company, which focuses on restructuring projects and crisis management. He worked also as sales manager in international industrial company and was also a crisis manager in several Slovenian companies. He is verified expert of Slovene Economists' Association and judicial expert; he is a member of several Supervisory Boards and has a licence for managing insolvency proceedings. His research interests are in crisis management and corporate renewal, strategic alliances, mergers and acquisitions, and international business. He gives regular lectures at several Slovene faculties. He is author of 8 books and 80 articles from the above-mentioned fields.
e-mail: linnair@siol.net

İlknur Eskin has graduated from the Faculty of Business Administration and Economics, Muğla University, Muğla Turkey. She also has Masters and Ph.D. in Business. Her research interests are in accounting, internal control, social responsibility and international financial reporting. She has 4 years of work experience as an accounting supervisor at a private company.

Anastasia Filiou holds a Ph.D. from the Athens University of Economics and Business. Her research interests are focused on corporate social accounting, corporate governance, management accounting and financial management.

Assoc. Prof. Seyhan Bilir Güler fulfills duty at Trakya University, Faculty of Economics and Administrative Sciences, Department of Business Administration, Major Field of Administration and Organization Studies.
    After completing her undergraduate study at İnönü University Faculty of Economics and Administrative Sciences, Department of Business Administration, in 1993 she took office as a research assistant at Trakya University, Faculty of Economics and Administrative Sciences, Department of Business Administration, Major Field of Administration and Organization Studies. She has completed her graduate study at Trakya University and her doctorate at Ankara University, Faculty of Political Sciences. After earning her Ph.D. in 2005, she was assigned as assistant

professor at Trakya University, Faculty of Economics and Administrative Sciences, Department of Business Administration.

She carries out the Board membership in Trakya University Quality and Strategy Development, Application and Research Center. Her research fields are women and gender in working life, organizational culture and organization theories.
e-mail: seyhanguler@trakya.edu.tr

Iliya Kereziev is a Chief Assistant Professor, Faculty of Management and Administration at the University of National and World Economy (UNWE). He is working for years on different aspects of entrepreneurship, in that number on social entrepreneurship in Bulgaria. He participated in different initiatives related to social entrepreneurship. His books and articles have been published by prominent publishers and high impact journals. He has presented her researches in various national and international conferences.

Diana Kopeva is a full time professor at the University of National and World Economy (UNWE), Sofia, Bulgaria. She gives lectures on Strategic management, Entrepreneurship, Business Planning, Cost-Benefit Analysis and Project Management. She has more than 100 scientific publications, based on his research interests. She is one of the leading researchers in the area of business economics and entrepreneurship in Bulgaria. Her research interests are in the field of start-ups, corporate social responsibility (CSR) and circular economy. She participated in numerous projects (national and international) focused on CSR and transition from linear to circular and regenerative economies. Her books and articles have been published by prominent publishers and high impact journals. She has presented her researches in various national and international conferences.

Fernando Benedicto Mainier holds a degree in Chemical Engineering from the Federal University of Rio de Janeiro (1967) and a doctorate in Education from the Federal University of Rio de Janeiro (1999). He was the Director of the Engineering School of Fluminense Federal University (UFF) from January 2012 to January 2016. He is currently a Professor and Advisor of the Graduate Courses in Engineering Civil, Chemical Engineering and Management (Latec). He has experience in the area of Materials Engineering and Metallurgy, with emphasis on Corrosion, working mainly on the following topics: corrosion, environment, corrosion tests, contaminations and corrosion inhibitor.

Marcelo Jasmim Meiriño Professor at Fluminense Federal University (UFF) in the School of Engineering; Professor in the Doctoral Program in Sustainable Management Systems (PPSIG UFF); Professor in the Master´s Program in Management Systems (MSG UFF); Ph.D. in Civil Engineering, emphasis on Management, Production, Quality and Sustainable Development. Architect and Urban Planner; Master in Civil Engineering; Occupational Safety Engineer; Coordinator in the Innovation Center and Technology for Sustainability (NITS/UFF); Specialist in Sustainability and Energy Efficiency in Buildings; Member of the Social Responsibility Commission of the Brazilian Institute of Oil, Gas and Biofuels (IBP); Coordinator of the

National Congress on Management Excellence (CNEG); Reviewer of journals and academic events; Researcher and Consultant.

Michail Nerantzidis (B.A., M.Sc., M.B.A., Ph.D., Postdoc.) is an Assistant Professor of Accounting at the Department of Accounting and Finance, School of Economics and Business at the University of Thessaly. He is an Associate Editor in *Corporate Governance: The International Journal of Business in Society*. His current research interests focus on financial accounting and reporting and corporate governance. His research work has been published in peer-reviewed journals, while he has participated in a number of international conferences.
e-mail: mnerantz@econ.duth.gr

İsmail Çağrı Özcan is an assistant professor at Ankara Yıldırım Beyazıt University. His research focuses on (i) transportation economics, finance, policy, and sustainability (ii) project finance and privatizations and (iii) regional economics. He has his work published in the *Journal of Air Transport Management*, *European Journal of Transport and Infrastructure Research*, *International Journal of Transport Economics*, and *Case Studies on Transport Policy*, among others.
e-mail: icozcan@ybu.edu.tr

Hilal Özen holds an honors degree in B.S. Business Administration from Hacettepe University (2004). Her M.S. (2007) and Ph.D. (2011) degrees are in Marketing from Istanbul University School of Business. She is currently an Associate Professor of Marketing in Trakya University. Her current research interests enthusiastically focus on digital marketing, e-health, social media marketing, tourism marketing, sustainability, and consumer decision making styles. She has published on these topics in various peer-reviewed journals and conference proceedings of international conferences. She has taught and still teaching courses: Principles of Marketing, Marketing Management, Research Methodology, Marketing Strategies, Current Issues in Marketing, Digital Marketing and Healthcare Marketing to all levels of business students: undergraduate, MBA and executive MBA students.
e-mail: hilalozen@trakya.edu.tr

Dilma Pimentel Ph.D. in Civil Engineering at Fluminense Federal University UFF, with emphasis on Management, Production, Quality and Sustainable Development, Master in Civil Engineering. Graduated in Biological Sciences at Santa Ursula University, she is also a Postgraduate in Sustainable Business Management (UFF) and Early Childhood Education at Catholic Pontifical University. Professor of Sustainability, Social Responsibility and Integrated Management System in Postgraduate courses. She is also a consultant for public and private companies in the implementation of Integrated Management Systems—Quality, Environment, Occupational Safety and Health, Governance and Community Relations.

Osvaldo Luiz Gonçalves Quelhas Coordinator of the Technology, Business and Environment Management Laboratory (LATEC UFF), Professor at Fluminense Federal University (UFF) in the School of Engineering; Coordinator and Professor in the Doctoral Program in Sustainable Management Systems (PPSIG UFF); Vice

Coordinator and Professor in the Master's Program in Management Systems (MSG UFF); Ph.D. in Production Engineering, graduated as a Civil Engineer; Member of the Social Responsibility Commission of the Brazilian Institute of Oil, Gas and Biofuels (IBP); Coordinator of the National Congress on Management Excellence (CNEG); He worked as an Engineer and Process Manager in several national and international organizations such as the Brazilian Naval Arsenal in Rio de Janeiro, Mills Cover Letter Equipamentos Ltda and Shell Brasil S.A. Reviewer of journals and academic events; Researcher and Consultant.

Sayed Mohamed Saeed Sayed Mohammed received his Bachelor's degree in Accounting and Finance from Ahlia University in 2012, and his MBA in 2017, also from Ahlia University. Sayed Mohammed is currently employed at Bahrain Accounting House and work as senior accountant in Bahrain Accounting House.

Mara Telles Salles Graduated in Civil Engineering (1981), Master in Civil Engineering (1992) and Ph.D. in Production Engineering (1998). She is currently Adjunct Professor and Researcher of the Production Engineering Department of Fluminense Federal University in the Exclusive Dedication Regime and Academic Coordinator of the Post-Graduation Course in Project Management at UFF. She has experience in the Production Engineering area, with emphasis on Product Development and Processes, and has worked in research and consultancy, mainly in the following subjects: Product and Process Engineering, Product Development, Sustainable Development, Quality, Management and Social Responsibility.

Dr. Adel Sarea is an Assistant Professor of Accounting at Ahlia University and Director of the MBA programme since 2013. He has a Master's degree in Accounting from Al al-Bayt University, Jordan, A Bachelor's degree in Accounting from Petra University, Jordan, and a Ph.D. in Economics and Business Administration (Accounting) from the Faculty of Economics and Business Administration at the Islamic Science University of Malaysia. He is a recognised Ph.D. supervisor at Brunel University, UK, and serves as a member of the editorial boards for a number of international journals. He has written more than 30 papers, many of which have been published or accepted in regional and international journals.

Nikolay Sterev is full time professor in Organization and Management of Marketing at the University of National and World Economy—Sofia (UNWE), Bulgaria. He is Head of Industrial Business Department at the Business Faculty. He is Chairman of Association of Professors of Industrial Economics and Management (APIUI). Main research field are: industrial growth, leadership and marketing leaders, START-Ups and entrepreneurship, CSR in industry, industrial marketing management. His books and articles have been published by prominent publishers and high impact journals. He has presented her researches in various national and international conferences.

Ioannis A. Tampakoudis is an Assistant Professor of Finance at the Department of Business Administration, School of Business Administration at the University of Macedonia. He holds a B.Sc. and a Ph.D. in Finance from the University of

Macedonia and an M.Sc. in Banking and International Finance from the Business School of City University, London, UK. His research is focused on mergers and acquisitions, corporate governance, credit markets and FDIs. His research work has been published in peer-reviewed journals, while he has participated in a number of international conferences.

Mehmet Kenan Terzioğlu received his M.Sc. degree in Actuarial Sciences from Hacettepe University. He studied at Tilburg University in the Department of Econometrics and Operations between 2008 and 2009 while working in the Department of Actuarial Sciences at Hacettepe University between 2006 and 2009 as a Research Assistant. He worked as a Risk Analyst Assistant (Assistant Specialist) in Ziraat Bank Risk Management Department and got his Ph.D. degree in Econometrics from the Department of Econometrics at Gazi University. Since 2018, he has been working as an Associate Professor in the Econometrics Department at Trakya University. He takes part in the management team of the Risk Management and Corporate Sustainability Application and Research Center at Trakya University.
e-mail: kenanterzioglu@trakya.edu.tr

Stéphane Trébucq is Full Professor in Management and Accounting at the University of Bordeaux, France. He is in charge of the chair "Human Capital and Global Performance" in Bordeaux. His research deals with human capital and SCR. He has written many scientific articles and has coordinated a book dedicated on the subject of Human Capital.

Bahar Yaşin is an Associate Professor of Marketing at Istanbul University School of Business. She graduated with a B.Sc. degree in Business (2001) from Ege University in İzmir, Turkey. Bahar Yasin obtained her M.Sc. degree in Marketing (2003) and Ph.D. degree in Marketing (2007) from Social Sciences Institute of Istanbul University in Istanbul, Turkey. She is a Marketing Associate Editor of *Istanbul Business Research Journal* since 2015. Her research interests are largely directed towards understanding consumer behavior. She has number of publications in international peer-reviewed journals and conference proceedings that focus on corporate social responsibility, corporate reputation, brand equity, brand relationship quality, consumer innovativeness, e-health, destination image, tourism information search, service quality and consumer decision-making styles.
e-mail: bkarciga@istanbul.edu.tr

List of Figures

List of Tables

Part I
New Approaches in CSR, Sustainability

Chapter 1
Sustainable Buildings and Biodiversity: A Critical Analysis

Dilma Pimentel, Mara Telles Salles, Marcelo Jasmim Meiriño, Osvaldo Luiz Gonçalves Quelhas, and Fernando Benedicto Mainier

Abstract Biodiversity can be a complex subject. However, ignoring the negative impacts that it has been suffering shows that the current mechanisms for identifying environmental aspects and analyses of significance have been flawing and will eventually confront us in the future with situations which, if not irreversible, will be extremely costly to society. In this context, the aim of the thesis is to discuss adjustments to the existing indicators, and/or insertion of new indicators related to the biological diversity in the sustainable building tool: LEED ND "Neighborhood Development". Initially, biodiversity and ecosystem services are conceptualized. Then, the conceptual basis for the framework of the existing pre indicators, the four environmental aspects that guided the proposed changes and the validation phase with experts are presented: Mirrored Facade, Green Roofs and Walls, Public Lighting and Wind Energy. Given the achieved results, it is believed that the dissemination of new indicators will support Brazil regarding its responsibility as a very important world player in terms of Biodiversity, besides representing a supporting basis for the national entrepreneurs, through a coherent, constructive and sustainable model.

Keywords Sustainable building · Urban planning · Biodiversity · Aspects and environmental impacts · Performance indicators

D. Pimentel · M. J. Meiriño (✉) · O. L. G. Quelhas
Civil Engineering Department, Fluminense Federal University UFF, Niterói, Rio de Janeiro, Brazil
e-mail: marcelojm@id.uff.br

O. L. G. Quelhas
e-mail: osvaldoquelhas@id.uff.br

M. T. Salles
Production Engineering Department, Fluminense Federal University UFF, Niterói, Rio de Janeiro, Brazil
e-mail: marasalles@id.uff.br

F. B. Mainier
Graduate Courses of Civil Engineering, Chemical Engineering and Management, Fluminense Federal University UFF, Niterói, Rio de Janeiro, Brazil
e-mail: fmainier@uol.com.br

© The Author(s), under exclusive license to Springer Nature Singapore Pte Ltd. 2021
K. T. Çalıyurt (ed.), *New Approaches to CSR, Sustainability and Accountability, Volume II*, Accounting, Finance, Sustainability, Governance & Fraud: Theory and Application, https://doi.org/10.1007/978-981-33-6808-8_1

1.1 Introduction

The concept of country of megadiversity was created by the president of Conservation International, Russell Mittermeier, during a field research on primates. In 2006 he observed that 75% of the primate species were concentrated in only 4 countries: Brazil, Congo (former Zaire), Indonesia and Madagascar. He concluded that the same way there is the G7, group consisting of the seven countries that concentrate the economic wealth of the planet, there is the G17, group formed by 17 countries distributed across the 4 continents, which concentrates the biodiversity richness. The criteria that characterize the concept are the number of endemic plants and the total number of mammals, birds, reptiles and amphibian.

As a member of the select group, Brazil is the absolute champion of terrestrial biodiversity, having, according to the data from Conservation International (CI) in Brazil, almost 12% of all the natural life of the planet. Besides, the country has 55 thousand species of superior plants (22% of all the existing plants in the world), many of them endemic; 524 species of mammals; more than 3 thousand species of fresh water fishes; between 10 and 15 million of insects (the vast majority yet to be described); and more than 70 species of psittaciformes: macaws, parrots and parakeets.

It is important to emphasize that four of the richest biomes in the world are in Brazil, at serious risk of biodiversity loss: the Atlantic Forest, Cerrado, Amazon and Pantanal. Thus, it is important for our country to intensify research aiming at a better use of the Brazilian biodiversity—at the same time guaranteeing the access to the exotic genetic resources, also essential to the improvement of the national agriculture, cattle farming, silviculture and pisciculture.

The biodiversity value, whether it is direct or indirect, is incalculable, and showing it is a complex issue, because it is determined by a variety of economic and ethical factors.

Its mitigation endangers environmental sustainability, the availability of natural resources, but also life on earth itself. Its conservation and sustainable use, on the contrary, result in incalculable benefits to humankind.

The thesis, from which the content of this article was extracted, had the macro-objective of proposing adaptations and/or new indicators to the most updated and relevant assessment tools for sustainable buildings in Brazil, which are The Sustainable Cities Program, AQUA Process, QUALIVERDE and LEED Certification. The environmental aspects analyzed in such tools were the wind turbines, public street lightning, mirrored glass and green roofs and walls.

The indicators linked to the main assessment tools used in Civil Construction and Urban Planning are effective for monitoring or mitigating diversity loss. From such analysis, it was opted to focus the research on the management development tool—LEED ND—a standard developed by the institution known as Green Building to assess condominiums and cities. Regarding the ecosystemic services, the focus of the approach comprehended: pollination, biological control, genetic diversity and habitats.

1.2 Material and Methods

Before talking about the material and research methods discussed in this article, it is necessary to emphasize that there was an initial phase of the study where, in an exploratory research model, answers from 157 students and 22 professors of the Post-graduation sustainable building courses offered by the Catholic University of Petrópolis and Fluminense Federal University were analyzed.

The questionnaire applied to the interviewees was divided in three parts:

- Personal data,
- A conceptual part separated in diversity, impact and ecosystem and
- A part focused on management issue, divided in development and certification.

The objective of such phase was to know how effectively people were aware of the biodiversity issue, in order to relate it with the objective of the research. As for the objective, it was opted for an exploratory research type. Such research has the purpose of providing more familiarity for the problem, aiming to make it more explicit in face of the raised questions. As for the used techniques, it was necessary: bibliographic research, documental research and two types of data collection, one of exploratory character and the other aiming at the validation of the proposition that guides the study. The descriptive exploratory investigation involved, primarily, research through electronic means or via the Internet and bibliographic data collection focused on environmental management articles—environmental aspects and impacts, ecology and economy of nature.

The keywords were turned into sub-areas and new keywords were inserted. The search process was also altered by starting to insert the connection "E" into the keywords string. The purpose was that, through such restrictive action, the research only identified articles on two or three themes simultaneously. The search was performed in the CAPES—Coordination for the Improvement of Higher Level—or Education—Personnel—Periodical Portal.[1] In this second phase, 1079 articles from the 18 keywords related to the issue were catalogued (Table 1.1).

Through the reading of the summaries of the articles, however, the quantity decreased abruptly, summing up only 20 articles with relevant information about the concepts related to Biologic Diversity, Ecosystemic Services, Entrepreneurial References and Public Policies. Among the authors considered relevant, the works of Fernandes and Coelho (2010), Klein (2002), Barros (2010), Beatrice (2011), McGuire et al. (2013), Oliveira and Rosin (2013), Bogard (2013), Arnett et al. (2013), Ferraz and Leite (2011) and Ogden (2014) stand out.

Yet, in the research on the Validation phase, the survey technique, which consists of the application of structured and standardized questionnaires to a restricted representative sample of the investigation universe, was adopted. The applied questionnaire aimed to identify the "Relevance" and "Viability" of the propositions, besides validating the proposed adaptations and indicators.

---

[1] http://www.periodicos.capes.gov.br/.

Table 1.1 Articles and keywords related to biodiversity

Keywords	Total of articles	Relevant articles
Biodiversity + sustainable building	124	6
Civil construction impact + biodiversity	56	0
Sustainable building + negative environmental	53	4
Biologic diversity + negative environmental impacts	122	1
Impacts	145	3
Nagoya protocol + biodiversity	199	0
LEED ND certification + biodiversity	21	1
AQUA certification + biodiversity	0	0
QUALIVERDE certification + biodiversity	0	0
Sustainable cities program + biodiversity	72	0
Pollination + sustainable building	2	0
Green roofs and walls + invasive species	81	2
Sustainable building + bats	3	0
Bat mortality + sustainable building	0	0
Bird mortality + sustainable building	72	2
Bird mortality + mirrored glass	**0**	**0**
Sustainable building + facade	**9**	**0**
Sustainable building + public lighting	**16**	**0**
Invasive species + sustainable building	**19**	**0**
Sustainable building + wind power energy	**26**	**0**
	1079	**20**

Source Elaborated by the authors

1.3 Results and Discussion

After the presentation of the alteration and insertion propositions, the analyses of two categories considered fundamental by the author for the acceptance and incorporation of sustainable building tools were required from the respondents:

- "Relevance"—related directly to the understanding of the subject;
- "Viability"—practical aspect, aiming at the operationalization of the proposition.

The proposed changes were classified in four ways: (i) simple exchange of words, (ii) insertion of words, (iii) insertion of a new indicator, (iv) insertion of a new development criterion for a pre-existent indicator.

The suggested propositions for each one of the four dimensions of LEED ND (LEED Neighborhoods) will be presented next, followed by the "Relevance" and "Viability" analyses by part of the participants of the research in the Validation phase.

A. Alteration and Insertion Proposition and Relevance Analysis
1. Dimension—Smart Location and Linkage (SLL)

In relation to the alteration and insertion proposition, it was identified that it is necessary to take the ecosystems services into consideration, by including amphibians and
insects, as it is presented in Table 1.2.

As to the "Relevance" analysis of the SMART LOCATION and LINKAGE, 60%
of the respondents considered it highly relevant; 33% average relevant and 7% little
relevant (Fig. 1.1).

Gráfico: azul: little relevant/vermelho: average relevent/verde: highly relevant.

2. Dimension—Neighborhood Pattern and Design (NPD)

Regarding the alteration and insertion proposition, the following research points were
considered (Table 1.3).

The analysis of the relevance presented the following results (Fig. 1.2):

Gráfico: azul: little relevant/vermelho: average relevent/verde: highly relevant.

Table 1.2 Smart location and linkage (SLL) proposition

Leed neighborhoods original text	Alteration and/or insertion proposition
SLL pre-requisite: conservation of species and ecological communities at risk Objective: conserving the endangered species and ecological communities	The analysis will have to take the ecosystem services into consideration, including amphibians and insects
SLL credit: steep hillside protection Objective: minimizing erosion, protecting the habitat and diminishing the pressure on the natural water systems, preserving the steep hillsides in their natural state, with vegetation	Using only native species if planting is needed

Source Elaborated by the authors

Fig. 1.1 Relevance
percentage—LEED
ND–SLL. *Source* Elaborated
by the authors

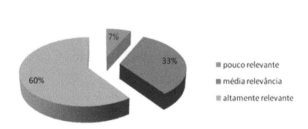

Table 1.3 Neighborhood pattern and design (NPD) proposition

Leed neighborhoods original text	Alteration and/or insertion proposition
NPD pre-requisite: peaceful streets Objective: promoting public transportation efficiency and reducing the distance traveled by the vehicle. Providing safe, attractive and comfortable street environments that stimulate daily physical activities and avoid pedestrian-car accidents to improve public health	Aiming also at the use at night, fighting light pollution by installing a public lighting system that should have protected bulbs and luminaries that avoid the inadequate light dispersion
NPD credit: woody and shaded streets Objective: stimulating walking and cycling and discouraging speeding. Improving air quality, increasing evapotranspiration and reducing the cooling loads of buildings to diminish the effects of the urban heat island	Using only native plants. However, in case of an anthropized environment, presenting an action plan for the gradual substitution of the exotic species

Source Elaborated by the authors

Fig. 1.2 Relevance percentage—LEED ND—NPD. *Source* Elaborated by the authors

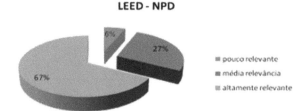

LEED - NPD

- pouco relevante
- média relevância
- altamente relevante

The Neighborhood Pattern and Design (NPD) was considered highly relevant by the majority of the interviewees (67%), while only 6% disregarded its importance.

3. **Green Infrastructure and Buildings (GIB)**

As to the alteration and insertion proposition, the following results were obtained (Table 1.4).

Regarding the analysis of its relevance, the following results were obtained (Fig. 1.3):

Gráfico: azul: little relevant/vermelho: average relevent/verde: highly relevant.

The majority of the interviewees (73%) consider the Green Infrastructure and Buildings (GIB) Proposition highly relevant.

4. **Regional Priority (RP)**

Regarding the alteration and insertion proposition, the following results were obtained (Table 1.5).

Table 1.4 Green infrastructure and buildings (GIB) proposition

Leed neighborhoods original text	Alteration and/or insertion proposition
GIB credit: energetic performance optimization Objective: stimulating the conception and construction of energetically efficient buildings that reduce the air, water and soil pollution and adverse environmental effects from the production and consumption of energy	Installing gadgets that avoid the avifauna and chiropterans mortality in case of mirrored facade buildings
	Guaranteeing the use of native species in case of green roofs and walls
	Implementing a suitable residue management so the wood waste, especially pine, do not attract vectors like cockroaches, beetles and termites
EA credit: renewable energy production Objective: reducing the economic and environmental damages associated with fossil energy fuels, increasing the self-supply of renewable energy	Confirming if the wind power farm took the specific precautions to avoid barotraumas and the avifauna and chiropterans mortality in case of wind power purchase
SS credit: light pollution reduction Objective: increasing night sky access, improving nocturnal visibility, and reducing the development consequences for the wildlife and people	Installing illumination systems that do not disperse light, avoiding predatory imbalance

Source Elaborated by the authors

LEED - GIB

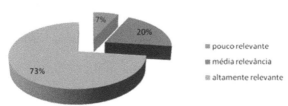

- pouco relevante
- média relevância
- altamente relevante

Fig. 1.3 Relevance percentage—LEED ND—GIB. *Source* Elaborated by the authors

Table 1.5 Regional priority (RP) proposition

Leed neighborhoods original text	Alteration and/or insertion proposition
RP credit: regional priority Objective: Providing an incentive for the achievement of the credits that approach the specific geographic equity: environmental, social and public health priorities	Inserting a protection belt into the project in case of proximity with conservation units of integral protection
	Developing the neighborhood project by considering migration routes and priority areas for the biodiversity conservation

Source Elaborated by the authors

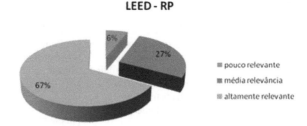

Fig. 1.4 Relevance percentage—LEED ND—RP. *Source* Elaborated by the authors

In relation to the analysis of the "relevance", it was observed that the big majority of the respondents (67%) believe in the relevance of the tool. While just one interviewee considers it irrelevant (Fig. 1.4).

Gráfico: azul: little relevant/vermelho: average relevent/verde: highly relevant.

B. **Analysis of Viability**

As to the analysis of the "Viability", it was questioned in a unified way, taking all the propositions into consideration: Regarding the viability criterion, how do you define the suggestions for LEED Neighborhoods? The following result was obtained (Fig. 1.5):

Gráfico: Si = Yes/Não = No.

Thus, it is possible to consider that 93% of the respondents adopt and believe in the viability of the tool.

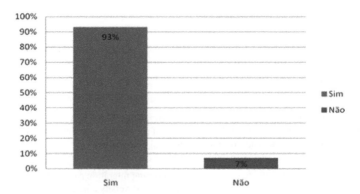

Fig. 1.5 Viability percentage of the presented propositions—LEED ND. *Source* Elaborated by the authors

1.4   Comments

The "Neighborhood Development" ND version—named LEED Neighborhoods in this chapter, presents Requirements and Credits from LEED® that allow regional specificities. Such possibility adjusts to the necessary adaptation of the Brazilian context, not only due to the continental dimension of the country, but also the biological diversity.

The suggested propositions aimed to insert differentiated analyses into each neighborhood project. The result surprises, because in the four dimensions in which the suggestions were presented, the answers "little relevant" appeared in all of them. It can be understood as a result of the unawareness of the ecosystem interactions (Table 1.6).

In the **SLL** dimension, for example, the proposition that the analyses consider the ecosystemic services, including amphibians and insects, may have been a surprised. Even that empirically, the relation between the reduction of the populations of amphibians is diametrically in opposition with the increase of illnesses transmitted by insect vectors—dengue, Ebola, chikungunya; yet, the necessity for city growth superimposes.

The insertion of actions that minimize light pollution might also have been the justification for the identification of little relevance in the **NPD** and **GIB** dimensions. It is important to remind that one of the results of the Exploratory phase questionnaire, which requested that the respondent list the types of pollution that he or she knew about; light pollution was not cited by any professor, and neither was cited by 85% of the students.

Despite the fact that LEED ND already has a credit that aims at light pollution reduction, the goal for its insertion is the human comfort, and not the risk of predatory imbalance of insects and bats that end up interfering in the food web.

In the **RP** dimension, also aiming to avoid judicial imbroglios, the proposition includes the necessity of a protection belt when the enterprise is close to Integral Protected areas according to demands from the Ministry of Environment of Brazil.

One stimulating result is that all propositions had percentages higher than 50% in the "highly relevant" category. Another encouraging point is related to the "Viability" category, because all propositions had results higher than 90%.

Table 1.6 Consolidated results in the validation phase

Development tool		Leed			
Indicator		SLL	NPD	GIB	RP
% Relevance	Highly relevant	60	67	73	67
	Average relevant	33	27	22	27
	Little relevant	7	6	7	6
% Viability		93%			

Source Elaborated by the authors

The productive system strong pressure on natural resources has been altering the environment significantly, in one or more of its components. And the vertiginous increase of public policies and assessment tools for sustainable buildings is visible. However, unfortunately, there is the concentration of indicators focused on eco-efficiency, mainly water, energy and materials.

Such policies and tools, many times based on indicators, translate, in a measurable format, a reality aspect in a way to operationalize behaviors and strategies. Such verification was decisive for the motivation of this research and for the definition of the questions that were confirmed after the result analyses of the Exploratory phase questionnaire.

The demands of the market, society, science and technologies are the references for what to teach and learn today, putting aside systemic analyses of the limited support capacity of the planet, in a schizophrenic game of life and death, where decisions are postponed and responsibilities are fled.

1.5 Conclusion

From the cited aspects of the impacts on biodiversity, a long way has been traveled since the initial proposition for the discussion of adaptations or insertions of the indicators of the most relevant assessment tools for building performance in Brazil. A construction enterprise, be it a simple building, an infrastructure work or a neighborhood planning, may have negative impacts—primary or secondary—on the local, regional or global biodiversity.

There is an endless number of themes that must be introduced in national debates. It is not only about defending ecosystems, species and genetic material, it is about the implementation of policies and practices that discuss the objectives of conservation, the urgency for the sustainable use of natural resources and the equitable distribution of the benefits offered by the environment, even gratuitously, with society.

The challenge is not only in developing a compiling spreadsheet for environmental aspects that includes the biological diversity, but getting rid of the anthropocentric short-term view that insists on putting the most urgent needs of the human beings as more important than the needs of the other living beings, as it was possible in face of the ecosystemic interactions.

Treating the human being and the environment as if they belonged to two different worlds is a legacy of our culture, disseminated by the educational institutions, the companies, the media and the public policies. Fortunately, however, such scenario seems to be changing. We hope that the change comes at the pace the planet needs it.

The configuration of a coherent and quite sustainable building model, points out the need to create methodological instruments that minimize, in a systemic and concomitant way, the negative environmental impacts linked to regional problems and characteristics of the ecosystems, but also the global problems and characteristics of the ecosystems.

References

Arnett EB, Hein CD, Schirmacher MR, Huso MMP, Szewczak JM (2013) Evaluating the effectiveness of an ultrasonic acoustic deterrent for reducing bat fatalities at wind turbines. PLoS ONE 8(6):e65794. https://doi.org/10.1371/journal.pone.0065794

Barros LC (2010) Morte de pássaros por colisão com vidraças. Revista Ciências do Ambiente On-Line Dezembro, vol 6, Número 3 58. Disponível em: http://sistemas.ib.unicamp.br/be310/index.php/be310/article/view/265/208. Acesso em 15 de setembro de 2013

Beatrice CC (2011) Avaliação do potencial de uso de três espécies vegetais como cobertura leve de telhados em edificações. Dissertação de mestrado, Universidade de São Carlos. Disponível em: https://www.google.com.br/url?sa=t&rct=j&q=&esrc=s&source=web&cd=1&cad=rja&uact=8&ved=0CB8QFjAA&url=http%3A%2F%2Fwww.teses.usp.br%2Fteses%2Fdisponiveis%2F18%2F18139%2Ftde-22092011-151752%2Fpublico%2FDissertacaoCaioCuryBeatrice.pdf&ei=0cpyVP3LHcapgwSbhoGoDg&usg=AFQjCNGEu58IBZzSW4WTPszud5NtFywMBg&sig2=pt36pWa1QXmdzHIaroIQ6g&bvm=bv.80185997,d.eXY. Acesso em: 23 de fevereiro de 2014

Biodiversity Values Disponível em: http://www.biodiversitya-z.org/pages/22. Acesso em 15 de setembro de 2013

Bogard P (2013) Bringing back the night: a fight against light pollution. Disponível em: http://e360.yale.edu/feature/bringing_back_the_night__a_fight_against_light_pollution/2681/. Acesso em 07 de fevereiro de 2014

Colding J, Barthel S (2013) The potential of 'urban green commons' in the resilience building of cities. Ecol Econ 86:156–166. Disponível em: http://www.phytoremediation.be/wp-content/uploads/2013/07/Urban-green-commons.pdf. Acesso em 15 de setembro de 2013

Conservation International do Brasil (2005) Mapa Hotspot. Disponível em: http://www.conservation.org.br/arquivos/Mapa%20Hotspots%202005.pdf. Acesso em: 10 de março de 2010

Davies TW, Bennie J, Inger R, Gaston KJ (2013) Artificial light alters natural regimes of night-time sky brightness. Environment and Sustainability Institute, University of Exeter, Penryn, Cornwall TR10 9EZ, U.K. CIENTIFIC REPORTS, 3, 1722. https://doi.org/10.1038/srep01722

Davies TW, Duffy JP, Bennie J, Gaston KJ (2014) The nature, extent, and ecological implications of marine light pollution. Frontiers Ecol Environ 12(6):347–355. Disponível em: https://doi.org/10.1890/130281. Acesso em 21 de setembro de 2014

Espínola A, Júlio HF (2007) Espécies invasoras: conceitos, modelos e atributos. Interciencia, vol 32, núm. 9, septiembre, pp 580–585, Asociación Interciencia. Disponível em: http://www.redalyc.org/articulo.oa?id=33932902. Acesso em 13 de setembro de 2013

Fatal Light Awareness Program—FLAP. Disponível em: http://www.flap.org/index.php. Acesso em 26 janeiro de 2014

Fatal Light Awareness Program—Flap. Bird-Friendly Development Rating System and Acknowledgement Program. Disponível em: http://www1.toronto.ca/city_of_toronto/city_planning/zoning__environment/files/pdf/rating_system_form_jan18.pdf. Acesso em 26 janeiro de 2014

Fernandes GW, Coelho MS (2010) Desequilíbrio. O impacto ambiental da poluição luminosa. Scientific American Brasil, 2, pp 41–47

Fernandes GW, Coelho MS, Caires T O impacto ambiental da poluição luminosa. Disponível em: http://www.amda.org.br/imgs/up/Artigo_01.pdf. Acesso em 25 de janeiro de 2014

Ferraz LL, Leite BCC (2011) Amendoim no telhado: O comportamento da grama-amendoim (Arachis repens) na cobertura verde extensiva. VI Encontro Nacional e IV Encontro Latino-americano sobre Edificações e Comunidades Sustentáveis—Vitória. Disponível em: http://www.elecs2013.ufpr.br/wpcontent/uploads/anais/2011/2011_artigo_016.pdf. Acesso em: 23 de fevereiro de 2014

Green Building Council Brasil. LEED® ND "Neighborhood development". Disponível em: http://gbcbrasil.org.br/leed-neighborhood.php?doc=LEEDND.pdf. Acesso em: 23 de fevereiro de 2014

International Organization for Standardization. ISO 14004:2004. Sistemas da gestão ambiental—Requisitos com orientações para uso

International Organization for Standardization. ISO 14044 (2009) Gestão ambiental—Vocabulário
Instituto Horus. Código de conduta voluntário para horticultura ornamental sustentável.
Disponível em: http://www.institutohorus.org.br/download/ornamentais/codigodecondutavolunt
ario.pdf. Acesso em 15 de setembro de 2013

Instituto Horus. Base de dados nacional de espécies exóticas invasoras, I3N Brasil, Instituto Hórus
de Desenvolvimento e Conservação Ambiental, Florianópolis—SC. Disponível em: http://i3n.
institutohorus.org.br. Acesso em 15 de setembro de 2013

Klein SE (2002) Scheidemantel. Diretrizes de Gestão Ambiental na Indústria da Construção Civil de
Edificações, 1v, 84p. (Mestrado em Engenharia Ambiental). Universidade Regional de Blumenau

Lonsdale WM (2004) Global patterns of plant invasions and the concept of invasibility.
Ecology 80:1522–1536. Disponível em: http://www.esf.edu/efb/parry/lonsdale.pdf . Acesso em:
6 setembro de 2013

Mcguire KL, Payne SG, Palmer MI, Gillikin CM, Keefe D et al (2013) Digging the New York City
skyline: soil fungal communities in green roofs and city parks, Anthony J (ed) Gilbert, Argonne
National Laboratory, United States of America. Disponível em: http://www.plosone.org/article/
info%3Adoi%2F10.1371%2Fjournal.pone.0058020. Acesso em: 23 de fevereiro de 2014

Mcneely J (2001) Invasive species: a costly catastrophe for native biodiversity. Land use water
resource. Disponível em: http://www.luwrr.com/uploads/paper01-02.pdf. Acesso em 13 de
setembro de 2013

Meadows R (2008) Pollination crisis in biodiversity hotspots. Disponível em: http://conservation
magazine.org/2008/07/pollination-crisis-in-biodiversity-hotspots/. Acesso em: 15 de setembro
de 2013

Mittermeier RA et al Uma breve história da conservação da biodiversidade no Brasil. Disponível
em: http://www.conservation.org.br/publicacoes/files/04_Mittermeier_et_al.pdf. Acesso em 06
de setembro de 2012

Mittermeier RA et al (2005) Hotspots Revisitados. As regiões biologicamente mais ricas e
ameaçadas do planeta. Disponível em: http://www.conservation.org.br/publicacoes/files/Hotspo
tsRevisitados.pdf. Acesso em: 6 setembro 2012

Myers N et al Biodiversity hotspots for conservation priorities. Disponível em: http://www.equali
sambiental.com.br/wp-content/uploads/2013/02/My042.pdf. Acesso em 15 de setembro de 2013

Ogden LE (2014) Does green building come up short in considering biodiversity? BioScience.
https://doi.org/10.1093/biosci/bit019. First published online: January 15, 2014. Disponível
em: http://bioscience.oxfordjournals.org/content/early/2014/01/14/biosci.bit019.full.pdf+html.
Acesso em 07 de setembro de 2014

Oliveira MVM, Rosin JARG (2013) Telhados Verdes e sua Contribuição para a
Sustentabilidade das Cidades. Revista Nacional de Gerenciamento de Cidades, 1(4), pp
60–66. Retrieved from http://www.amigosdanatureza.org.br/publicacoes/index.php/gerenciam
ento_de_cidades/article/view/535. Acesso em: 23 de fevereiro de 2014

Petenon D, Pivello VR (2008) Plantas invasoras: representatividade da pesquisa dos países trop-
icais no contexto mundial. Artigos Técnico-Científicos—Natureza & Conservação, vol 6, no
1, pp 65–77. Disponível em: http://ecologia.ib.usp.br/lepac/conservacao/Artigos/invasoras.pdf.
Acesso em: 06 de maio de 2012

Primack RB (2001) Biologia da conservação. E. Planta, Londrina, 328 p

Secretariado da Convenção Sobre Diversidade Biológica—CDB. O Panorama da Biodiversidade
Global 3. Disponível em: http://www.mma.gov.br/estruturas/sbf_chm_rbbio/_arquivos/gbo3_72.
pdf. Acesso em 13 de setembro de 2013

Silva VG (2003) Avaliação da sustentabilidade de edifícios de escritórios brasileiros: diretrizes
e base metodológica, 210 f. Tese (Doutorado em Engenharia Civil)—Escola Politécnica da
Universidade de São Paulo, São Paulo

TEEB (2004) Economic instruments in biodiversity-related multilateral environmental agreements.
Disponível em: http://www.unep.ch/ETB/publications/EconInst/ecoInstBioMea.pdf. Acesso em:
15 de setembro de 2013

TEEB (2008) The economics of ecosystems and biodiversity—an interim report. Disponível em: http://www.teebweb.org/media/2008/05/TEEB-Interim-Report_Portuguese.pdf. Acesso em: 24 maio 2010

TEEB (2011a) Manual for cities: ecosystem services in urban management. Disponível em: http://www.teebweb.org/publication/teeb-manual-for-cities-ecosystem-services-in-urban-man agement/. Acesso em: 11 abril 2012

TEEB (2011b) National and international policy making. Disponível em: http://www.teebweb.org/ publication/teeb-in-national-and-international-policy-making/. Acesso em: 11 abril 2012

TEEB (2012a) Local and regional policy and management. Disponível em: http://www.teebweb. org/publication/the-economics-of-ecosystems-and-biodiversity-teeb-in-local-and-regional-pol icy-and-management/. Acesso em: 08 agosto 2013

TEEB (2012b) Business and enterprise Disponível em: http://www.teebweb.org/publication/the-eco nomics-of-ecosystems-and-biodiversity-teeb-in-business-and-enterprise/. Acesso em: 08 agosto 2013

TEEB (2012c) Nature and its role in the transition to a green economy. Disponível em: http://www. teebweb.org/publication/nature-and-its-role-in-a-green-economy/. Acesso em: 08 agosto 2013

TEEB (2012d) Implementation guide for Aichi target 2: a TEEB perspective. Disponível em: http://www.teebweb.org/publication/implementation-guide-for-aichi-target-2-a-teeb-perspe ctive/. Acesso em: 08 agosto 2013

TEEB (2012e) Implementation guide for Aichi target 3: A TEEB perspective. Disponível em: http://www.teebweb.org/publication/implementation-guide-for-aichi-target-3-a-teeb-perspe ctive/. Acesso em: 08 agosto 2013

TEEB (2012f) Implementation guide for Aichi target 11: A TEEB perspective. Disponível em http://www.teebweb.org/publication/implementation-guide-for-aichi-target-11-a-teeb-perspe ctive/. Acesso em: 08 agosto 2013

TEEB (2013) Valuation database manual. Disponível em: http://www.teebweb.org/wp-content/upl oads/2014/03/TEEB-Database-and-Valuation-Manual_2013.pdf. Acesso em: 2 fevereiro 2014

United Nations Environment Programme—UNEP (2005) Relatório-Síntese da Avaliação Ecos- sistêmica do Milênio. Disponível em: http://www.unep.org/maweb/documents/document.446. aspx.pdf. Acesso em 6 de novembro de 2012

Vamosi JC, Knight TM, Steets JA, Mazer SJ, Burd M, Ashman TL (2006) Pollination decays in biodiversity hotspots. Proc Natl Acad Sci U S A 103(4):956–961. Disponível em: http://www. pnas.org/content/103/4/956.full. Acesso em: 15 de setembro de 2013

World Resources Institute (2003) Ecossistemas e o bem-estar humano: Estrutura para uma avali- ação. Disponível em: http://www.millenniumassessment.org/documents/document.63.aspx.pdf. Acesso em 29 de setembro de 2011

Chapter 2
Business Model of Social Entrepreneurship: Bulgarian Experience

Diana Kopeva, Iliya Kereziev, and Nikolay Sterev

Abstract For two decades, the European institutions have recognized the ability of social entrepreneurship to correct social and economic imbalances and achieve objectives of common interest. The European Parliament has defined it as the basis of the European social market model. The EU's interest in social entrepreneurship stems from its link with several autonomous development policies: social inclusion, employment policy, the social economy and civil society. According to the European Economic and Social Committee in 2012, social entrepreneurship plays an important role in the EU: • 2 million social enterprises/10% of all European enterprises, • produces 10% of Member States' GDP, • an employer is 11 million or 6% of the employed, • accelerated creation of social enterprises—1 out of 4 new companies are social enterprises. Contribution of social enterprises to key EU objectives in the social field: active inclusion of people out of the labour market; quality services of general interest; social innovation in the context of social change. Social entrepreneurship is a driver for regional development. It occupies market niches in which the state fails to offer enough services and the market fails to make enough profits. Social entrepreneurship encourages the dissemination of good practices at local level by: reinvesting profits in geographic areas where they are created; mobilizing local actors and local resources; creating an entrepreneurial culture; linking activities to local needs/services in a community/; keeping activities at risk of disappearing because they are not profitable/crafts/; creating social capital. Over the last 10 years, social entrepreneurship in Bulgaria has undergone a strong development. Different forms of social entrepreneurship are implemented in practice, and we can already talk about experience in different sectors. This report aims to present the applied business models of social entrepreneurship in agriculture and small businesses in urban environment. The advantages and disadvantages of used business

D. Kopeva (✉) · I. Kereziev · N. Sterev
University of National and World Economy (UNWE), Sofia, Bulgaria

I. Kereziev
e-mail: iker@unwe.bg

N. Sterev
e-mail: apiui@abv.bg

© The Author(s), under exclusive license to Springer Nature Singapore Pte Ltd. 2021   17
K. T. Çalıyurt (ed.), *New Approaches to CSR, Sustainability and Accountability,*
Volume II, Accounting, Finance, Sustainability, Governance & Fraud: Theory
and Application, https://doi.org/10.1007/978-981-33-6808-8_2

models are presented and analysed. The report presents the effects and impact of these models on the respective communities and for the development of the region.

Keywords Social entrepreneurship · Business models · Social enterprises · Bulgaria

2.1 Social Entrepreneurship: Definition and Boundaries

Despite the widespread popularity of the term social entrepreneurship, there are still ambiguities about its nature, characteristics and scope. This often leads to confusion, and a wide variety of activities, whether deserved or not, are defined as social entrepreneurship. In addition, social entrepreneurship as a phenomenon does not find a clear and theoretically grounded definition (Barendsen and Gardner 2004) taking into account its specific characteristics. Moreover, the scientific area of social entrepreneurship is still not clearly defined and is at a very early stage of development compared to the wider entrepreneurial science field. There are numerous research studies, focused on social entrepreneurship, but they are poorly interrelated, which prevents consensus and the accumulation of systematic knowledge.

Social entrepreneurship is a form of entrepreneurial activity, and for this reason, it is necessary to take into account its relation to entrepreneurship when revealing its nature (Dees 1998). According to Dees (1998), the concept of entrepreneurship can be applied in the social sector. The initial legitimacy of social entrepreneurship is a result of the vast public interest in inspirational stories of entrepreneurs who have achieved tremendous success in treating complex social problems. We can find such examples not just in developed countries, but also in developing world. Even we can assume that where the most severe social needs are observed, the soil and environment for the emergence and development of social entrepreneurs are most favourable. In this regard, the concept of entrepreneurship, which is used mostly within business organizations, now is increasingly being applied in seeking solutions to a number of social problems and deficiencies (Thake and Zadek 1997).

The social entrepreneur is a key element in the social entrepreneurship process. The public and academic interest towards social entrepreneurs is based on their mission to make the world better place for living and their courage to take the responsibility to fight with problems often considered as unsolvable (Zahra et al. 2008). According to Bornstein (2004), the social entrepreneur is a pioneer, totally obsessed with his vision of change. Driven by a social cause, he finds a creative and innovative solution to a significant social problem and implements it in compliance with the established ethical norms. These are a wide variety of social problems, such as poverty, illness, disability, illiteracy, environmental destruction, human rights abuses and corruption. Thompson (2002) emphasizes the social commitment and the emotional workload of social entrepreneur. He stands out by meeting social needs for which the state social system and markets offer no solution. Due to a limited access to capital, social entrepreneurs mobilize human, financial and political resources.

Leadbeater (1997) highlights the management skills of social entrepreneurs who besides their entrepreneurial behaviour create and manage an organization through which they bring social change.

One of the most commonly cited definitions is that of Dees (1998), according to which the *social entrepreneur is an agent of change in the social sector*. Social entrepreneurs build and develop new business models that are entirely dedicated to delivering a social value through solving significant social and environmental problems. They implement social mission without focusing on their own interests or the profit potential of their organization. Bornstein and Davis (2010) further defines social entrepreneurship "as a process by which citizens build or transform institutions to advance solutions to social problems".

The founder of Ashoka considers the social entrepreneurship as a provider of innovative solutions to society's most pressing social, cultural and environmental challenges. The most important aim is production of systems-level change, not just improvement of the problem. In Europe, social entrepreneurship most often takes place within the third sector, and the attention has been mainly devoted to the concept of "social enterprise" (Defourny and Nyssens 2010). The term social enterprise is embedded in the field of social economy and includes any company aiming at serving society. According to European Economic and Social Council (EESC), the concept of social enterprise is broader and includes social entrepreneurship. The opinion of EESC (2014) stated that definitions of social enterprises in different countries and geographic areas differ substantially. For this reason, instead of a definition, the EESC proposes a description of social entrepreneurship, based on the identification of common and often quoted characteristics. The aim is to reduce the ambiguity about the nature of social entrepreneurship and thus to promote it as a legitimate and promising area of academic research and driver for socially oriented market economy.

In this regard, its distinctive features have been identified, such as the existence of social objectives and the creation of social benefits in the interest of society, the reinvestment of profits predominantly in the social mission, the use of a variety of legal forms and business models, application of social innovations, transparent and cooperative decision-making and management.

Most common characteristics of social entrepreneurship can be summarized as follows:

- It is mission focused, not profit-driven, that reflects its values;
- Address social problems or needs not met by private markets or government;
- Combine profit-oriented activities and social purposes to achieve financial sustainability, through entrepreneurial and market based approaches;
- Focusing on generating and maximizing positive social returns and achieving large scale social change;
- Profit is reinvested rather than being distributed among the stakeholders and founders;
- Decision-making power is not based on capital ownership, but on the participatory and collaborative principles.

Comparing the essence and characteristics of social entrepreneurship with those of business sector entrepreneurship, it can be concluded that mission-related impact becomes the core of social entrepreneurship, not wealth creation (Dees 1998). Also an important aspect of the social entrepreneurship is its innovative nature, which gives it the power to transform the social sector. Last but not least, social entrepreneurship requires simultaneous implementation of social activities delivering social benefits and, on the other hand, economic activities that generate income and profitability. In this way, social enterprises are able to achieve financial stability and relatively independent of public and private grants and subsidies (Bacq and Janssen 2011).

Further unique features of the social entrepreneur can be highlighted its emotional engagement and sensitivity to social problems, ability to attract public subsidies and to mobilize voluntary resources, ethical behaviour, and social impact and change attainment.

2.2 European Approach to Social Entrepreneurship

European approach to social entrepreneurship is found as quite different from the leading approaches in other regions especially USA. The main characteristics that define the European case in understanding and applying social entrepreneurial measures and instruments could be found in three main pillars.

First, European Commission defines own understanding on social enterprises and social economy in order to put in order different EU-members' practices in that field. As the social entrepreneurship is not a new approach in EU inside the social economy understanding, its legal concepts is linked to the beginning of 1990s (Defourny and Nyssens 2010). The different speed of development of the social enterprises, different law requirements and, respectively, different schemes for financing them among EU Member' States allow the EC to set a definition of social enterprise in 2011 used for establishment of EU Social initiative. It is based on adopted Resolution on Social Economy in 2009. The main definitions on the EU-level are as follows:

a. **Social economy** is based on a social paradigm which is in line with the fundamental principles of the European social and welfare model, and it combines profit with solidarity, aim at creating high-quality jobs, strengthening social, economic and regional cohesion, generating social capital, promoting active citizenship, solidarity and economics, in which people are set on the first place. (EC 2009, 2017)

b. **Social enterprise** is main actor in the social economy whose main objective is to have a social impact rather than make a profit for their owners or shareholders. It operates by providing goods and services for the market in an entrepreneurial and innovative fashion and uses its profits primarily to achieve social objectives. It is managed in an open and responsible manner and, in particular, involves employees, consumers and stakeholders affected by its commercial activities (EC 2011).

Social enterprises are ventures in the business of creating significant social value, and do so in an entrepreneurial, market-oriented way, that is, through generating own revenues to sustain themselves (EC 2013a, b).

The recognized forms of social (economy) enterprises are: associations, foundations and mutual societies (EC 2009) The main characteristics of business activities of social enterprises are given the next (EC 2015): (1) enterprises with social or societal objectives, (2) enterprises which reinvest their profits to achieve social objectives and (3) enterprises with democratic or participatory principles of operating or focusing on social justice.

In 2016, the EC focused on start-ups and innovations as a result of social enterprise activities and started the Start-up and Scale-up Initiative (EC 2016) as a financial instrument for boosting the social economy and social enterprises and encourage social start-ups to scale up.

Thus, it can be summarized that social entrepreneurship is used to describe the behaviours and attitudes of individuals involved in creating new ventures for social purposes, including the willingness to take risks and find creative ways of using underused assets (EC 2013a, b).

Second, the history of EU social enterprise establishment is given by Defourny and Nyssens (2010):

c. In 1991, Italian social cooperatives are used for inspiring model's concept of social enterprises incl. enterprises focused on social, health and educational services ("A-type" social cooperatives), and enterprises providing integration for disadvantaged people ("B-type" social cooperatives).

d. The Portuguese "social solidarity cooperative" was created in 1997 to foster the integration of vulnerable groups, such as children, people with disabilities and socially disadvantaged families and communities.

e. In 1999 was put on legal form Spanish "social initiative cooperative" and Greek "limited liability social cooperative" targeting social inclusion groups and aiming integration of social excluded persons.

f. French law widens the definition of social enterprises in 2002 as it defines the "collective interest cooperative society" to bring together employees, users, volunteers, local and regional authorities and any other partners wishing to work together on a given local development project.

g. In most of the countries, the social enterprise definition was adopted in 2010s as there a few EU Member States without such definition (Austria, Cyprus, Czech, Denmark, Estonia, Luxemburg, Swiss).

The main differences are summarized as follows (EC 2015).

a. At least 10% of the revenues of a social enterprise should come from market sources (Czech) or must generate at least 25% of its income from entrepreneurial activity or trade (UK and Croatia) up to 70% of the income will be from entrepreneurial activities (Italy).

b. The interpretation of what constitutes a social aim varies from a narrow focus on work integration (Finland, Lithuania, Poland, Slovakia and Sweden) to broader societal and environmental goals (UK, Greece).

Third, as the European Commission adopted The Social Business Initiative (SBI) in 2011 (EC 2011), the main financial schemes cover:

c. Financial access for up to EUR 500,000 investments via public and private investors at national and regional level, as part of the EU Programme for Employment and Social Innovation (EASI).
d. Financial support through pilot equity investments under the European Fund for Strategic Investments (EFSI). Equity instrument are linked to incubators/accelerators and co-investments with social Business Angels.
e. Access to co-funds projects focussing on boosting the development of the demand and supply side of social finance markets in Europe (21 pilot projects were selected under a call for proposals in 2013 and further 20 projects were selected under a call for proposals in 2016).

2.3   Social Enterprise Concept

Understanding the social (economy) entrepreneurship and social enterprises, we should define the specific business model of them.

As the main goals of the social enterprises are towards the social economy introduction to different excluded persons and groups as well as social enterprises boost the scale-up of innovative start-ups (resp. via financing resources of social business angels), the social enterprises business model is quite different from the traditional for-profit business model.

Carvalho (2016) summarized the researches on added value of social enterprises:

- the creation of social and shared value (see Austin and Seitanidi 2012);
- co-creative networking (see Chatterjee 2013; Zott et al. 2011);
- multiple value creation that refers to ecological, social, economic (or financial) and psychological value (see Carvalho and Jonker 2015).

According to summary of new social business models, they are focused on establishment of added values (e.g., economic, social, ecological and psychological) offered to the different social stakeholders (Carvalho and Jonker 2015).

The specific place of social enterprises among the non-profit organizations and for-profit enterprises is explained by Gandhi and Raina (2018). The compromise between society needs and business goals encompasses the business and commercial techniques along with not-for-profit managerial approaches and business and social goals fulfilment (Fig. 2.1).

So, according to Fig. 2.1, the boundaries between non-profit social organizations (resp. social economy enterprises) and profit-oriented business become more flexible with inclusion of society into the for-profit enterprises. As EC (2016) accepted, the

Fig. 2.1 Different types of business from not-profit to for-profit

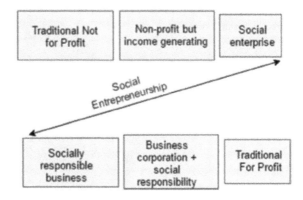

Fig. 2.2 Types of enterprises and social entrepreneurship

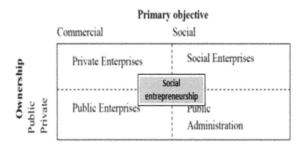

innovations and their scales-up are the crossing point between social enterprises and for-profit enterprises—the key element of the social entrepreneurship.

Additionally, the explanation of the place of social entrepreneurship business model could be done on the graph of the business types (Fig. 2.2).

The importance of social entrepreneurial business model increases as the contemporary economy is focused on understanding the market rather than understanding business social needs and projects. Accordingly, the social entrepreneurship has a dual goal—at the microeconomic level to pursue projects that address specific social needs, and at the macroeconomic level to advance the market economy.

Thus, the main issues describing the market-oriented business could be quite different for the social entrepreneurial business:

- Market: a social entrepreneur marketing environment usually implies that the costs are not fully covered by the revenue of the social enterprise.
- Market failure: a social entrepreneur emerges when there is a social market failure of the traditional market business. For example, the social enterprises are oriented to social and societal needs that are not covered by the for-profit business.
- Profit: as the profit is not driver for development of social entrepreneurs, they could focus on diversity of social quality measurements.
- Business strategy: social entrepreneurship is focused on cooperative approach rather than on the individual value creation approach.

Fig. 2.3 Social
entrepreneurship model.
Carvalho (2016)

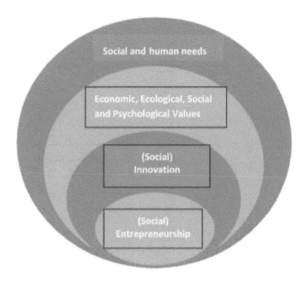

- Mission: The essential purpose of social entrepreneurship is creating social value for the greater public good.

The social entrepreneurship establishment model is also quite different form the traditional for-profit market business model (Carvalho 2016). It starts with identification of specific social or human needs, then creating a product (good, service, idea) primary based on (social) innovation that satisfies better the users and society. On the next level, the added values except economic are revealed (e.g., ecological, social and psychological) and finally, introduction to the market is needed to sustain the social entrepreneur activities (Fig. 2.3).

2.4 Juridical Framework for SE in Bulgaria

Until 2018, there is no unified law in Bulgarian legislation regulating the activity of social enterprises. There are multiple laws affecting individual aspects of the business, the legal form or taxation. Bulgarian national legislation offers a comprehensive legal basis[1] for the development of activities that have a relation to the characteristics of social economy:

(1)   **Commercial Law**[2]—SG 48, 18.06.1991, effective from 01.07.1991, last suppl. SG. No. 33 of 19 April 2019—related to social enterprises engaged in trade in the part for determining a Trader within the meaning of the law,

---

[1] National Concept of Social Economy. Ministry of Labor and Social Policy, Sofia 2011.

[2] https://lex.bg/laws/ldoc/-14917630—available 07.2019.

defining the types of traders and types of companies, state and municipal enterprises, their registration, way of functioning and closure of its activities;

(2) **Cooperatives Act**[3]—Effective from 1999, SG 113, 28.12.1999, last amend.—SG 42, 22.055.2018—related to social cooperatives and cooperatives performing social activities in the part determining a cooperative within the meaning of the law, their registration, way of functioning and closure of its activities;

(3) **Non-Profit Legal Entities Act**[4]—Effective from 01.01.2001, SG 81, 06.10.2000, last suppl.—SG 98, 27.11.2018—related to social enterprises operating as non-profit organizations in the part determining a Non-Profit Legal Entity within the meaning of the law, their registration, way of functioning and closure of its activities; Non-Profit Legal Entity is the most common form of registration of social enterprises in Bulgaria;

(4) **Law on Integration of People with Disabilities**[5]—Effective from 01.01.2005, SG 81, 17.09.2004, last amend. and suppl. SG 60, 20.07.2018, annulled SG 105, 18.12.2018—related primarily to Section III. Employment of People with Disabilities, in particular registration, establishment, operation and financing of specialized enterprises and cooperatives of people with disabilities;

(5) **Employment Promotion Act**[6]—Effective from 01.01.2002, SG 112, 29.12.2001, last amend. SG 24, 22.03.2019—This law governs public relations in (1) promoting and preserving employment; (2) vocational guidance and adult education and (3) mediation of information and recruitment. In exercising of rights and obligations under this law, direct or indirect discrimination, privileges or limitations based on nationality, background, ethnicity, personal status, sex, sexual orientation, race, colour, age, political and religious beliefs, membership in trade unions and other public organizations and movements, family, social and material situation and the presence of mental and physical disabilities. A direct relation to social enterprises has chapter six. Employment promotion—Section VI. Promoting entrepreneurship, as well as Section VIII. Programs and measures providing equal opportunities through socioeconomic integration of disadvantaged groups on the labour market;

(6) **Social Assistance Act**[7]—Effective from 1998, SG 56, 19.05.1998, last amend. and suppl. SG 35, 30.04.2019—sets out the rules for the allocating/granting of social aid and the provision of social services;

(7) **Small and Medium Enterprises Act**[8]—Effective from 1999, SG 84, 24.09.1999, last amend. SG 30, 03.04.2018—This law regulates the public relations related to implementation of the state policy for encouragement

---

[3] https://www.lex.bg/laws/ldoc/2134696966—available 07.2019.

[4] https://www.lex.bg/laws/ldoc/2134942720—available 07.2019.

[5] https://lex.bg/bg/laws/ldoc/2135491478—available 07.2019.

[6] https://lex.bg/laws/ldoc/-12262909—available 07.2019.

[7] https://lex.bg/laws/ldoc/2134405633—available 07.2019.

[8] https://www.lex.bg/laws/ldoc/2134682112—available 07.2019.

of creation and development of small and medium enterprises as well as measures and programs for encouragement of development of small- and medium-sized enterprises—in particular, the provisions of this law also apply to small and medium-sized social enterprises;

(8) **Crafts Act**[9]—Effective from 28.05.2001, SG 42, 27.04.2001, last amend. SG 17, 26.02.2019—many social enterprises operate in the production of various souvenirs, works of art and handmade household goods and accordingly fall under the provisions of the Craft Act;

(9) In 2011, a **National Concept for Social Economy**[10] was adopted. It outlines the vision, objectives, principles, conditions and the framework for the development of social economy and in particular of the social entrepreneurship in Bulgaria;

(10) From 2014 by decision of the Council of Ministers, a **two-year Action Plan For Social Economy** is accepted, respectively, for 2014/15; 2016/17 and 2018/19 periods

- For 2014/15 period, the **Action Plan For Social Economy**[11] sets five priorities, respectively, (1) raising stakeholder awareness on the nature and functioning of the social economy with three objectives—improving the visibility of social entrepreneurship; creating partnerships and disseminating good practices in the sphere of the social economy, and developing an active supportive environment for the development of the social economy subjects; (2) creating supporting structures for the social economy and social enterprises with one objective—providing institutional support for the social economy; (3) information provision of the social economy with one objective—supporting the information environment for the development of social economy; (4) creating favourable conditions for education, training and research in support of the social economy with two objectives—Development and implementation of educational and training programs in the field of social economy and assessment of the economic and social impact of the social economy subjects on employment, inclusion and achievement of social and territorial cohesion; (5) creating a favourable environment stimulating the development of the social economy with one objective—facilitating access to public procurement

- For the period 2016/17, the priorities and objectives set by the **Action Plan For Social Economy**[12] remain the same as for 2014/15 period, except for the objective of fifth priority—for this period, it is aimed at optimizing the

---

[9] https://lex.bg/laws/ldoc/2135184905—available 07.2019.

[10] National Concept for Social Economy was adopted. Ministry of Labor and Social Policy, Sofia 2011.

[11] Action Plan for Social Economy, 2014/15 http://seconomy.mlsp.government.bg/upload/docs/2014-02//RESENIE_NA_MS_N_43.pdf.

[12] Action Plan For Social Economy, 2016/17 http://seconomy.mlsp.government.bg/upload/docs/2016-03//16RH146.pdf.

national regulatory and strategic framework for the development of the social economy

- For the period 2018/19, the priorities and objectives set by the **Action Plan For Social Economy**[13] remain the same as for 2016/17 period.

(11)   In 2018 in Bulgaria has been promulgated a **Law for Enterprises of the Social and Solidarity Economy**,[14] Prom. SG, no. 91 from 2.11.2018, in force from 2.05.2019, amend. SG 17 of 26.02.2019, in force from 2.05.2019, amend and supplements, SG num. 24 of 22.03.2019, in force since 22.03.2019 and **Regulation No 115 of 13 May 2019**[15] for the Application of the Law on Enterprises of the Social and Solidarity Economy. The law regulates the social relations to social and solidarity economy, the types of subjects and the measures for their promotion, as well as the terms and conditions for the activity of the social enterprises. It aims to promote the development of the social and solidarity economy as an economic sector. It gives the definition that social and solidarity economy is a form of entrepreneurship aimed at one or more social activities and/or social objectives pursued by enterprises, including through the production of different goods or the provision of services in cooperation with state or local authorities or independently. It sets the principles of the social and solidarity economy as (1) advantage of social-economic goals; (2) association for public and/or collective benefit; (3) publicity and transparency; (4) independence from state authorities; (5) participation of members, employees in making managerial decisions.

2.5   Measurement of Social Enterprises in Bulgaria

Bulgaria has been introducing the European experience and practice in the sphere of social economy over the last 15 years. However, there was no exclusive definition of the term social enterprise until the end of 2018, and therefore, there were not established criteria for the identification of the social enterprises. The strategic documents regulating the development and support of social economy and social entrepreneurship use different interpretations for the terms social enterprise and social entrepreneurship. Although their meanings are very similar on conceptual level, in practice, the different definitions lead to different mapping of social sector. As a result, the statistical assessment of the social sector is hampered, and at present, there is no precise statistical data that allows the tracing and analyses of the size and development of the social economy in Bulgaria. **There are no official estimates of the scale of social enterprise in Bulgaria**.

---

[13] Action Plan For Social Economy, 2018/19 http://www.seconomy.mlsp.government.bg/page.php?c=38&d=125.

[14] http://dv.parliament.bg/DVWeb/showMaterialDV.jsp?idMat=131143—available 07.2019.

[15] http://dv.parliament.bg/DVWeb/showMaterialDV.jsp?idMat=137575—available 07.2019.

Table 2.1 Statistical estimation of social enterprise number in Bulgaria

Type of organization	Total number	Estimated number of social enterprises
Non-profit legal entities	35,000	Unknown—it is needed assessment of fulfilling the criteria for social enterprises based on a case-by-case basis
Commercial companies setup by NPLEs	85	85
Workers production cooperatives (specialized cooperatives of people with disabilities are excluded)	221	221
Specialized enterprises and cooperatives for people with disabilities	125	125

Source EC (2014), A map of social enterprises and their ecosystems in Europe: Country Report: Bulgaria, ICF Consulting Services, Limited Watling House, London

Specifically, social enterprises in Bulgaria adopt a variety of legal forms. The EC country report from 2014 (EC 2014) identifies three most common ones that meet the criteria of the European operational definition of social enterprise. These are non-profit legal entities (NPLEs) such as associations and foundations, workers production' cooperatives (including cooperatives of people with disabilities) and specialized enterprises for people with disabilities (using legal forms of commercial companies). According to the report, over 35,000 NPLEs and 346 cooperatives and specialized enterprises are operating in the country (see Table 2.1).

NPLE is the most suitable legal and organizational form for social entrepreneurship development, but despite their large number, just a small fraction of them could be defined as social enterprises. This is because most of them rely predominantly on external financing and do not generate income from market sources. The data for 2012 shows that only 85 NPLEs could be determined as social enterprises with certainty, because they have set up their own commercial enterprise and carry out business activities for income generation and self-sustaining.

Bulgarian National Statistical Institute (NSI) officially started to collect statistical data for Bulgarian social enterprises in 2012. In order to resolve the above-mentioned identification problem, NSI introduced guiding criteria on the basis of which the respondents were able to determine whether they are a social enterprise. According to the statistical survey carried out in 2013, organizations must self-declare themselves as social enterprise if meeting one of the following criteria:

- They regularly invest more than 50% of the profit in the achievement of social aims, such as: assistance to socially vulnerable groups and/or individuals in isolation; environmental protection with impact on society; social innovation activities; other activities, provision and/or production of goods and services with a social purpose; and/or
- Over 30% of their staff comprises vulnerable people.

The NSI survey for 2013 shows that the number of social enterprises is 3612. About 3/5-th of all organizations (2046 number) are registered as trading companies and cooperatives, 1381 of them being profitable. 2/5-th (1566 number) of the self-identified social enterprises are registered as NPLEs, with only 197 of them being profitable.

The most reliable is the statistical data regarding specialized enterprises for people with disabilities, as they are registered at a special register of the Agency for People with Disabilities. As of August 2015, 281 specialized enterprises and cooperatives of people with disabilities were present in the Register of the Disabled Persons, employing 3,364 people with disabilities. All of them are SMEs in size.

The data shows that the different types of cooperatives for work integration of people with disabilities are still predominant forms for social entrepreneurship in Bulgaria. Cooperatives are the oldest and traditional form of social enterprises. In the same time, social enterprises are increasingly being set up by associations and foundations in recent years.

The Economic and Social Council (ESC 2013) reports that the main field of activity of Bulgarian social enterprises is provision of social and educational services, including employment of people with disabilities, provision of assistance in finding a suitable position and going back to work, encouragement of self-employment and entrepreneurship, provision of social and health care services, education and life-long learning, etc. Production and trade are less developed. Specialized enterprises and cooperatives are engaged in provision of commercial services such as utilities, transport, web advertising and design, publishing and advertising. Manufacturing companies make clothes, food (bread, honey), carpentry, herbal cosmetics, souvenirs, decorations, greeting cards, ventilation and air-conditioning filter installations, filters for clean premises, HEPA-filters, etc.

Obviously the activities of Bulgarian social enterprises are usually in areas not particularly attractive to the business, which implies lower profits, slower returns on investments and difficult sustainability.

The main target groups served by social enterprises in Bulgaria are elderly people, young people and children, people with disabilities, long-term unemployed people and marginalized groups in society such as ethnic minorities.

According to the data presented, it seems that the social sector in Bulgaria is well developed, but only in quantitative terms. In addition, the social enterprises have achieved significant results in terms of creating employment and provision of social services to vulnerable groups of society. However, it is unclear what part of the produced social value is the result from sustainable initiatives and organizations which are more compliant to the concept of social entrepreneurship. Also, the available information does not make it possible to determine the effectiveness of the social sector or the extent to which the invested financial funds contributed to achieved social impact.

According to social stakeholder and experts' opinions, the majority of NPLEs rely on external funding through donations or funds attracted from foreign foundations and European programmes. They do not have their own revenues as a result of well-organized and innovative business activities. This outlines an unfavourable picture.

Many of the organizations could not survive without or with limited external support and funding.

Still occasional and rare are the cases of social enterprises that manage to develop innovative business models, offer products and services that have a good market acceptance and thus achieve financial independence.

As a positive trend over the past few years can be highlighted the growing number of implemented socially and community-oriented initiatives. Usually, they are organized and realized by proactive young people, who possess the main features of the social entrepreneur. Usually, they are young, well-educated, often occupying managerial position and have significant professional experience. Driven by strong motivation, they apply original approaches, attract followers and volunteer resources in order to implement bold causes. Good example is the organization of sports tournaments that cover their expenses through donations and voluntary work and generate revenues through participants' fees. The whole earnings are directed to patients needing expensive medical care.

Such kind of initiatives often manages to attract the attention of the society, to generate strong public response and even to change public attitudes and perceptions. However, these examples often remain out of the statistics because they are not always implemented in the form of any formal organization. With proper support, they can become the main source of powerful social entrepreneurs and enterprises able to develop social entrepreneurship in difficult and severe environment.

2.6 Common Business Forms of Social Enterprises in Bulgaria

Social enterprises in Bulgaria[16] exist as commercial companies, cooperatives and non-profit legal entities. All of them have socially significant results for vulnerable groups. The most popular form is NGOs.

There are three **main applied models**[17] of social enterprises in Bulgaria:

(1) Model for creating employment and developing the workforce—the economic logic of the business initiative is based on the possibility of creating jobs for disadvantaged people. The model is associated with so-called "Protected employment" where the social enterprise is an employer of people with disabilities.

---

[16] http://www.socialnet-bg.com/index.php/bg/social-ent-bottom—project "Establishing a network of social enterprises for implementing innovative marketing strategies", implemented by the Association of Southwest Municipalities in partnership with South Western Coalition, United Kingdom, and financed under the Operational Program "Human Resources Development"—available 07.2019.

[17] http://www.socialnet-bg.com/index.php/bg/social-ent-bottom—project "Establishing a network of social enterprises for implementing innovative marketing strategies", implemented by the Association of Southwest Municipalities in partnership with South Western Coalition, United Kingdom, and financed under the Operational Program "Human Resources Development"—available 07.2019.

(2) An entrepreneurial model where the social enterprise is a mediator between disadvantaged people and the market. In this model in the form of occupational therapy, people with disabilities participate in the production of products for which the social enterprise provides distribution.

(3) Direct service model—This model is most directly related to social service providers. Here, the social enterprise provides social services against payment to external clients, and at the same time, it is a provider of social services for its members, as the payment is being made with a contract with the municipality or the state. It is important to note that under this model, a social enterprise develops the same services but targets different consumers and customers.

According to the registered social enterprises in Bulgaria, they operate mainly in the **following areas**[18]:

(1) **Production and trade**—Most social enterprises operate in production and trade activities, mostly cosmetics, souvenirs, household goods, clothing, food, etc. After realizing their production on the market, the generated earnings are reinvested in the economic activity.

(2) **Social services**—Under the Social Assistance Act, "social services" are activities that support and expand the ability of individuals to live independent life. They take place in specialized institutions or in the community. Social services are based on purposeful social work in support of individuals to carry out day-to-day activities, as well as their social inclusion and guaranteeing independent living.

(3) **Educational services**—Legislation in Bulgaria does not impose special rules on educational services provided by social enterprises but entitles non-profit organizations and commercial companies or cooperatives to register as schools and vocational training centres and to issue valid diplomas for education or acquired professional qualification. Social enterprises providing education services may hire persons from socially vulnerable groups as trainers or organize training for such persons. Fees for these trainings are the profits from this activity.

(4) **Health services**—In the provision of health services and consultations mainly non-profit organizations are involved. Most commonly, these services include blood pressure or blood glucose measurement, medical assistance, rehabilitation services, prophylactic examinations, psychiatric and sex advising, free AIDS testing, and more. They are usually provided together with social services.

Agriculture, eco- and rural tourism—One of the promising areas in which social enterprises can develop is agriculture and rural tourism. Similar businesses exist in many EU countries. Taking into consideration the natural and cultural assets of Bulgaria, the development of such activity is also a possibility. In addition to the

---

[18] https://socialenterprise.bg/resources-1/faq.html—available 07.2019.

production and sale of environmentally friendly agricultural products, social enterprises can also work in the field of rural tourism, production and trade of traditional
objects, etc. 7. Bulgarian examples of social entrepreneurship.

Some of the best examples of social enterprises in Bulgaria could be summarized
in the next points:

(1) **Social shops,**[19] **Varna, Bulgaria**—In 2013, the first Social Shop in Varna,
    located in the Palace of Culture and Sports started offering products made by
    people with disabilities from Workers Production Cooperative Rodina, as well
    as handmade souvenirs by blind people. Products that are available in the social
    store are hand-crafted by socially vulnerable groups. The initiative is part of the
    project "Social Shop—Live Heritage", which was implemented by "My City"
    Association with the financial support of the Municipality of Varna. Another
    Social Shop, financially supported by the Workshop for Civic Initiatives Foun-
    dation under project "Institutional Strengthening of the Public Donors Fund
    for Varna" is operating at 7 Dragoman Str. in which handmade souvenirs—
    ornaments, postcards and other articles made by disabled people are displayed,
    as well as unique jewellery made of people with mental difficulties, cards with
    interesting elements created by children deprived of parental care, many other
    jewellery, magnets and souvenirs made by the hands of people with special
    needs. This initiative, called the Dreamwork Workshop, will allow the social
    service centres in the city, as well as many people from socially vulnerable
    groups, to show their abilities through their craft products. The funds received
    in the donation box placed in the store will be used to purchase materials and
    support training in labour and art therapies in social service centres.
(2) **"Green" Laundry**[20]—**social enterprise for adults with mental problems,
    Sofia, Bulgaria** (Global Initiative in Psychiatry (GIP) Foundation)—The
    Laundry is a social enterprise founded in 2009 with the support of the
    MATRA—KAP programme. Since then, more than 20 people with mental
    problems have acquired work skills through the training program and work in
    the laundry. GIP also actively pays attention of employers to the myths asso-
    ciated with people with mental health problems. Work-based training helps
    people with severe mental illnesses develop work skills, learn how to adapt to
    work and keep their jobs.
(3) **The Social Teahouse**[21]—**jobs for young people who grew up in institutions,
    Varna, Bulgaria**—The Social Teahouse is a social enterprise set up in 2014

[19] https://www.dfbulgaria.org/2019/socialen-magazin-varna/ and http://www.moreto.net/novini.
php?n=222742—available 07.2019.
[20] www.gip-global.org and http://open-mind-project.eu/wp-content/uploads/2018/03/Open-
Mind_E-book_BG.pdf—E-book "50 Inspiring Examples of Social Entrepreneurship and Women
Entrepreneurs" prepared in the framework of Project No: 2016-1-BG01-KA203-023,754—available 07.2019.
[21] http://thesocialteahouse.bg/en/ and http://open-mind-project.eu/wp-content/uploads/2018/03/
Open-Mind_E-book_BG.pdf—E-book "50 Inspiring Examples of Social Entrepreneurship and
Women Entrepreneurs" prepared in the framework of Project No: 2016-1-BG01-KA203-023,754—
available 07.2019.

in Varna, which provides opportunities for disadvantaged young people who have grown up in institutions to practice social skills, start a job and build an independent life. The Teahouse proposes a three-year mentoring program based on three main stages:

- Mentoring program that helps young people develop social and communication skills, knowledge of their civil rights and duties, emotional intelligence.
- Practical training in the Teahouse where they acquire professional competences in customer service.
- First job, which helps young people have a chance to work and improve their quality of life.

The given examples explain the social business model that supports the development of economic initiatives undertaken by disadvantaged (socially and economically) families. Access to financial resources for such families is restricted as they are not eligible for loans/credits from financial institutions. The target group of the model mainly includes families who:

- do not have sufficient assets to guarantee a steady income;
- take the risk of doing their own business;
- want to become independent producers by acquiring ownership over resources for business activities;
- they may offer their own financial contribution for the acquisition of tangible assets;
- participate with their own labour input and make independent management decisions.

The main goal of the explained social business model is families to become independent economic units by turning accumulated assets into income-generating capital. This is achieved by enabling them to develop a sustainable business by owning tangible assets and acquiring skills to use them effectively. In long run, this increases their chances of access to the instruments offered by financial institutions and to EU business support and development programs. The model is made up of two main components—development of human potential and access to tangible assets. The first component develops skills for efficient use of resources, while the second helps families to accumulate assets. The two components are applied simultaneously.

To ensure development of human potential by introducing the social business model, it is necessary to organize and to support specialized expert assistance in three fields:

(1) specialized consultations/advising;
(2) specialized training;
(3) access to information.

Specialized advising (learning by doing) is the most active field used in the model. Through it, technological knowledge is formed and skills by solving specific practical problems. The specialized trainings are conducted in the form of thematically focused courses and seminars. This pursues longer-term goals related to acquaintance with new manufactures and technologies, methods and means of payment business development and management. Access to up-to-date information is provided through the distribution of specialized technological, economic, legal and legal publications. They are used to promote self-the broad extension of knowledge.

Access to tangible assets is provided through financial schemes. The funds are provided under condition to be returned/repaid and with own financial contribution to assisted families. There are several advantages to this approach.

- Firstly, the conditions under which families work approach the real market conditions in the country.
- Second, the risk is shared between the donor organization and the model participants. There are two main schemes: a scheme for fixed assets that is reused in the production process (land, machinery, buildings); and disposable short-term assets scheme (fertilizers, preparations, supplies). For scheme participants, periodic on-site consultations provide opportunities for continuous monitoring of their activities.

The main role in the model is played by the financial scheme for the acquisition of tangible fixed assets. It is realized with the following parameters:

(1)   funds initially provided by the families for their own contribution;
(2)   annual appreciation;
(3)   repayment period not exceeding 5 years;
(4)   the purchased fixed assets are used as a guarantee for reimbursement.

A condition for providing access to funds for the purchase of non-tangible assets requires the prior participation in the fixed assets scheme. The main features of the financial scheme for accessing current assets are: a minimum participation of at least 30%; annual appreciation; and repayment term—one production cycle, but not more than 1 year.

The scheme will only start if: (1) the family can guarantee the funds provided through its own tangible assets, or if it participates in the financial scheme for the purchase of tangible assets. In the second case, the maximum amount of aid provided is the value of the already paid share of tangible assets. The requirement for own financial contribution contributes to the proper choice of families and ensures the stability of financial schemes. Securing one's own participation indicates a willingness to take risks in the production activity. Accrual of annual appreciation is aimed at preserving financial resources from inflationary processes, approaching the requirements of the credit market and possibly partial or full maintenance of the model. It is desirable to bring the price closer to the market interest rate or at least to the percentage of similar business support programs implemented in a normal market environment.

The model integrates two types of support—training and financial, aimed at achieving a comprehensive and sustainable improvement in the business practices of assisted families. This requires the use of three types of organizational forms with specific functions and tasks:

- for full implementation and management of the model;
- to develop human potential;
- to ensure access to tangible assets.

This business model of social entrepreneurship has been tested in agricultural production (Plovdiv Region) and in urban areas in different cities of the country for starting a small business (car services and repairing, blacksmith shops, hair salons, bakeries, pastry shops, tailoring workshops and others).

2.7 Conclusion

Social enterprises are accepted form of social and business activities in Bulgaria for more than 25 years. Nevertheless, there fully recognition by the Bulgarian law and authorities is not finished yet.

The main needs of the existence of such type of social entrepreneurship is accepted to be part of social incentives of the social market economy across Europe and EU Member States. As there a huge difference in practices in that field, the EC has accepted different strategic documents harmonising these practices. So, the Bulgarian law recognizes the definitions of social enterprises, social entrepreneurship and social entrepreneurs given by the European Social Business Initiative.

Although the application of social enterprise model is used from 1990s, the real boost of social enterprises is found after 2014 with acceptance of **Bulgarian Action Plan for Social Economy**. They are fully based on the **Bulgarian National Concept for Social Economy** from 2011.

The main sectors that are covered by the social enterprises in Bulgaria are: **Production and trade**; **Social Services**; **Educational services**; **Health services** and **Agriculture, eco- and rural-tourism**.

Although there are a lot of good examples of social enterprises in Bulgaria after 2014, they are based on the social business model that supports the development of economic initiatives undertaken by disadvantaged (socially and economically) families. The different examples cover three **main applied models**:

(1) creating employment and developing the workforce;
(2) social enterprise is a mediator between disadvantaged people and the market; and
(3) direct Service Model.

Some of the recommendations of the GECES (2016) for development social economy and social enterprises across EU Member States are fully recommended for the Bulgaria:

- to promote a culture of policy co-creation with social enterprises and their representative organizations;

- to promote participation of social enterprises in different financial schemes as a part of investment and capacity building funding programmes to help social enterprises;
- to enabling National public financial for raising the quality of (newly) established social enterprises;
- to launching national programmes for training social entrepreneurs on how to apply state aid for social enterprises.

References

Austin JE, Seitanidi MM (2012) Collaborative value creation: a review of partnering between nonprofits and businesses: part I. Value creation spectrum and collaboration stages. Nonprofit Voluntary Sect Quart 41(5):726–758

Barendsen L, Gardner (2004) Is the social entrepreneur a new type of leader? Leader to Leader, 34(Fall), October 2004, pp 43–50

Bacq S, Janssen F (2011) The Multiple Faces of Social Entrepreneurship: A Review of Definitional Issues Based on Geographical and Thematic Criteria. Entrepreneurship and Regional Development 23(5):373–403. https://doi.org/10.1080/08985626.2011.577242

Bornstein D (2004) How to change the world: Social entrepreneurs and the power of new ideas. New York: Oxford University Press. ISBN: 0195138058 9780195138054; (OCoLC)607759498

Bornstein D, Davis S (2010) Social Entrepreneurship: What Everyone Needs to Know New York: Oxford University Press; ISBN-10: 0195396332; ISBN-13: 978-0195396331

Carvalho JMS (2016) Social innovation and entrepreneurship: the case of Porto Region. In: Cagica LC (ed) Handbook of research on entrepreneurial success and its impact on regional development, 2 vols. Hershey, USA, IGI Global, pp 542–576

Carvalho JMS, Jonker J (2015, in press) Creating a balanced value proposition exploring the advanced business creation model. J Appl Manage Entrepreneurship 20(2)

Chatterjee S (2013) Simple rules for designing business models. Calif Manage Rev 55(2):97–124

Dees J (1998) The meaning of "social entrepreneurship." Comments and suggestions contributed from social Entrepreneurship Funders Working Group Center for the Advancement of Social Entrepreneurship. Fuqua School of Business: Duke University. http://faculty.fuqua.duke.edu/centers/case/files/dees-SE.pdf

Dees JG (1998) "Enterprising nonprofits", Harvard Business Review, Vol. 76, January-February, pp 55–67

Defourny J, Nyssens M (2010) Conceptions of social enterprise and social entrepreneurship in Europe and the United States: convergences and divergences. J Social Entrepreneurship 1(1):32–53

EC (2009, 2011, 2017) Social Enterprises. EC nternal Market, Industry, Entrepreneurship and SMEs. https://ec.europa.eu/growth/sectors/social-economy/enterprises_en

Economic and Social Committee (2013) Analysis of social enterprises and social entrepreneurship. http://www.esc.bg/documents/category/3 (in Bulgarian language). Accessed on 13 July 2019

European Commission (2011) Social business initiative creating a favourable climate for social enterprises, key stakeholders in the social economy and innovation Brussels, 25.10.2011 COM, 682 final

European Commission (2013a) Guide to social innovation. European Commission, Brussels. https://ec.europa.eu/eip/ageing/library/guide-social-innovation_en

European Commission (2013b) Social economy and social entrepreneurship. Social Europe guide vol 4. European Commission, Brussels. http://www.fngis.pt/wp-content/uploads/Economia-e-Empreendedorismo-Sociais-_-Guia-A-Europa-Social-_-Vol-4.pdf

European Commission (2014) A map of social enterprises and their eco-systems in Europe, Country report, Bulgaria. ICF Consulting Services, Limited Watling House, London

European Commission (2015) A map of social enterprises and their eco-systems in Europe: synthesis report. Publications Office of the European Union, Luxembourg

Gandhi and Raina (2018) Social entrepreneurship: the need, relevance, facets and constraints. J Glob Entrepreneurship Res 8:9

GECES (2016) Social enterprises and the social economy going forward, European Commission, Commission Expert Group on Social Entrepreneurship (GECES). http://ec.europa.eu/growth/sec tors/social-economy/enterprises/expert-groups_en

Khatiwada P Social entrepreneurship as an approach to community development, a case study of social entrepreneurship in Kathmandu, Nepal, Diaconia University of Applied Sciences

Leadbeater C (1997) The Rise of the Social Entrepreneur, London: Demos. ISBN 1 898309 53 1

Thake S, Zadek S (1997) Send in the social entrepreneurs [Electronic version]. New Statesman, 26(7339), 31

Thompson J (2002) The world of the social entrepreneur. September 2002, International Journal of Public Sector Management 15(5):412–431. https://doi.org/10.1108/09513550210435746

Zahra et al (2008) Globalization of Social Entrepreneurship Opportunities. June 2008, Strategic Entrepreneurship Journal 2(2):117–131. https://doi.org/10.1002/sej.43

Zott C, Amit R, Massa L (2011) The business model: recent developments and future research. J Manag 37(4):1019–1042

Chapter 3
Mapping the Intersection Between Corporate Governance and (Strategic) Management

Michail Nerantzidis, Evangelos Drimpetas, Anastasia Filiou, Ioannis Tampakoudis, and Stavros Apostolakis

Abstract The aim of this paper is twofold. Firstly, to illustrate the connection between corporate governance and (strategic) management and secondly to explore their inter-relationship. Our analysis indicates that although corporate governance and management are two separate fields, their structures/shapes are intersected at the strategic management level. Based on this argument, we develop a conceptual framework to illustrate the dynamic relationship among three pillars: corporate governance, management and strategic management. Our "mapping" approach explains that strategic decisions are shaped under complex, and non-linear processes. This perspective highlights the important need of future studies to apply multimethodologies to capture the contribution of boards in strategic decision making.

Keywords Corporate governance · Strategic management · Internal mechanisms · External mechanisms

3.1 Introduction

> Social history faces the twenty-first century as the Corporate Governance era, as opposed to the twentieth century that was seen as the era of management. Tricker (2009, p. 4)

M. Nerantzidis (✉) · E. Drimpetas
Department of Economics, Democritus University of Thrace, Komotini, Greece
e-mail: nerantzidismike@yahoo.gr

A. Filiou
Department of Accounting and Finance, Athens University of Economics and Business, Athens, Greece

I. Tampakoudis
Department of Business Administration, University of Macedonia, Thessaloniki, Greece
e-mail: tampakoudis@uom.edu.gr

S. Apostolakis
Department of Tourist Enterprises, Technological Educational Institution of Western Greece, Patras, Greece
e-mail: airapo@yahoo.gr

The purpose of any organization is to create value, which is to provide earnings to entrepreneurs, compensation to employees and rewards to clients and society (Lepak et al. 2007, p. 185; Post et al. 2002). This implies that the dominant paradigm today, both in corporate governance (hereafter CG) and in management is profit maximization in a transparent and ethical manner. To put it differently, regardless of how someone may see organization, i.e., under the lenses of shareholder or stakeholder model, good governance adds value by improving the performance of the organization through more efficient management and strategy (i.e., the long-term direction of an organization).

However, what should be mentioned is that CG and management are, in essence, separate fields but this doesn't mean that their boundaries are hard and fast (IEG World Bank 2007). Consequently, the aim of this paper is to highlight the intersection between CG and management, which is strategic management, and to illustrate their inter-relationship.

In practice, we firstly combine the governance and management pyramid and we elevate the role of boardroom as a mean to "manage" strategy in action. This helps us to answer the widespread question of who directs and affects strategy. Then, we develop an analytic framework of how board impact strategic decisions through the various CG systems. To do so, we present the dynamics of internal and external mechanisms and how these two interact and impact on the board involvement in strategy. This leads us to the conclusion that CG affects strategic management through the interaction of these mechanisms and strategic management influence CG through the ability of managers to affect the firm's ownership structure.

The rest of the paper is organized as follows. Section 3.2 defines the concept of CG. Section 3.3 describes the separate role of CG and management and presents their intersection, which lies into the field of strategic management. Section 3.4 discusses the dynamic relationship between CG and strategic management. Section 3.5 provides concluding remarks.

3.2 Defining the Concept of Corporate Governance

CG is a quite new concept and came into the spotlight in the 1970s when various business scandals took place (e.g., Enron, Tyco, Adelphia, WorldCom, Xerox, etc.). However, CG issues are not new. They date back to the eighteenth century when the "corporate" entity as a form of business activity was emerging, and the ownership of an enterprise was separated from management (Goergen 2012, p. 7; Tricker 2009, p. 8).

Thus, the need for CG results from the problems arising from the separation of ownership and control (Berle and Means 1932). This illustrates the conflict of interest between those making decisions and those who own the company, the so-called principal-agent model of Jensen and Meckling (1976). This model relies on the assumption that, as companies grow, ownership eventually separates from control and the company is run by "professional" managers[1] who may have little or no equity ownership (Goergen 2012, p. 13). Therefore, there is a need to ensure that the decisions which managers make will serve the shareholders' interests instead of their own (Fama and Jensen 1983; Shen and Gentry 2012), since as Adam Smith (1776) characteristically mention, the managers of a business are not able to manage the money of others with the same willingness (*"The directors of such companies, however, being the managers rather of other people's money than of their own, it cannot well be expected that they should watch over it with the same anxious vigilance which the partners in a private copartnery frequently watch over their own"*, Smith 2009, p. 439).

Therefore, in order to reduce this additional cost that the separation causes to shareholders, it is proposed to implement the appropriate control mechanisms (for more, see Denis and McConnell 2003), contributing to the creation of a strong CG system.[2] More generally, there is a growing awareness of shareholders in promoting international best practices[3] as a key factor in enhancing the CG system, as well as the efficiency of financial market.[4]

However, although CG has become central issue in the running and regulating enterprises, it still lacks a generally accepted definition. In particular, as Goergen (2012, p. 4) refers this may be explained by the fact that most definitions are based on the role that each corporation should have in society; a quite vague issue since this objective(s) depend(s) on the institutional framework of each country. Or, to put it another way: there is a dilemma in corporate objective between the maximization of shareholder's or stakeholder's welfare (Staikouras 2006, p. 1138).

Brickley and Zimmerman (2010) mention that there is a myth that a common definition of CG exist. They acknowledge that many textbooks do not define CG explicitly. Practically speaking, while some researchers argue that the role of governance is shareholders' wealth maximization, others take a broader perspective. To shed light on this debate, Nerantzidis et al. (2012) applied a content analysis to a sample of 22 definitions, dated from 1992 to 2010 to better understand the CG term. Their analysis revealed that there is no consensus on how CG is defined. This is based on the different perspective that each researcher has regarding the firm's objective (for instance, some give more emphasis on the shareholder's dimension, while others on the stakeholder's dimension). As a more representative definition, they proposed that CG is the plethora of internal and external mechanisms that ensure a minimum fair value to shareholders and at the same time protect those who have a direct legitimate interest (Nerantzidis 2012). More generally, Larcker et al. (2007, p. 964) define the CG as *"the set of mechanisms that influence the decisions made by managers when there is separation of ownership and control"*. However, one of the most commonly used definitions is that of Shleifer and Vishny (1997, p. 737) according to which: *"Corporate governancedeals with the ways in which suppliers of finance to corporations assure themselves of getting a return on their investment"*.

In conclusion, CG, more as a practice than as a concept, does not have common features in its application throughout the world, as it consists of a set of rules that vary from one country to another, and this makes it difficult to form a general structure. Nevertheless, it is a general agreement that its purpose is the alignment of managers and shareholders' interests; a task that board is responsible for.

3.3 Separation of Corporate Governance and Management

It is well known that the genesis of management is preceded by that of CG, as the first coincides with the development of scientific management by Taylor (1911), while the latter is found in published text for the first time in the 1980s.[5] However, these two concepts are usually confused. It is therefore necessary to study their similarities and clarify the difference between the concepts of administration and management. In particular, management[6] refers to how the organizational goals are attained *"in an effective and efficient manner through planning, organizing, leading and controlling organizational resources"* (Daft 2006, p. 8). Accordingly, the administration (i.e., middle managers and first line managers) refers to all the actions that take place to execute or make a specific decision. As a result, management takes decisions, while the administration processes and executes them. We could, therefore, illustrate the hierarchy of individuals who contribute to the operation of a business, in the following way (pyramid of management) (Fig. 3.1).

On the first three levels, we can see the company's top managers [Chief Executive Officer (CEO), president, executive directors and top executive managers] who are generally responsible for setting organizational goals, defining strategies and making decisions. On the next level, we can see the middle managers (e.g., business unit head, department manager) who apply the defined strategies and policies. Finally, we have the first line managers (e.g., supervisor, line manager, office manager) who are accountable for the production line as well as for the nonmanagement employees

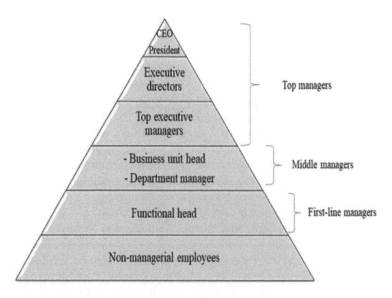

Fig. 3.1 The management pyramid. *Source* Adapted from Bonoma and Lawler (1989) and Daft (2006, p. 15)

(Daft 2006, pp. 15–17). Subsequently, first line managers acting as a link between top/middle managers and nonmanagement employees.

At this point, one wonders, "How do these concepts relate to CG?" And if there is any connection, "how this relationship is interpreted?". Taking into consideration that CG defines the relationship among the three pillars of the firm (i.e., shareholders, managers and board of directors), the common section of the concepts of management and CG is at the level of "strategic management" and could be illustrated as in Fig. 3.2.

This means that top managers define the strategic decisions while the board of directors assess and approve, the main strategies and projects of the firm (Monks and Minow 2004, p. 200). In other words, we may say that boards can add to the firm's strategic plan (e.g., Brauer and Schmidt 2008, p. 649; Goold and Campbell 1990; Rindova 1999; Zahra 1990) or to put it differently, they are having the potential role to change its strategy (Goleden and Zajac 2001, p. 1087). However, the concepts of management and CG should not be confused and perceived as the same because they have a different objective.[7] As Tricker (2009, p. 36) says management runs the firm while the board assures the quality of decision making. Consequently, boards are the

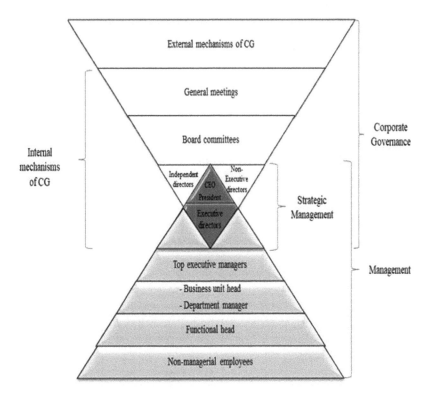

Fig. 3.2 Distinction between management and CG. *Source* Adapted from Tricker (2009, p. 36) and Lazarides and Drimpetas (2011, p. 108)

overlap between a few influential people who runs the company and an enormous passive group of people (i.e., shareholders) who expects to see a well-run firm (Monks and Minow 2004, p. 195).

3.4 The Dynamic Relationship Between Corporate Governance and Strategic Management

The function of CG in any company is generally affected by internal and external mechanisms which induce managers to make decisions that are consistent with the maximization of firm value (Denis and McConnell 2003, p. 2). This means that these mechanisms could be either implemented on the initiative of the firm or enforced "externally" by society and government or both (Karamanis 2008, p. 127). In fact, this constitutes the framework of the CG which includes: (i) the board of directors (i.e., board composition and executive compensation), (ii) the ownership structure, (iii) the internal audit, (iv) the board committees, (v) the market for mergers and acquisitions, (vi) the labor market, (vii) the market of goods and services and (viii) the legal system of each country and which aims at maximizing the wealth of shareholders and stakeholders (Agrawal and Knoeber 1996; Denis and McConnell 2003).

However, one may wonder: *Which is the purpose of these mechanisms?* According to the agency theory, it is the alignment of managers and shareholders' interests and the minimization of the separation cost between ownership and control. Consequently, these mechanisms (both internal and external) interact and affect strategic decisions (see Fig. 3.3), to ensure that managers will make decisions that serves on shareholders' interests. Therefore, the first direction of the relationship between CG and strategic management is the way that the former affects the later through the interaction between the internal and external mechanisms of CG.

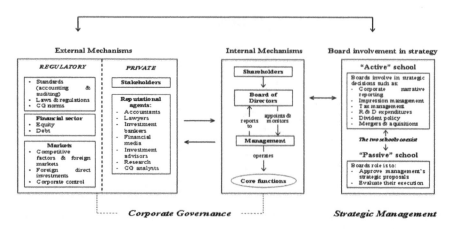

Fig. 3.3 The dynamic relationship between CG and strategic management. *Source* Inspired from Muir and Saba (1995)

Consider, for instance, the labor market in any country. Since competitiveness is a crucial factor for the efficiency of CG system, the more intense it is the better managers are selected. On the same direction Hoskisson et al. (2004) argue that external mechanisms (e.g., the market for mergers and acquisitions and the market of goods and services) complements the market-based system. Indeed, John and Senbet (1998) indicate that external devices for managerial control substitutes internal mechanisms for control. Also Cremers and Nair (2005, p. 2859) examine how the market for mergers and acquisitions interacts with shareholder activism (internal governance) and they provide evidence that the complementarity effect is confirmed for low leveraged and small firms. Needless to say that there is some evidence that substitution effects between alternative internal CG mechanism also exist (for more, see Rediker and Seth, 1995). This means that a level of any mechanism could be influenced by the level of other mechanisms (Rediker and Seth 1995) (see, Fig. 3.3).

The main argument in strategic management literature is that top managers have a significant role in strategy development process (Westphal and Fredrickson 2001, p. 1113). This indicates that board members define the upcoming corporate strategies. However, as McNulty and Pettigrew (1999) argue, although executives should participate in strategy formulation, there is a lack of primary data about their active role in practice. In other words, boar members' contribution to strategy is considered as highly important but our perception on this role fulfillment is limited (Hendry et al. 2010, p. 33). Nevertheless, some recent studies propose that boards can indeed have some influence over strategic decisions. Particularly, recent empirical research that use agency lens on boards have examined how boards may influence strategic decisions when agency costs are high and directors have the intention to protect shareholders, (Bergh 1995; Gibbs 1993; Johnson et al. 1993; Westphal and Fredrickson 2001, p. 1114).

Golden and Zajac (2001, p. 1087) indicate that there are two distinct perspectives regarding the role that board plays in strategy formulation, the "passive perspective" and the "active perspective". The "passive perspective" considers board members as "rubber stamps" (Herman 1981) or, as "mechanisms" of top managers (Pfeffer 1972, p. 219), who have no effect on boards' strategy or changes in that strategy. According to this perspective, their role is to approve all the managers plans based on the law requirements and to evaluate their achievement according to the data provided by management (Hendry et al. 2010, p. 34). On the other hand, the "active perspective" views boards members as free thinkers who have a vital role in formulating the strategic plan and running of the business (Brauer and Schmidt 2008, p. 650; Davis and Thompson 1994; Finkelstein and Hambrick 1996; Walsh and Seward 1990). Consequently, this active perspective implies that board and management collaborate in strategy formulation, then management performs this strategy and finally both of them assess the results. This reveals that board's involvement relies on contextual components as for example the internal and external mechanisms of CG (Hendry et al. 2010, p. 34). However, we should consider the dynamic nature of the organizations, and therefore, we believe that there is a reconciliation between the two "schools". In particular, as Carter and Lorsch (2004) characteristically mention *"A board cannot be a pilot (active) without also being a watchdog (passive) ...*"; an argumentation which has also been acknowledged by Hendry et al. (2010).

In practice, McNulty and Pettigrew (1999) developed a conceptual model to show that non-executive directors (i.e., outside—or else—part-time board members) influence the processes of strategic choices, as well as change and control these by forming the content of the organization strategy (i.e., shaping the ideas, methodologies and processes). They report that their involvement in strategy relies on several components such as CG norms, the firm's history/environment and the "communication" of the directors in the board meetings. On the same direction, Westphal (1999) found that boards can affect strategic preference through advice and counsel interactions with CEOs. Fiegener (2005, p. 627) document that board's participation in strategic decision exists when the company is large, the board has significant proportion of outside directors or the power of CEO is low. Similarly, Ruigrok et al. (2006, p. 1201) report that board participation in strategic decision is lower when boards are highly interlocked. In addition, they present weaker evidence that this involvement is lower when there is a combination of roles of CEO and chair. Pugliese et al. (2009), using content analysis methodology of 150 articles, found that studies on boards and strategy have developed from normative and structural viewpoint to behavioral and cognitive one. This highlights the perspective that boards are decision-making groups and thus their internal and external mechanisms should be better understood.

Aside of the theoretical argumentation, in practice the board of directors impact on a wide spectrum of strategic decisions such as corporate narrative reporting, impression management, tax management, R&D expenditures, dividend policy, mergers, acquisitions, etc. To begin with, Allen and Caillouet (1994) argue that individual and companies use common strategies to defend their image, with equivalent outcomes (Elsbach and Sutton 1992). This implies that companies use strategic management impressions to enhance their social attractiveness. For instance, in corporate reporting (i.e., accounting literature), impression management is considered as a mean "*to control and manipulate the impression conveyed to users of accounting information*" (Clatworthy and Jones 2001, p. 311). Consequently, it is assumed that managers use corporate reports as impression management tools to "*strategically ... manipulate the perceptions and decisions of stakeholders*" (Yuthas et al. 2002, p. 142). This illustrates that managers as well as boards are *responsively* participating in these processes (Merkl-Davies and Brennan 2007). To put it differently, it is assumed that these parties strategically prefer "*the information to display and present that information in a manner that is intended to distort readers' perceptions of corporate achievements*" (Godfrey et al. 2003, p. 96).

Minnick and Noga (2010) hypothesize that directors and CEOs play a vital role in the selection of tax management[8] strategy. Under this view, CG could constitute a significant role in long-run tax management strategy of an organization. Indeed, their results confirm the hypothesis, meaning that firms that adopt a different CG model have the tendency to choose different tax management strategies. More specifically, they found that (i) the most significant factor of tax management is the pay-performance-sensitivity (PPS) for both directors and CEOs, (ii) governance is the major factor of the company that leads its tax management strategy. On the same direction, Lanis and Richardson (2011) report that as the proportion of outside members on the board increases, then the likelihood of tax aggressiveness reduces. This evident is largely consistent with the view that board composition affects tax strategy (Erle 2008).

The R&D expenditures are also strategic decisions and they are important for the competitiveness of organizations (especially for technologically intensive industries). Kor (2006a, b, p. 1081) indicates that both the composition of top managers and board directly affect and adds-on R&D strategies. She also documents that a healthy conversation between management and board team is crucial for their success. Other evidence indicates that the percentage of independent directors is positively related to R&D investment (see, Dong and Gou 2010, p. 180). Patel and Chrisman (2014) find that family firms have the tendency to choose different R&D investments than non-family firms as a mean to protect socioemotional wealth. They point out that family firms reconcile their economic and noneconomic purposes by making investments in exploitative R&D projects which move into more credible sales levels.

Brickley and Zimmerman (2010, p. 239) highlight that boards are also important in formulating and ratifying dividend payouts. They suggest that boards need to evaluate the dividend policy (i.e., if it is too high or too low) by understanding the firm's investment choices, as well as managers' motives. Abor and Fiabor (2013) investigate the relationship between CG and dividend payout policy in sub-Saharan Africa. They found a positive relationship between independent board members and dividend payout ratio in Kenya. In addition, they reported that institutional shareholders can influence the high-dividend payouts both in South Africa and Kenya. Chen et al. (2017) presented positive relationship between the proportion of female directors and dividend payouts. In addition, they found that boards with female directors have the tendency to use dividend as a monitoring mechanism when CG is weak.

Boards can also have an important strategic role on potential of merger and acquisition (M&A) success (Armout 2002). Piana and Hayes (2005) assert that top managers and directors have the tendency to use M&A as a mean to enhance the organizational scale, expand the scope and improve the productivity. McDonald et al. (2008) investigate if outside directors with prior experience on M&As have a positive impact on the firm's performance. Their empirical evidence supports the hypothesis that experience, and knowledge are positively related to the performance of a focal firm's acquisitions. In addition, they reported that outside director knowledge may provide more benefits when the board and the management of the focal firm are not related. Also, Redor (2016) using literature by different disciplines highlights that in the field of M&As the effect of board characteristics on shareholder's wealth is distinctive to each company.

Finally, we should also explain the relationship between CG and strategic management according to which the latter affect and formulate CG mechanisms. In particular, as Shen and Gentry (2012) outline, this influence stems from the effect of strategic management in firm's ownership structure, which then impacts on CG. On the one hand, according to agency theory, top managers have the tendency to switch strategy and also the ownership structure of the company (Bethel and Liebeskind 1993; Brunninge et al. 2007), since ownership dispersion is an important strategic decision.

This means that managers can influence investors' decisions to buy or sell their stocks through their strategic decisions and therefore changes in corporate strategy may have impact on the firm's composition (Shen and Gentry 2012).[9] On the other hand, ownership structure affects CG, since it is an important source of motivation for managers, boards, and outside shareholders (Chen 2001; Milgrom and Roberts 1992). Particularly, when the ownership share is widely dispersed, shareholders have practically no incentives to spend money to monitor and influence managers (Denis and McConnell 2003). This means that diffuse ownership leads to weak monitor of the managers' decisions (Hitt et al. 2007), since as the size and the ownership stake increases the access to the CEO and the board is higher[10] and the influence over governance changes is stronger (Shen and Gentry 2012). Consequently, the actual pattern of ownership has an influence on CG, since ownership concentration increases the active role of the shareholders, who are interested in adopting more effective CG mechanisms to control managerial decisions (Hitt et al. 2007; Tricker 2009).

3.5 Conclusion

On this paper, we try to bring together CG and (strategic) management to illustrate their connections. Combining their different structures/shapes, we highlight their intersection (i.e., strategic management) and we elevate the role of boardroom as a mean to "manage" strategy in action.

Based on this argument, we develop a conceptual framework to present the dynamic relationship among three pillars: CG, management and strategic management. We bring together the various CG mechanisms (i.e., internal and external mechanisms) and we describe how board impact strategic decisions through the various CG systems. Our analysis indicates that researchers may find new ways of looking CG to really understand the impact of the role of boards in strategic decision making. This will help us to move to the next level and find meaningful solutions about what are the prerequisites for an effective strategy. We hope that this conceptual framework will contribute to this direction.

Notes

1. However, there are also some benefits from the separation of ownership and control, as highlighted by Denis and McConnell (2003, p. 1) who mention that owners do not necessarily combine expertise and knowledge.
2. Weimer and Pape (1999) in their study "A Taxonomy of Systems of Corporate Governance" proposed the distinction of four types of CG systems based on eight characteristics.
3. International best practices (CG codes) are designed and implemented in a country, either to enhance the technical efficiency of a CG system or to address issues of institutional framework improvement (Aguilera and Cuervo-Cazurra 2004, p. 417).

4.   Inappropriate CG practices, combined with abusive market practices, lead to distortions in stock prices and inefficient allocation of productive assets of listed companies.
5.   The first appearance of CG in published text is determined in the 1980s, as Earl (1983) also states, while the first published CG code dates back to January 1978 by the Business Roundtable of the USA entitled "The Role and Composition of the Board of Directors of the Large Publicly Owned Corporation".
6.   It comes from the verb manage and has its root in the Latin word manus.
7.   For instance, some of the functions of the board of directors are: to select top managers and to provide advice, to determine management compensation and to approve the financial objectives (for more, see Monks and Mino 2004, p. 200).
8.   *"Tax management is defined as the ability to pay a low amount of taxes over a long period of time"* (Minnick and Noga 2010).
9.   This is explained by the fact that different investors have different risk preferences (Hoskisson et al. 2002), position toward CSR and investment strategies (Bushee 1998; Porter 1992). For more, see Shen and Gentry (2012).
10. We should note that the members of the firm's board are elected by the shareholders with the duty to act on their behalf and protect their interests by monitoring and controlling the firm's top managers (Hitt et al. 2007).

References

Abor J, Fiabor V (2013) Does corporate governance explain dividend policy in Sub-Saharan Africa? Int J Law Manage 55(3):201–225

Agrawal A, Knoeber ChR (1996) Firm performance and mechanisms to control agency problems between managers and shareholders. J Finan Quant Anal 31(3):377–397

Aguilera RV, Cuervo-Cazurra A (2004) Codes of good governance worldwide: what is the trigger? Organ Stud 25:415–443

Allen MW, Caillouet RH (1994) Legitimation endeavours: impression management strategies used by an organization in crisis. Commun Monogr 61(1):44–62

Armour E (2002) How boards can improve the odds of M&A success. Strat Leadership 30(2):13–20

Bergh DD (1995) Size and relatedness of units sold: an agency theory and resource-based perspective. Strat Manag J 16(3):221–239

Berle A, Means GC (1932) The modern corporation and private property. Transaction Publishers, New York

Bethel JE, Liebeskind J (1993) The effects of ownership structure on corporate restructuring. Strat Manag J 14(S1):15–31

Bonoma TV, Lawler JC (1989) Chutes and Ladders: Growing the General Manager. Sloan Management Review 30(3):27–37

Brauer M, Schmidt SL (2008) Defining the strategic role of boards and measuring boards' effectiveness in strategy implementation. Corporate Govern Int J Bus Soc 8(5):649–660

Brickley JA, Zimmerman JL (2010) Corporate governance myths: comments on Armstrong, Guay, and Weber. J Account Econ 50(2–3):235–245

Brunninge O, Nordqvist M, Wiklund J (2007) Corporate governance and strategic change in SMEs: the effects of ownership, board composition and top management teams. Small Bus Econ 29(3):295–308

Bushee BJ (1998) The influence of institutional investors on myopic R&D investment behavior. Account Rev 73(3):305–333

Carter CB, Lorsch JW (2004) Back to the drawing board: designing corporate boards for complex world. Harvard Business School Press, Boston, MA

Chen J (2001) Ownership structure as corporate governance mechanism: evidence from Chinese listed companies. Econ Plan 34(1):53–72

Chen J, Leung WS, Goergen M (2017) The impact of board gender composition on dividend payouts. J Corp Finan 43:86–105

Clatworthy M, Jones MJ (2001) The effect of thematic structure on the variability of annual report readability. Account Audit Account J 14(3):311–326

Cremers KJM, Nair VB (2005) Governance mechanisms and equity prices. J Finan 60(6):2859–2894

Daft RL (2006) The new era of management, Thomson South-Western, United Kingdom

Davis GF, Thompson TA (1994) A social movement perspective on corporate control. Adm Sci Q 39(1):141–173

Denis DK, McConnell JJ (2003) International corporate governance. J Finan Quant Anal 38(1):1–36

Dong J, Gou YN (2010) Corporate governance structure, managerial discretion and the R&D investment in China. Int Rev Econ Finan 19(2):180–188

Earl MJ (1983) Perspectives on management: a multidisciplinary analysis. Oxford University Press, Oxford

Elsbach KD, Sutton RI (1992) Acquiring organizational legitimacy through illegitimate actions: a marriage of institutional and impression management theories. Acad Manag J 35(4):699–738

Erle B (2008) Tax risk management and board responsibility. In: Tax and Corporate Governance, pp 205–220

Fama EF, Jensen MC (1983) Separation of ownership and control. J Law Econ 26(2):301–325

Fiegener MK (2005) Determinants of board participation in the strategic decisions of small corporations. Entrep Theory Pract 29(5):627–650

Finkelstein S, Hambrick DC (1996) Strategic leadership: top executives and their effects on organizations. West Publishing Co., Minneapolis, St. Paul, MN

Gibbs PA (1993) Determinants of corporate restructuring: the relative importance of corporate governance takeover threat, and free cash flow. Strat Manag J 14(S1):51–68

Godfrey J, Mather P, Ramsay A (2003) Earnings and impression management in financial reports: the case of CEO changes. Abacus 39(1):95–123

Goergen M (2012) International corporate governance. Pearson Education Limited, Essex, England

Golden B, Zajac E (2001) When will boards influence strategy? Inclination x power = strategic change. Strat Manag J 22(12):1087–1111

Goold M, Campbell A (1990) Brief case: non-executive directors' role in strategy. Long Range Plan 23(6):118–119

Hendry KP, Kiel GC, Nicholson G (2010) How boards strategise: a strategy as practice view. Long Range Plan 43(1):33–56

Herman E (1981) Corporate control, corporate power. Cambridge University Press, New York

Hitt MA, Ireland RD, Hoskisson RE (2007) Strategic management: competitiveness and globalization (concepts and cases), 7th edn. Thomson South-Western Publishing Co., Canada

Hoskisson RE, Hitt MA, Johnson RA, Grossman W (2002) Conflicting voices: the effects of institutional ownership heterogeneity and internal governance on corporate innovation strategies. Acad Manag J 45(4):697–716

Hoskisson RE, Yiu D, Kim H (2004) Corporate governance systems: effects of capital and labor market congruency on corporate innovation and global competitiveness. J High Technol Manage Res 15(2):293–315

Independent Evaluation Group (IEG)—World Bank (2007) Sourcebook for evaluating global and regional partnership programs. http://www.oecd.org/development/evaluation/dcdndep/379 81082.pdf. Accessed 10 Jan 2018

Jensen MC, Meckling W (1976) Theory of firm: managerial behavior, agency costs and ownership structure. J Financ Econ 3(4):305–360

John K, Senbet LW (1998) Corporate governance and board effectiveness. J Bank Finan 22(4):371–403

Johnson RA, Hoskisson RE, Hitt MA (1993) Board of director involvement in restructuring: the effects of board versus managerial controls and characteristics. Strat Manag J 14(S1):33–50

Karamanis K (2008) Modern audit: Theory and practice in line with the International Auditing Standards (in Greek). Athens University of Economics and Business Publications, Athens, Greece

Kor (2006) Direct and interaction effects of top management team and board compositions on R&D investment strategy

Kor YY (2006) Direct and interaction effects of top management team and board compositions on R&D investment strategy. Strat Manag J 27(11):1081–1099

La Piana D, Hayes M (2005) M&A in the nonprofit sector: managing merger negotiations and integration. Strat Leadership 33(2):11–16

Lanis R, Richardson G (2011) The effect of board of director composition on corporate tax aggressiveness. J Account Publ Pol 30(1):50–70

Larcker D, Richardson S, Tuna I (2007) Corporate governance, accounting outcomes, and organizational performance. Account Rev 82(4):963–1008

Lazarides T, Drimpetas E (2011) Evaluating corporate governance and identifying its formulating factors: the case of Greece. Corporate Governance: Int J Bus Soc 11(2):136–148. https://doi.org/10.1108/14720701111121010

Lepak DP, Smith KG, Taylor MS (2007) Value creation and value capture: a multilevel perspective. Acad Manag Rev 32(1):180–194

McDonald ML, Westphal JD, Graebner ME (2008) What do they know? The effects of outside director acquisition experience on firm acquisition performance. Strateg Manag J 29(11):1155–1177

McNulty T, Pettigrew A (1999) Strategists on the board. Organ Stud 20(1):47–74

Merkl-Davies DM, Brennan NM (2007) Discretionary disclosure strategies in corporate narratives: incremental information or impression management? J Account Lit 27:116–196

Milgrom P, Roberts J (1992) Economics, management and organisation. Prentice Hall, Englewood Cliffs, NJ

Minnick K, Noga T (2010) Do corporate governance characteristics influence tax management? J Corp Finan 16(5):703–718

Monks RAG, Minow N (2004) Corporate governance, 3rd edn. Blackwell Publishing, United Kingdom

Muir R, Saba JP (1995) Improving state enterprise performance: the role of internal and external incentives. http://documents.worldbank.org/curated/en/489021468186871150/Improving-state-enterprise-performance-the-role-of-internal-and-external-incentives. Accessed 12 Jan 2018

Nerantzidis M (2012) Delphic hierarchy process (DHP): a methodology for the resolution of the problems of the evaluation of corporate governance quality. http://www.iacmaster.it/iacgconfe rence2012/wp-content/uploads/2012/04/Nerantzidis-Michail.pdf. Accessed 12 Jan 2018

Nerantzidis M, Filos J, Lazarides TG (2012) The puzzle of corporate governance definition(s): a content analysis. Corporate Board Role Duties Comp 8(2):13–23

Patel PC, Chrisman JJ (2014) Risk abatement as a strategy for R&D investments in family firms. Strat Manag J 35(4):617–627

Pfeffer J (1972) Size and composition of corporate boards of directors: the organization and its environment. Adm Sci Q 17:218–228

Porter M (1992) Capital choices: Changing the way America invests in industry. Council on Competitiveness, Harvard Business School, Boston, MA

Post J, Preston L, Sachs S (2002) Redefining the corporation: stakeholder management and organizational wealth. Stanford University Press, Stanford CA

Pugliese A, Bezemer PJ, Zattoni A, Huse M, Van den Bosch FA, Volberda HW (2009) Boards of directors' contribution to strategy: a literature review and research agenda. Corp Govern Int Rev 17(3):292–306

Rediker KJ, Seth A (1995) Boards of directors and substitution effects of alternative governance mechanisms. Strat Manag J 16(2):85–99

Redor E (2016) Board attributes and shareholder wealth in mergers and acquisitions: a survey of the literature. J Manage Govern 20(4):789–821

Rindova VP (1999) What corporate boards have to do with strategy: a cognitive perspective. J Manage Stud 36(7):953–975

Ruigrok W, Peck SI, Keller H (2006) Board characteristics and involvement in strategic decision making: evidence from Swiss companies. J Manage Stud 43(5):1201–1226

Shen W, Gentry RJ (2012) A cyclical view of the relationship between corporate governance and strategic management. J Manage Govern 18(4):959–973

Shleifer A, Vishny RW (1997) A survey of corporate governance. J Finan 52(2):737–783

Smith A (1776) The wealth of nations. W. Strahan and T. Cadell, UK

Smith A (2009) An inquiry into the nature and causes of the wealth of nation. Digireads.com Publishing, USA

Staikouras PK (2006) Corporate (Mis)governance? A critical and comparative analysis for the case of Greece. European Bus Law Rev 17(4):1129–1167

Taylor FW (1911) The principles of scientific management. Harper and Brothers, New York

Tricker B (2009) Corporate governance: principles, policies and practices. Oxford University Press, New York, USA

Walsh JP, Seward JK (1990) On the efficiency of internal and external control mechanisms. Acad Manag Rev 15(3):421–458

Weimer J, Pape JC (1999) A taxonomy of systems of corporate governance. Corp Govern Int Rev 7(2):152–166

Westphal JD (1999) Collaboration in the boardroom: the consequences of social ties in the CEO/board relationship. Acad Manag J 42(1):7–24

Westphal JD, Fredrickson JW (2001) Who directs strategic change? Director experience, the selection of new CEOs, and change in corporate strategy. Strat Manag J 22(12):1113–1137

Yuthas K, Rogers R, Dillard JF (2002) Communicative action and corporate annual reports. J Bus Ethics 41(1–2):141–157

Zahra SA (1990) Increasing the board's involvement in strategy. Long Range Plan 23(6):109–117

Part II
New Approaches in Corporate Governance and New Technologies

Chapter 4
A Pathway to Sustainable Health During COVID-19 Pandemic: Digital Health Services

Hilal Özen and Bahar Yaşin

Abstract In this paper, we aim to examine the effect of health information orientation on attitudes toward using digital health services and explore the mediating role of e-health literacy in this relationship. We also tested the impact of attitudes toward using digital health services on digital health service use intention. We collected data through an online survey method. A total of 520 respondents participated, and data were analyzed using structural equation modeling. The results showed that people who are health information oriented and capable of finding and utilizing e-health information have positive attitudes and intention toward using digital health service. Variables in the model explain 60% of the variance in digital health service use intention. This study confirmed the partial mediating role of e-health literacy on the relationship between health information orientation and attitudes toward using digital health services. Future research is needed to explore whether these relationships are confirmed in a specific health context. Furthermore, comparing the digital health service usage attitudes and intentions of people who have and do not have chronic illnesses can also be insightful. Cross-cultural comparisons may also add to the knowledge related to the adoption of digital health services. We conducted this study during the early phase of COVID-19 pandemic in Turkey and explored the digital health service use intention partly within the Theory of Reasoned Action framework. We have also tried to contribute to Sustainable Development Goals with our research results.

Keywords Attitude toward using digital health service · Digital health service use intention · e-health · e-health literacy · Health information orientation · Structural equation modeling · Sustainability · Turkey

H. Özen
Department of Business Administration, Faculty of Economics and Administrative Sciences, Trakya University, Edirne, Turkey
e-mail: hilalozen@trakya.edu.tr

B. Yaşin (✉)
Department of Marketing, School of Business, Istanbul University, Istanbul, Turkey
e-mail: bkarciga@istanbul.edu.tr

4.1 Introduction

Digital health service, mostly mentioned as telemedicine in the literature, is a convenient and 7/24 accessible system that allows the physicians to offer some healthcare services remotely with the help of a webcam-enabled media such as smartphones, tablets and personal computers. It is especially useful for diagnosing symptoms and taking preventive care actions.

The importance of providing health services digitally has become clear during the pandemic since many people with chronic diseases do prefer not to go in-person visits, even scheduled ones, in order to protect themselves from COVID-19, as a result, the probability of encountering serious health problems other than COVID-19 has arisen. Within this context, if the public healthcare system of a country and/or the private hospitals and clinics are able to provide health services digitally, it would be beneficial for the patients, healthcare professionals and society as it is a method that protects everyone from disease exposure. Digital health service is also consistent with social distance and self-quarantine measures. Physicians who must be in quarantine, but healthy can still provide their services remotely. It may help to reduce the number of patients visiting hospitals and to decrease workload of health professionals.

In Turkey, a few numbers of private hospitals, psychologists and dentists announced that they offer digital health services through their webpage, social media accounts, short message service (SMS) and e-mail during the pandemic. Unfortunately, public health institutions, where the most of the population get health services, could not offer it as an option.

In this unprecedented time of the COVID-19 pandemic, understanding how the potential customers of digital health service approach the issue is thought to be important and this led to the execution of this study. This study aims to answer following research questions:

RQ1: How is the consumers' attitudes toward using digital health service?
RQ2: What factors affect the consumers' attitudes toward using digital health service?
RQ3: Do consumers have an intention to use digital health service?

Digital health service is not a new but evolving concept since 1975 (Bashur et al. 1975). There are a number of studies in the literature related to digital health service, but most of these studies were published before the emergence of COVID-19 pandemic. In todays' context, studies examining digital health service from consumers' point of view are limited (Pappot et al. 2020). As Pappot et al. (2020) mentioned, one of the first studies after COVID-19 pandemic is a commentary and focuses on the benefits of digital health service for the general health system. The book chapter by George et al. (2020) discusses how digital health service can strengthen the healthcare system during the COVID-19 crisis. Khilnani et al. (2020) examined the issue from the perspective of social inequalities in the delivery and reach of digital healthcare during the COVID-19 pandemic. They reported that the digitally disadvantaged part of the population is less likely to use digital health services to meet their healthcare needs during the pandemic in the USA. The study of Cheng et al. (2021) examined the digital health service experience during the COVID-19 pandemic for the US population. Authors confirmed the empowering role of hospitable digital health service experience in reducing isolation and anxiety of patients. The study of Serrano et al. (2021) is also one of the few studies that examines digital health service from a consumers' point of view, but the data of this research were collected during October and November 2019 in Brazil, before the measures to cope with COVID-19 pandemic became apparent. In that study, authors utilized the UTAUT model to assess the digital health service acceptance for younger generations.

As seen, the number of studies published related to the digital health service that examines the issue from the consumers' perspective during the COVID-19 pandemic is limited, and they were mostly conducted in developed countries. One of these studies also incorporated variables from the UTAUT model as an antecedent of digital health service adoption.

The current study is designed in order to fill the gap of understanding consumers' use intention of digital health service in a developing country after the negative impacts and preventive measures of COVID-19 pandemic spread all over the world. In relation with the Theory of Reasoned Action, the variables that constitute the research model of the study are health information orientation, e-health (electronic health) literacy, attitudes toward using digital health service and digital health service use intention. The Theory of Reasoned Action (TRA) implies that a person's behavior is determined by their intention to perform the behavior and the intention is a function of a person's attitude toward the behavior and his/her subjective norms (Ajzen and Fishbein 1975). As there are only few private hospitals that offer digital health service in Turkey right now, this study focused only on attitudes and intentions, whereas health information orientation and e-health literacy were treated as the determinants of attitudes toward using digital health service. As using digital health service requires e-health literacy, the ability to cope with the challenges in finding, understanding and using health information and health services, this study also examined if e-health literacy mediates the effect of health information orientation on customers' attitudes toward using digital health service.

Accessing and using digital health service is also possible only if the people can access Information Communication Technologies (ICTs). This study conducted in Turkey, an emerging country where the rate of usage and access to internet (Internet usage: 79% among the people ages between 16 and 74; Internet access from home: 90.7% of households), computers (household that have desktop computer 16.7%, portable computer 36.4%, tablet computer 22%) and mobile smart phones (99.4%) are high (Tuik 2020). Because of the broad ICT coverage in Turkey, spreading potential of the use of digital health service was thought to be promising and worth exploring.

This study also takes sustainability as an important determiner and interprets the results of the study in light of it. Today, sustainability is an important issue in most of the industries throughout the world. It also had gained importance and attracted the attention of academic researchers. Digital healthcare sector is one of the areas in which sustainability is being studied as a new topic (Asi and Williams 2018; Novillo-Ortiz et al. 2018; Faggini et al. 2018; Presti et al. 2019). Since there is an incredible development in digital health services such as telemedicine, wearable technologies, remote monitoring tools and mobile health applications, its connection with sustainability is also being discussed.

UN Department of Economic and Social Affairs announced 17 goals for sustainable development (https://sdgs.un.org/goals). When the goals are examined carefully, digital health services have relationship with some of them obviously. One of them is "Goal 3: Good Health and Well-Being" which tries to ensure healthy lives and promote well-being for all at all ages. On the other hand, Sherman et al. (2020) state in their paper that conventional healthcare services are major emitters of environmental pollutants which adversely affect our health. That is also related to "Goal 13: Climate Action" which tries to take urgent action to combat climate change and its impacts.

This study therefore takes UN's Sustainable Development Goals into consideration, especially Goal 3 and Goal 13, during COVID-19 pandemic and focuses on digital health services. Measuring the attitudes and intentions for using digital health services in the population, and defining the factors affecting attitudes could trigger the efforts for Sustainable Development Goals and contribute to their achievement.

4.2 Conceptual Background

4.2.1 Digital Health Service and e-Health

Providing health services digitally is a new service for healthcare service users (patients) and providers (hospitals, clinics and individual doctors and dentists) in Turkey. Nevertheless, digital health service is not a new but evolving concept. One of the first definitions of digital health service is from Bashur et al. in 1975 as cited in the study of House and Roberts (1977). According to Bashur et al. (1975), the meaning of the term is as follows:

> Situations in which health care professionals use telecommunications channels to communicate with each other or with their patients, with the goal of improving in some way the delivery of health care service.

Some recent definitions of digital health service are as follows. Wernhart et al. (2019) define it as the provision of health services with the support of Information Communication Technology (ICT) while the patients and physicians are not present at the same place. For Swan et al. (2019) it is "a platform that allows patients to be seen by health-care providers from any location using a smartphone, tablet, and/or computer with audio and video capabilities".

In some studies, digital health service is used as a synonym of e-health and in some it is covered as a subcomponent of e-health and/or medical informatics. Pagliari et al.

(2005) provide 36 different definitions of e-health, and according to their study, 99 of the 392 published articles that use e-health term is related to digital health service (for detailed information, see Pagliari et al. 2005, Table 4.4). Current study embraces e-health as a generic umbrella term for describing the use of Information and Communication Technologies (ICTs) in health-related services and processes (Wernhart et al. 2019; Pagliari et al. 2005) and digital health service as its subcomponent.

4.2.2 Health Information Orientation

Health information orientation focuses on people's willingness to look for health-related information, in other words their tendency to search for health-related information. Health orientation is also defined as individuals' proactive behaviors of taking care of their health conditions (Cho et al. 2014). Health-oriented people are more eager to search for health information from different resources, nowadays especially from online sources. Previous studies inform that health information orientation is positively associated with e-health literacy (Cho et al. 2014; Dutta-Bergman 2004; Lwin et al. 2020). This is meaningful because if a person feels that he/she can find, understand and utilize online health information without difficulty, inevitably apply for online health information when he/she needs as the online health information is readily available and easily accessible for everyone.

Sheng and Simpson (2013) utilized health information orientation as a motivating factor and e-health literacy as an ability factor in their research model for explaining seniors' likelihood of using the Internet as a source of health information and tested the effect of health information orientation on e-health literacy. Analysis results showed support for their hypotheses. The Updated Integrative Model of eHealth Use by Bodie and Dutta (2008) also assumes an association between health literacy and health information orientation. Based on these empirical results and theoretical assumptions, this study hypothesizes that:

H_1: Health information orientation affects e-health literacy.

Health information orientation reflects the intrinsic consumer interest toward health issues and motivates consumers to use information technologies for health purposes (Dutta-Bergman 2004). As providing digital health service is only possible through the help of ICT, the attitudes toward using digital health services are expected to be affected by health information orientation. Accordingly, this study hypothesizes that:

H_2: Health information orientation affects attitudes toward using digital health services.

4.2.3   e-Health Literacy

According to Martin (2008), digital literacy is a mind-set that enables users to perform intuitively in digital environments while accessing the wide range of knowledge embedded in such environments easily and effectively. Digital literacy for the health domain is conceptualized as e-health literacy in the related literature.

In 1998, Nutbeam explained health literacy as an ability to cope with the challenges in finding, understanding, using and assessing health information and health services. E-health literacy is a kind of digital version of health literacy. It is related to finding and evaluating health information from online sources (Norgaard et al. 2015). Today, online health information is easily accessible, but unfortunately most of the online health information is criticized to be inaccurate, misleading and difficult to understand (Lwin et al. 2020; Holmberg et al. 2019; Huhta et al. 2018). People with high e-health literacy may benefit from online health information more, but if they are not literate in evaluating e-health sources that could result with harmful health decisions.

The term e-health literacy has been proposed by Norman and Skinner (2006a), and they defined it as "the ability to seek, find, understand, and appraise health information from electronic sources and apply the knowledge gained to addressing or solving a health problem" (Norman and Skinner 2006a, b). These researchers also suggested Lily Model to explain the e-health literacy and the eHEALS scale to measure the e-health literacy. Lily Model of e-health literacy includes six types of literacies (traditional reading and arithmetic, information, media, health, computer and scientific) that are depicted as petals of a lily. The eHEALS scale measures consumers' combined knowledge, comfort and perceived skills at finding, evaluating and applying electronic health sources to health problems. The eHEALS is the most cited scale in the measurement of e-health literacy, and its validity has been checked across different populations (Lwin et al. 2020; Chang and Schulz 2018; Chung et al. 2018; Paige et al. 2018; Van der Vaart et al. 2011).

Related literature has many studies on e-health literacy, but most of them make comparisons between old and young people (Choi and Dinitto 2013; Paige et al. 2018; Neter and Brainin 2012; Tennant et al. 2015), countries (Athanasopoulou et al. 2017), males and females (Corrarino 2013; Robb and Shellenbarger 2014), racial/ethnic minorities (Paasche-Orlow and Wolf 2007). There are also studies that examine the role of e-health literacy on health apps use. For instance, Bol et al. (2018) studied the factors associated with mobile health application use, and they found that e-health literacy positively affects health application use. They interpreted that e-health literacy could be considered a prerequisite of mobile health app use. Likewise, Cho et al. (2014) examined e-health literacy as a cognitive factor that affects health apps use. They found that e-health literacy affects health apps use through health app use efficacy. Neter and Brainin (2012) also argue e-health literacy as a strong predictor of technology use.

As the digital health service necessitates ICT usage capability, like the situation in online shopping, online banking and online distance education, users' attitudes toward using digital health service are considered to be affected by their digital health literacy. Studies conducted in different but related contexts support this claim. For instance, Huang et al., (2019) confirmed the positive impact of health literacy on attitude toward staying in hospice care. In another study, Panahi et al., (2017) found a positive correlation between health literacy and attitudes toward the harm of smoking. Ri et al., (2020) questioned the role of health literacy on dementia attitude and found that health literacy plays an important role in fostering a positive dementia attitude. In a different study where digital literacy in general concept was associated with attitude, Ryder and Machajewski (2017) found digital literacy was associated with students' attitude toward using Information and Communication Technology (ICT).

Since the effect of literacy on attitude is examined in various studies, this study tested e-health literacy's effect on attitude toward using digital health services. Currently, there is a gap in the literature examining the role of e-health literacy on attitudes toward using digital health service. Since, e-health literacy is considered to have an amplifier affect between information orientation and attitude, this study aims to understand direct and mediator effect of e-health literacy on consumers' attitudes toward using digital health services and hypothesizes that:

H_3: e-health literacy affects attitudes toward using digital health service.

H_4: e-health literacy mediates the relationship between health information orientation and attitudes toward using digital health service.

4.2.4   Attitudes Toward Using Digital Health Services and Use Intention Relationship

For Menachemi et al. (2004), digital health service involves the use of ICT for delivering or supporting direct medical care to patients and promoting collaboration between physicians although they are physically distant. Recent literature consists of many studies that examined the perception and adoption of digital health service from physicians' perspective and for some specific type of disease such as diabetes (Farmer et al. 2005a, b; Farmer et al. 2005a, b; Guljas et al. 2014); child and adolescent psychiatry (Mitchell et al. 2009; Grealish et al. 2005; Schulze et al. 2019); allergy services (Taylor et al. 2019); rehabilitation (Ullah et al. 2020); psychotherapy services (Békés and Aafjes-van Doorn 2020).

Number of studies that shed light on patients' attitudes toward using digital health service among the general population is only a few and conducted before the COVID-19 pandemic (Call et al. 2015; Stankova and Mihova 2019; Zobair et al. 2019; Sørensen 2008).

Studies that examine the effect of usage attitude on use intention mostly employs Technology Acceptance Model and/or Theory of Reasoned Action Model approach. For example, Choi et al. (2009) found attitude toward using mobile TV positively influences intention to use mobile TV. Mena et al. (2017) tried to examine the factors affecting teachers' behavioral intentions to use educational video games in their courses using a Technology Acceptance Model approach and found that attitude toward educational video games had a positive effect on intention to use educational video games. Attitude toward using mobile health services was found to be a positive determinant of mobile health adoption intention in a study made by Zhao et al. (2018).

Thus, understanding the impact of attitudes toward using digital health service on use intentions of consumers in general is thought to provide important insights for the providers of these kinds of services. Accordingly, this study hypothesizes that:

H_5: Attitudes toward using digital health service affect use intention of digital health services.

4.3 Research Methodology

This study proposes an integrative model to explain consumers' use intentions of digital health service as seen in Fig. 4.1. Accordingly, "health information orientation" affects "e-health literacy" and "attitudes toward using digital health service"; "e-health literacy" mediates the relationship between "health information orientation" and "attitudes toward using digital health service" and "attitudes toward digital health service" have a direct positive effect on "intention to use digital health service".

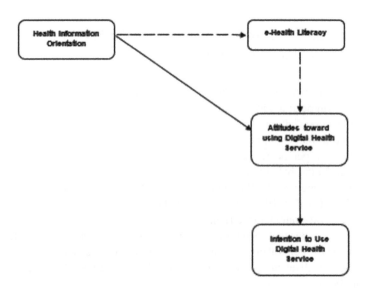

Fig. 4.1 Conceptual model

So, the objectives of the study are twofold, first to test the overall direct effects, second to find if "e-health literacy" has a mediator (full, partial) role on the relationship between health information orientation and e-health literacy.

4.3.1   Measures

In this study, multiple-item 5-point Likert-type scales, ranging from strongly disagree (1) to strongly agree (5), were used for measuring each of the variables in the research model. All the measurement items were derived from previously validated scales and adopted to digital health service context. "Health information orientation" was measured by eight items derived from Dutta-Bergman (2004). "e-Health literacy" was measured by eight items derived from Norman and Skinner (2006a, b). "Attitudes toward using digital health service" were measured by eight items derived from Call et al. (2015). "Digital health service use intention" was measured by three items derived from Van Slyke et al. (2004).

4.3.2   Data Collection and Participant Characteristics

The data of the study were collected through an online survey from Turkish consumers who are older than 18 and who reported that he/she went to a public or private hospital/clinic in the last 12 months. A URL link was generated after uploading the survey form on Google Forms, and the target respondents were reached through snowball sampling. Researchers shared URL link through WhatsApp with their contacts and WhatsApp groups and requested receivers to share the survey link with their own contacts and groups as well as on their social media accounts and with the network of their workplace if it exists.

The survey was conducted in May 2020 during COVID-19 pandemic. On those days, people were generally staying at home and working from home in Turkey, in effect, the targeted respondents were quickly reached within a week. In total, 520 valid questionnaire forms were filled by the Turkish consumers.

In the survey form, the definition of digital health service was given before asking the respondents their previous experience in using digital health service. Given definition is as follows:

> Digital health service is a service that enables remote patient-physician interview from any location through webcam of digital communication media like computer, tablet, smartphone.

The sample of this study consists of participants who have and do not have an experience in using digital health service, but the number of respondents who tried it previously was only a few.

Demographic profiles of the respondents were summarized in Table 4.1. Majority of the respondents are female (70.6%) and highly educated (65.4% graduated from university and 15.2% had master/doctorate degrees).

The income level of the respondents is mostly above the minimum wage (at the time of this study, the minimum wage in Turkey was 2324.70 ₺whereas exchange rate of Euro was 7.6 ₺and US Dollar was 6.8 ₺), but the 19.6% of the respondents has an income below 3000 ₺. Among the respondents, 22.7% are at the ages of 34

Table 4.1 Demographic profiles of the respondents

	n	%
Age		
18–25	64	12.3
26–33	89	17.1
34–41	118	22.7
42–49	111	21.3
50–57	82	15.8
58–65	49	9.4
66 and above	7	1.3
Total	520	100.0
Gender		
Female	367	70.6
Male	153	29.4
Total	520	100.0
Education		
Have not completed high school	13	2.5
High school	88	16.9
University	340	65.4
MS/Doctorate	79	15.2
Total	520	100.0
Income level		
3.000₺ and below	102	19.6
3.001–6.000₺	214	41.2
6.001–9.000₺	123	23.7
9.001–12.000₺	35	6.7
12.001–15.000₺	13	2.5
15.001–18.000₺	11	2.1
18.001–21.000₺	12	2.3
21.001₺ and above	10	1.9
Total	520	100.0

and 41; 21.3% are at the ages of 42 and 49; and 17.1% are at the ages of 26 and 33. In sum, the majority of the respondents (61.1%) are at the ages of 26 and 49.

4.3.3   Analysis and Results

Before testing the hypothesis, the overall means of all constructs were calculated. The "Health Information Orientation" construct has an overall mean of 4.02 which shows that the respondents take their health seriously and think that they should have information about health issues to stay healthy. The overall mean of the e-health literacy, attitudes toward and intention of using digital health service constructs are 3.5, 3.35 and 3.22, respectively.

Causal relations among the constructs were tested with structural equation modeling (SEM). A two-step approach (Anderson and Gerbing 1988) was followed for constructing the measurement model and testing the structural model with the help of AMOS18.

4.3.4   Measurement Model

In the first step, the measurement model was tested to validate the unidimensionality of the scales through confirmatory factor analysis (CFA). Unidimensionality explains the concept that the measured indicators are strongly associated and represent a single construct. Unidimensionality is the necessary condition for construct validity and reliability (Devaraj et al. 2002).

Through the measurement model, coefficients exceeding the acceptable limits and the model fit were checked. Initial results for the fit indices demonstrated poor fit and necessitated revisions in the measurement model. The items with either low factor loadings or large error variances (Broekhuizen 2006) were eliminated from the model. One item of "Health Information Orientation" construct (HIO8) and two items of "Attitudes toward using Digital Health Service" construct (ATUDHS1 and ATUDHS4) were deleted. After deleting the three items, the measurement model was assessed again, and the model showed an acceptable fit to the data and all the standardized loading estimates of the items exceeded the threshold value of 0.7 with the significant t-values.

The measurement model was assessed by using several fit indices. The minimum recommended threshold for GFI, CFI, NFI, AGFI and TLI is 0.9, and values greater than 0.95 for these indices indicate good fit to the data (Hu and Bentler 1999). All these fit indices for the measurement model of this study were above the recommended level as seen in Table 4.2.

For normed chi-square (X^2/df), the recommended cutoff point is 3 (Hair et al. 2014) and X^2/sd value for the measurement model of this study was 2.05. For a well-specified model, a root mean square of approximation (RMSEA) of 0.06 or

Table 4.2 Goodness-of-fit statistics for the measurement model

	X^2/df	GFI	CFI	NFI	AGFI	TLI	RMSEA
Goodness of fit measures	2.05	0.936	0.98	0.962	0.911	0.975	0.045
Recommended levels	<3.00	>0.90	>0.90	>0.90	>0.90	>0.90	<0.06

less represents a good fit (Hu and Bentler 1999). RMSEA value was also below the recommended level for the measurement model. So, the measurement model had a well fit with the data.

After evaluating the model fit, for the further check of construct validity, the convergent and discriminant validity were tested following the suggestions by Fornell and Larcker (1981), and reliability of the scales was evaluated by using Cronbach's alpha coefficient. The convergent validity of the constructs was tested using average variance extracted (AVE). The AVE estimates of the constructs ranged from 0.635 for attitudes toward using to 0.844 for use intention. AVE of all constructs exceeded the 0.50 rule of thumb (Fornell and Larcker 1981). These results provided evidence for the convergent validity (see Table 4.3).

Discriminant validity was assessed by comparing the square root of AVE of each construct with the correlations of the latent variables. According to Fornell and Larcker (1981), the square root of AVE for a latent construct should be greater than the correlations among the latent variables. Table 4.4 shows that discriminant validity was also met since the square roots of AVE are greater than the correlations.

After the convergent and discriminant validity checks, the composite reliability of the indicators was tested. The reliabilities of all items were higher than 0.70 and suggested good reliability (Hair et al. 2014). So, it can be concluded that each construct has fulfilled the reliability of the model.

4.3.5 Estimation of Structural Relationships

The structural relationships between the constructs were tested by SEM through AMOS. Table 4.5 summarizes the model fit estimates of the structural model. According to the estimates, the proposed structural model indicated a good model fit ($X^2/df = 2.22$ GFI = 0.930 CFI = 0.977 NFI = 0.959 AGFI = 0.904 TLI = 0.971 RMSEA = 0.049).

First, the effect of HIO (health information orientation) on EHL (e-Health literacy) was tested. According to the test results, Health information Orientation affects e-health Literacy significantly ($\gamma 1 = 0.513, p = 0.001$), supporting H1.

Then, the direct effects of the HIO and EHL on ATUDHS (Attitudes toward using Digital Health Service) were examined. Results (see the Table 4.6) revealed that HIO and EHL had positive effects on ATUDHS ($\gamma_2 = 0.117, p = 0.035; \gamma_3 = 0.342, p = 0.001$), supporting H2 and H3.

Table 4.3 Standardized factor loadings and average variance extracted (AVE) and reliability estimates

Scale items*	Factor loadings	Average variance extracted (AVE)	Composite reliability
HIO1	0.840	0.657	0.930
HIO2	0.869		
HIO3	0.857		
HIO4	0.836		
HIO5	0.875		
HIO6	0.724		
HIO7	0.643		
EHL1	0.794	0.713	0.952
EHL2	0.866		
EHL3	0.919		
EHL4	0.931		
EHL5	0.841		
EHL6	0.837		
EHL7	0.762		
EHL8	0.789		
ATUDHS2	0.787	0.635	0.912
ATUDHS3	0.816		
ATUDHS5	0.864		
ATUDHS6	0.771		
ATUDHS7	0.771		
ATUDHS8	0.767		
DHSUI1	0.895	0.844	0.942
DHSUI2	0.962		
DHSUI3	0.897		

*Details of the items are listed in the Appendix
HIO Health information orientation; *EHL* E-health literacy; *ATUDHS* Attitudes toward using digital health service; *DHSUI* Digital health service use intention

Table 4.4 Correlation matrix

	HIO	EHL	ATUDHS	DHSUI	Square root of AVE
Health information orientation (HIO)	1.00				0.810
e-Health literacy (EHL)	0.513	1.00			0.844
Attitudes toward using digital health service (ATUDHS)	0.286	0.394	1.00		0.797
Digital health service use intention (DHSUI)	0.265	0.364	0.771	1.00	0.919

Table 4.5 Model fit for the structural model

	X²/df	GFI	CFI	NFI	AGFI	TLI	RMSEA
Goodness-of-fit measures	2.22	0.930	0.977	0.959	0.904	0.971	0.049
Recommended levels	<3.00	>0.90	>0.90	>0.90	>0.90	>0.90	<0.06

Table 4.6 Parameter estimates for the structural model

	Standardized path coefficients	p-value	Hypothesis
Health information orientation → e-health literacy	0.513	0.001	Supported
e-Health literacy → attitudes toward using digital health service	0.342	0.001	Supported
Health information orientation → attitudes toward using digital health service	0.117	0.035	Supported
Attitude toward using digital health service → digital health service use intention	0.775	0.001	Supported

The proposed research model of this study assumes that e-health literacy has a mediator role between health information orientation and attitudes toward using digital health service. The mediator role of e-health literacy on attitudes toward using digital health service was tested with the bootstrap method in AMOS. Results after bootstrapping showed that e-health literacy has a significant effect (γ: 0.346; $p < 0.01$) on attitudes toward using digital health service. By the way, the effect of health information orientation on attitudes toward using digital health service is still significant. Since the direct effect from health information orientation to attitudes toward using digital health service (H$_2$) is significant, e-health literacy was found to have a partial mediator role between them (See Table 4.7). This result showed support for H4.

Finally, H$_5$ indicates the effect of ATUDHS on DHSUI. Results showed that attitudes toward using digital health service had a positive and relatively high effect on the use intention of digital health service ($\gamma_5 = 0.775, p = 0.001$), supporting H5.

Table 4.7 Standardized direct and indirect effect of health information orientation on attitudes toward using digital health service

Hypothesis	Direct effect	Indirect effect	Result
Health information orientation → e-health literacy → attitudes toward using digital health service	0.117*	0.176**	Partial mediation

*$p < 0.05$; **$p < 0.01$

The R^2 value for the digital health service use intention was found to be 0.6, which proves that the predictors of digital health service use intention in the model explain the 60 percent of its variance.

4.4 Discussion, Implications and Limitations

Studies on digital health service context conducted before COVID-19 pandemic report that there is a great potential to provide health services digitally; nevertheless, its adoption is expected to be slow. As everyone knows and experience, COVID-19 pandemic has changed the way of thinking and doing things. For instance, nowadays, people who have chronic diseases are afraid of going to hospitals for routine control interviews or continuing their regular treatments. In the presence of acute ailments, many people are preferring to ask treatment advice on Internet health forums instead of booking an appointment with their doctors. Even in some European countries, governments are prohibiting the general practitioner visits and general practitioners are mostly providing their services only on the phone. All these changes regarding the healthcare services are expected to fasten the adoption of digital health service so examining the issue during the pandemic was thought to be useful to shed light on the issue and this study was conducted.

The results of this study showed that health information orientation affects attitudes toward using digital health services, and this effect is partly mediated by e-health literacy. In addition, attitudes toward using digital health services strongly affects digital health service use intention. Based on the results of this study, several theoretical and practical implications can be advanced.

This study showed that Turkish consumers are highly health information oriented and health information orientation affects Turkish consumers' attitudes toward using digital health services. This means that Turkish consumers are eager to learn more and more about health issues. Besides, they enjoy learning about health issues, and they regard being informed about health issues as a need to keep their family and themselves healthy. To make informed decisions related to their health, actively seeking health related information as much as possible from various sources and channels is important for them. Accordingly, expecting people with a high level of health information orientation to utilize electronic health information sources and digital health services more than others to obtain health-related information is reasonable. Therefore, it can be said that, if health professionals and public and private health institutions focus on providing people with wide and reliable information about the health related issues on their digital channels (hospital website, hospital's social media, physician's personal website, mobile apps, etc.), they will most probably convince people to use their digital health service with the help of positive attitude people formed in effect with the previously provided health information on the digital channel.

This study confirmed that e-health literacy partially mediates the relationship between health information orientation and attitudes toward using digital health services. In other words, if people with high health information orientation also have high e-health literacy, the impact of health information on the attitudes toward using the digital health service will be boosted and they will form positive attitudes toward using digital health service as it is easy for them where and how to find, evaluate and use high-quality health information on the Internet. Therefore, working on the ways of increasing the e-health literacy of Turkish people can be recommended to the digital health service providers. For instance, giving public seminars/webinars, preparing booklets, attending TV programs, publishing videos on YouTube and other social media that explains how to find reliable health information sources on the Internet and how to understand if the information source (website, blog, forum, etc.) is reliable and has trustable content may help to increase e-health literacy of people.

On the other hand, the remote and digital health applications during COVID-19 pandemic also contribute to sustainability either directly or indirectly. One of the UN's Sustainable Development Goal (Goal-3) is good health and well-being. With this goal, it is aimed to ensure healthy lives and promote well-being at all ages. This SDG prioritizes health and well-being. Digital health services contribute to this goal by providing health services to all people regardless from their age. As stated above, people's positive attitudes toward using digital health services increase their use intention and informing them about digital health services will make them to create positive attitudes. In this way, more people will reach to health services in all ages. Since the use of digital health services is not common in some of the developing and underdeveloped countries, some interdisciplinary action is needed to be taken by governments, academic people and digital health service providers.

Another Sustainable Development Goal, Goal-13, tries to take urgent action to fight climate change and its impacts. Digital health services have also a positive contribution to the achievement of this goal. As more people adopt to using digital health services, less hospital visits and more electronic health records will take place. On the other hand by reducing visits, this will result in less carbon emissions. So, taking into consideration the results of this study and trying to increase the digital health service use intention will also contribute to UN's Sustainable Development Goals in Turkey.

Theory of Reasoned Action emphasizes the impact of attitudes toward using product/service on its use intention, and this study confirmed this relationship for the digital health service context. In Turkey, digital health service is an emerging service, and its popularity is increasing among the providers and users in effect with the COVID-19 pandemic. This study focused on the influence of personal health-related factors to explore the attitudes of using and intention to use digital health services. As it became widely available, future studies can follow the Technology Acceptance Model to explore how people perceive digital health service in terms of usefulness and ease of use or Unified Theory of Acceptance and Use of Technology (UTAUT) in explaining the antecedents of its adoption.

This study is one of the first studies that investigates the attitudes and intentions of using digital health service from the viewpoint of the general population in an emerging country during the COVID-19 pandemic. The findings based on the proposed research model provide rich insights to understand the role of personal health-related factors, health information orientation and e-health literacy in this case, on having positive attitudes toward using the digital health service. For practitioners (i.e., health service providers, health-related application designers, health information professionals, individual physicians), it seems logical to identify and target health information-oriented segments of the market in their go-to market strategy. In addition, it can be said that educating people on finding, evaluating and using online health information sources would be beneficial to create positive attitudes.

Future studies may employ more personal factors such as health consciousness, tech savviness, innovativeness as well as compare the attitudes and intentions of people who have chronic ailments, acute ailments and who are in good health condition.

Future studies may also recruit a larger and more diverse sample to broaden interpretation and verify if the findings hold for other samples and factors or not. In this study, only the use intentions of respondents were measured, and future studies may also test the model on the basis of actual use behavior. Cross-cultural comparisons may also add to the knowledge related to the adoption of digital health service.

Appendix: Scale Items Details

Health Information Orientation

HIO1 It is important to me to be informed about health issues.

HIO2 I need to know about health issues so I can keep myself and my family healthy.

HIO3 Before making a decision about my health, I find out everything I can about the issue.

HIO4 I really enjoy learning about health issues.

HIO5 To be and stay healthy it is critical to be informed about health issues.

HIO6 When I take medicine, I try to get as much information as possible about its benefits and side effects.

HIO7 I make a point to read and watch stories about health.

e-Health Literacy

EHL1 I know what health resources are available on the Internet.

EHL2 I know where to find helpful health resources on the Internet.

EHL3 I know how to use the health information I find on the Internet to help me.

EHL4 I know how to find helpful health resources on the Internet.

EHL5 I have the skills I need to evaluate the health resources I find on the Internet.

EHL6 I know how to use the Internet to answer my questions about health.

EHL7 I can tell high quality health resources from low quality health resources on the Internet.

EHL8 I feel confident in using information from the Internet to make health decisions.

Attitudes Toward Using Digital Health Services

ATUDHS2 Using a digital health service to meet with my doctor would be better than traveling long distances to see my doctor.

ATUDHS3 Using a digital health service to meet with my doctor would be better than traveling during bad weather conditions to see my doctor.

ATUDHS5 I would use digital health service if it allowed me to significantly reduce the time, I spend traveling to other communities to see my doctor.

ATUDHS6 I would prefer an interview through digital health service with my own specialist over an in-person visit with another physician.

ATUDHS7 Having digital health services in my community would mean that I would miss fewer appointments.

ATUDHS8 I would feel comfortable having digital health service interview with my doctor.

Digital Health Service Use Intention

DHSUI1 I would use digital services for health problems.

DHSUI2 Taking health services over digital platforms is something I would do.

DHSUI3 I could see myself using digital health services.

References

Ajzen I, Fishbein M (1975) A bayesian analysis of attribution processes. Psychol Bull 82(2):261–277
Amin M (2016) Internet banking service quality and its implication on e-customer satisfaction and e-customer loyalty. Int J Bank Market 34(3):280–306. https://doi.org/10.1108/IJBM-10-2014-0139
Anderson JC, Gerbing DW (1988) Structural equation modeling in practice: a review and recommended two-step approach. Psychol Bull 103(3):411–423
Asi YM, Williams C (2018) The role of digital health in making progress toward sustainable development goal (SDG) 3 in conflict-affected populations. Int J Med Inform 114:114–120. https://doi.org/10.1016/j.ijmedinf.2017.11.003
Athanasopoulou C, Välimäki M, Koutra K, Löttyniemi E, Bertsias A, Basta M, Vgontzas AN, Lionis C (2017) Internet use, eHealth literacy and attitudes toward computer/internet among people with schizophrenia spectrum disorders: a cross-sectional study in two distant European regions. BMC Med Inform Decis Making 17(136). https://doi.org/10.1186/s12911-017-0531-4
Bashur RL, Armstrong PA, Youssef ZI (1975) Telemedicine: explorations in the use of telecommunications in health care. Charles C Thomas Publisher Limited, Springfield, USA, p 309

Békés V, Aafjes-van Doorn K (2020) Psychotherapists' attitudes toward online therapy during the COVID-19 pandemic. J Psychother Integr 30(2):238–247. https://doi.org/10.1037/int0000214

Bodie GD, Dutta MJ (2008) Understanding health literacy for strategic health marketing: ehealth literacy, health disparities, and the digital divide. Health Market Quart 25(1–2):175–203. https://doi.org/10.1080/07359680802126301

Bol N, Helberger N, Weert JC (2018) Differences in mobile health app use: a source of new digital inequalities? Inform Soc 34(3):183–193. https://doi.org/10.1080/01972243.2018.1438550

Britt RK, Collins WB, Wilson K, Linnemeier G, Englebert AM (2017) eHealth literacy and health behaviors affecting modern college students: a pilot study of issues identified by the American College health association. J Med Internet Res 19(12). https://doi.org/10.2196/jmir.3100

Broekhuizen T (2006) Understanding channel purchase intentions: measuring online and offline shopping value perceptions, 1st ed. Labyrinth Publications

Call VR, Erickson LD, Dailey NK, Hicken BL, Rupper R, Yorgason JB, Bair B (2015) Attitudes toward telemedicine in urban, rural, and highly rural communities. Telemed e-Health 21(8):644–651. https://doi.org/10.1089/tmj.2014.0125

Chang A, Schulz P (2018) The measurements and an elaborated understanding of Chinese eHealth literacy (C-eHEALS) in chronic patients in China. Int J Environ Res Public Health 15:1–12

Cheng Y, Wei W, Zhong Y, Zhang L (2021) The empowering role of hospitable telemedicine experience in reducing isolation and anxiety: evidence from the COVID-19 pandemic. Int J Contemp Hosp Manag 33(3):851–872. https://doi.org/10.1108/IJCHM-07-2020-0786

Cho J, Park D, Lee E (2014) Cognitive factors of using health apps: systematic analysis of relationships among health consciousness, health information orientation, ehealth literacy, and health app use efficacy. J Med Internet Res 16(5):e125. https://doi.org/10.2196/jmir.3283

Choi NGI, DiNitto DM (2013) The digital divide among low-income homebound older adults: internet use patterns, ehealth literacy, and attitudes toward computer/internet use. J Med Internet Res 15(5):e93, 1–16. https://doi.org/10.2196/jmir.2645

Choi YK, Kim J, McMillan SJ (2009) Motivators for the intention to use mobile TV a comparison of South Korean males and females. Int J Advertising Quart Rev Market Commun 28(1):147–167. https://doi.org/10.2501/S0265048709090477

Chung S, Park BK, Nahm ES (2018) The Korean ehealth literacy scale (k-eheals): reliability and validity testing in younger adults recruited online. J Med Internet Res 20(4):e138, 1–10. https://doi.org/10.2196/jmir.8759

Corrarino JE (2013) Health literacy and women's health: challenges and opportunities. J Midwifery Womens Health 58:257–264. https://doi.org/10.1111/jmwh.12018

Devaraj S, Fan M, Kohli R (2002) Antecedents of B2C channel satisfaction and preference: validating e-commerce metrics. Inf Syst Res 13(3):317–333

Dutta-Bergman (2004) Health attitudes, health cognitions, and health behaviors among internet health information seekers: population-based survey. J Med Internet Res 6(2). https://doi.org/10.2196/jmir.6.2.e15

Eysenbach G, Jadad AR (2001) Evidence-based patient choice and consumer health informatics in the internet age. J Med Internet Res 3(2):1–11. https://doi.org/10.2196/jmir.3.2.e19

Faggini M, Cosimato S, Nota FD, Nota G (2018) Pursuing sustainability for healthcare through digital platforms. Sustainability 11:1–15. https://doi.org/10.3390/su11010165

Farmer AJ, Gibson OJ, Dudley C, Bryden K, Hayton PM, Tarassenko L, Neil A (2005) A randomized controlled trial of the effect of real-time telemedicine support on glycemic control in young adults with type 1 diabetes (ISRCTN 46889446). Diabetes Care 8(11):2697–2702

Farmer A, Gibson O, Hayton P, Bryden K, Dudley C, Neil A, Tarassenko L (2005) A real-time, mobile phone-based telemedicine system to support young adults with type 1 diabetes. Inform Prim Care 13:171–177

Fornell C, Larcker DF (1981) Evaluating structural equation models with unobservable variables and measurement error. J Mark Res 18(1):39–50

George B, Bucatariu L, Henthorne TL (2020) Technology in medicine: COVID-19 and the "coming of age" of "telehealth", tourism security-safety and post conflict destinations, International Case Studies in the Management of Disasters. Emerald Publishing Limited

Grealish A, Hunter A, Glaze R, Potter L (2005) Telemedicine in a child and adolescent mental health service: participants' acceptance and utilization. J Telemed Telecare 11(1):53–55. https://doi.org/10.1258/1357633054461921

Guljas R, Ahmed A, Chang K, Whitlock A (2014) Impact of telemedicine in managing type 1 diabetes among school-age children and adolescents: an integrative review. J Pediatr Nurs 29(3):198–204

Hair JF Jr, Black WC, Barry JB, Anderson RE (2014) Multivariate data analysis, Pearson Education, Edinburgh Gate, Harlow

Holmberg C, Berg C, Dahlgren J, Lissner L, Chaplin JE (2019) Health literacy in a complex digital media landscape: pediatric obesity patients' experiences with online weight, food, and health information. Health Inform J 25(4):1343–1357. https://doi.org/10.1177/1460458218759699

House AM, Roberts JM (1977) Telemedicine in Canada. Can Med Assoc J 117:386–388

Hu L, Bentler PM (1999) Cutoff criteria for fit indexes in covariance structure analysis: conventional criteria versus new alternatives. Struct Equ Modeling 6(1):1–55. https://doi.org/10.1080/10705519909540118

Huang HY, Kuo KM, Lu C, Wu H, Lin CW, Hsieh MT, Lin YC, Huang RY, Liu T, Huang CH (2019) The impact of health literacy on knowledge, attitude and decision towards hospice care among community-dwelling seniors. Health Soc Care Community 27:724–733. https://doi.org/10.1111/hsc.12791

Huhta AM, Hirvonen N, Huotari ML (2018) Health literacy in web-based health information environments: systematic review of concepts, definitions, and operationalization for measurement. J Med Internet Res 20(12):1–16

Khilnani A, Schulz J, Robinson L (2020) The COVID-19 pandemic: new concerns and connections between eHealth and digital inequalities. J Inf Commun Ethics Soc 18(3):393–403. https://doi.org/10.1108/JICES-04-2020-0052

Lwin MO, Panchapakesan C, Sheldenkar A, Calvert GA, Lim LK, Lu J (2020) Determinants of eHealth literacy among adults in China. J Health Commun 25:385–393. https://doi.org/10.1080/10810730.2020.1776422

Martin A (2008) Digital literacy and the "digital society". In: Lankshear C, Knobel M (eds) Digital literacies: concepts, policies & practices. Peter Lang, New York, pp 151–176

Mena AS, Parreño JM, Manzano JA (2017) The effect of age on teachers' intention to use educational video games: a TAM approach. Electron J e-Learn 15(4):355–366

Menachemi N, Burke DE, Ayers DJ (2004) Factors affecting the adoption of telemedicine—a multipleadopter perspective. J Med Syst 28(6):617–632

Mitchell SA, Maclaren AT, Morton M, Carachi R (2009) Professional opinions of the use of telemedicine in child & adolescent psychiatry. Scott Med J 54(3):13–16

Novillo-Ortiz D, Marin HDF, Saigí-Rubió F (2018) The role of digital health in supporting the achievement of the sustainable development goals (SDGs). Int J Med Inform 114:106–107. https://doi.org/10.1016/j.ijmedinf.2018.03.011

Neter E, Brainin E (2012) eHealth literacy: extending the digital divide to the realm of health information. J Med Internet Res 14(1):1–10

Norgaard O, Furstrand D, Klokker L, Karnoe A, Batterham R, Kayser L (2015) The e-health literacy framework: a conceptual framework for characterizing e-health users and their interaction with e-health systems. Knowl Manage E-Learn 7(4):522–540

Norman CD, Skinner HA (2006a) eHEALS: the eHealth literacy scale. J Med Internet Res 8(4):e27. https://doi.org/10.2196/jmir.8.4.e27

Norman CD, Skinner HA (2006) eHealth Literacy: essential skills for consumer health in a networked world. J Med Internet Res 8(2):1–10

Nutbeam D (1998) Health promotion glossary. Health Promot Int 13(4):349–364

Paasche-Orlow MK, Wolf MS (2007) The causal pathways linking health literacy to health outcomes. Am J Health Behav 31:19–26

Paige SR, Miller MD, Krieger JL, Stellefson M, Cheong J (2018) eHealth literacy across the lifespan: a measurement invariance study. J Med Internet Res 20(7):1–14

Pagliari C, Sloan D, Gregor P, Sullivan F, Detmer D, Kahan JP, Oortwijn W, MacGillivray S (2005) What is eHealth (4): a scoping exercise to map the field. J Med Internet Res 7(1):1–20

Panahi R, Ramezankhani A, Tavousi M, Koosehloo A, Niknami S (2017) Relationship of health literacy with knowledge and attitude toward the harms of cigarette smoking among university students. J Educ Community Health 3, No.12(4):38–44

Pappot N, Taarnhøj GA, Pappot H (2020) Telemedicine and e-health solutions for COVID-19: patients' perspective. Telemed e-Health 26(7):847–849

Presti LL, Testa M, Marino V, Singer P (2019) Engagement in healthcare systems: adopting digital tools for a sustainable approach. Sustainability 11:1–15. https://doi.org/10.3390/su11010220

Ri SH, Kyoung KS, Joo LH, Wool CS, Ho MS, Sun KY (2020) The moderating effect of health literacy on the association between dementia experience, social support and dementia attitude. J Korea Acad Industr Cooperation Soc 21(11):701–714

Robb M, Shellenbarger T (2014) Influential factors and perceptions of eHealth literacy among undergraduate college students. Online J Nursing Inform 18(3)

Ryder R, Machajewski S (2017) Investigating the relationship between students' digital literacy and their attitude towards using ICT. Int J Educ Technol 5(2):26–34

Schulze N, Reuter SC, Kuchler I, Reinke B, Hinkelmann L, Stoeckigt S, Tonn P (2019) Differences in attitudes toward online interventions in psychiatry and psychotherapy between health care professionals and nonprofessionals: a survey. Telemed e-Health 25(10):926–932

Serrano KM, Mendes GH, Lizarelli FL, Ganga GM (2021) Assessing the telemedicine acceptance for adults in Brazil. Int J Health Care Qual Assur 34(1):35–51

Sheng X, Simpson PM (2013) Seniors, health information, and the internet: motivation, ability, and internet knowledge. Cyberpsychol Behav Soc Netw 16(10):740–746

Sherman JD, Thiel C, MacNeill A, Eckelman MJ, Dubrow R, Hopf H, Lagasse R, Bialowitz J, Costello A, Forbes McG, Stancliffe R, Anastas P, Anderko L, Baratz M, Barna S, Bhatnagar U, Burnham J, Cair Y, Bilec MM (2020) The green print: advancement of environmental sustainability in healthcare. Resour Conserv Recycl 161:1–11. https://doi.org/10.1016/j.resconrec.2020.104882

Sørensen JF (2008) Attitudes toward telehealth use among rural residents: a Danish survey. J Rural Health 24(3):330–335

Stankova M, Mihova P (2019) Attitudes to telemedicine, and willingness to use in young people. intelligent decision technologies. Springer, Singapore, pp 329–336

Swan EL, Dahl AJ, Peltier JW (2019) Health-care marketing in an omni-channel environment exploring telemedicine and other digital touchpoints. J Res Interact Mark 13(4):602–618. https://doi.org/10.1108/JRIM-03-2019-0039

Taylor L, Waller M, Portnoy JM (2019) Telemedicine for allergy services to rural communities. J Allergy Clin Immunol Pract 7(8):2554–2559

Tennant B, Stellefson M, Dodd V, Chaney B, Chaney D, Paige S, Alber J (2015) eHealth literacy and web 2.0 health information seeking behaviors among baby boomers and older adults. J Med Internet Res 17(3):1–16

Türkiye İstatistik Kurumu (TÜİK) (2020) haber bülteni 2020 yılı hanehalkı bilişim teknolojileri (bt) kullanım araştırması sayı 33679" available at: https://data.tuik.gov.tr/Bulten/Index?p=Hanehalki-Bilisim-Teknolojileri-(BT)-Kullanim-Arastirmasi-2020-33679. Accessed 1 Sept 2020

Ullah S, Maghazil AM, Qureshi AZ, Tantawy S, Moukais IS, Aldajani AA (2020) Knowledge and attitudes of rehabilitation professional toward telerehabilitation in Saudi Arabia: a cross-sectional survey. Telemed e-Health. https://doi.org/10.1089/tmj.2020.0016

Van der Vaart R, Van Deursen AJ, Drossaert CH, Taal E, van Dijk JA, Van de Laar MA (2011) Does the eHealth literacy scale (eHEALS) measure what it intends to measure? validation of a Dutch version of the eHEALS in two adult populations. J Med Internet Res 13(4):1–11

Van Slyke C, Belanger F, Comunale CL (2004) Factors influencing the adoption of web-based shopping: the impact of trust. ACM SIGMIS Database DATABASE Adv Inform Syst 35(2):32–49

Wernhart A, Gahbauer S, Haluza D (2019) eHealth and telemedicine: practices and beliefs among healthcare professionals and medical students at a Medical University. Plos One 14(2):e0213067. https://doi.org/10.1371/journal.pone.0213067

Zhao Y, Ni Q, Zhou R (2018) What factors influence the mobile health service adoption? a meta-analysis and the moderating role of age. Int J Inf Manage 43:342–350

Zobair KM, Sanzogni L, Sandhu K (2019) Expectations of telemedicine health service adoption in rural Bangladesh. Social Sci Med 238:112485. https://doi.org/10.1016/j.socscimed.2019.112485

Chapter 5
Changing Culture and Ethics as an Integral Part of a Comprehensive Restructuring of a Company

Drago Dubrovski

Abstract In order for the company to be able to ensure its continued existence and development, it must constantly make changes, which may be evolutionary or revolutionary, depending on its actual position. Changing culture extends to both approaches and has some specific features in comparison to other methods. The article deals with the hypothesis that changing the culture due to its direct and indirect influence on ensuring the possibility of further existence and development is an integral part of a comprehensive renewal or restructuring of a company. Empirical data from a local survey show a gap between the declared need to change the culture in conditions of endangered further existence and development on the one hand and the actual implementation of these changes in practice on the other.

Keywords Culture · Ethics · Development · Crisis · Change · Restructuring

5.1 Introduction: Methods of Changing and Restructuring of a Company

The development of an organization (company) consists of the sum of various successive and parallel development phases (steps), which are a combination of life cycles of programmes (products and services or strategic business units) and intertwined periods of decline and growth, whereas the organization is supposed to reach a higher development level with every subsequent stage reached, measured by efficiency (the ratio between outcomes and inputs, which is reflected as the productivity of work resources and labour) and the business performance (the ratio between outcomes and the set objectives, which is reflected in profitability, marketability and flexibility). A company's development is driven by change, as it allows the company to achieve "organizational health". A company's development must, therefore, be based on

D. Dubrovski (✉)
International School of Social and Business Studies, Celje, Slovenia
e-mail: linnair@siol.net

Faculty of Management, University of Primorska, Koper, Slovenia

© The Author(s), under exclusive license to Springer Nature Singapore Pte Ltd. 2021   77
K. T. Çalıyurt (ed.), *New Approaches to CSR, Sustainability and Accountability,
Volume II*, Accounting, Finance, Sustainability, Governance & Fraud: Theory
and Application, https://doi.org/10.1007/978-981-33-6808-8_5

constant change, which always entails the collapse of existing internal and external balances and the establishment of new ones to improve performance and efficiency. If the company does not change, then it cannot develop, even though changes are risky, since the results are always uncertain.

More and more companies realize that once successful development formula implemented in the business model is now increasingly achieving its natural limitations, and therefore fundamental changes will be required. The business model defines the way in which an organization with a unique combination of programmes (products, services, knowledge, capital, information, technologies for targeted participants), sales conditions, distribution channels and market communication, and a unique combination of assets in a competitive environment creates value in their business processes (benefit) for customers, thus achieving its own fundamental goal and indirect goals of the participants in the organization. There are no best business models, but a decision on the selection of possibilities, suitable for a particular environment (Birkinshaw and Goddard 2009). Over time, business models become more resistant to change (Christensen et al. 2016). However, warning signals of the necessary changes do not come anymore from the financial and implementation areas, but from the structural indicators, which are hidden below the surface of the organization. Thus, the most successful examples of company renewal include the creation of a new core activity based on "hidden assets" of the organization (Zook 2007, 10), where it is possible to include *the design of an appropriate organizational culture.*

When a company's adjustment to changing environmental conditions is systematic, continuous, timely and appropriate given the circumstances, the change is evolutionary (small-step changes). However, if a business needs to change rapidly, radically and dramatically, because either it neglected a constant development-oriented change or there is a different external situation, then the changes have the character of discontinuous or revolutionary changes (big-step changes). Revolutionary change is necessary when it is too late for evolutionary (continuous) changes or they would not suffice given the changed circumstances (Table 5.1).

In the case of the ongoing analysis of events in the environment and particularly forecasting future directions, gradual changes can be adjusted in advance to the expected changed business conditions (active adjustment). If the company is

Table 5.1 Features of the changes

Revolutionary changes	Evolutionary changes
Strategic	Operational
Abrupt	Gradual
Broadly (integrally) oriented	Narrowly (locally) oriented
Periodic	Continuous and permanent
Transformational/turning	Transactional/transitional
Dramatic	Recognized as underway
Radical	Less thorough/moderate
Very noticeable	Less noticeable

sufficiently trained, and if the market position allows it to, it can also only influence (cause) changes in the environment (interactive adaptation). Revolutionary changes occur due to anticipation and forecasting of developments in a certain area, which will no longer be prospective or attractive for the company; therefore mission, vision and long-term business objectives or goals must be redefined, and often even *the culture of the organization*. However, if such a company is forced to make such a decision when the changes have already occurred, its position is much more difficult and requires a rapid, thorough reversal, especially if the company has already identified the state of the crisis.

If the extent of the progressive changes is insufficient or if they do not match the requirements of the changed environment, a phase of indecisive and unintended changes often follows without clear and elaborated directions and goals, which, in order to ensure the existence of the company, must be followed by the necessary phase of radical changes that, in cases of threats to further existence and development, are performed by the crisis management. The radical reforms usually come after years of deterioration in performance. When the time for a normal, planned, systematic and thus qualitative response is missed, we can talk about the concept of "crisis response", when it is necessary to adopt fast and crucial decisions for the existence and development of the company. However, they contain the highest degree of risk. Crisis management comprises planning, organizing, leading and monitoring companies (organizations) experiencing difficulties that directly endanger their existence (crisis elimination) and further development (crisis preventing) and its purpose is to stop negative trends by achieving a drastic change and providing the foundation for redevelopment (Dubrovski 2016).

It is possible to distinguish between the methods and concepts, with which these changes are being prepared and implemented (management or control of change), with evolutionary change methods and revolutionary change methods. Evolutionary change methods comprise the continuous measures taken to implement constant, daily changes in line with the company's mission and vision, long-term goals and core strategies, thereby ensuring a consistent and gradually increasing level of performance and operating efficiency. This can either be part of the company's normal strategic activity or a special effort aimed at achieving specific objectives on a project basis (e.g. bringing operations into compliance with the ISO 9000, ISO 14000, OHSAS 18000, ISO/TS 16949, VDA 6.1, DS 3027, HACCP, SA 8000, BS 7799, GMP, MDD or Qweb standard or implementing the 20 Keys methodology, Kaizen programmes, Six Sigma projects, CIP[2], business excellence or TQM projects, a learning organizational model or various other projects involving gradual change). Revolutionary change methods include restructuring (emphasis on extensive structural changes) and re-engineering (emphasis on extensive process changes), while the characteristics of both types of methods include the *changing of culture*, but there are some special features in comparison to other change methods.

The basic difference between the revolutionary change methods and the evolutionary attainment of change is that the first ones are used less often, they are comprehensive and broad-based, and they are conducted with greater intensity and in a shorter period, are much riskier and at the same time require certain sacrifices. Sacrifices may relate to material assets (sale of fixed assets and investments or "family silverware", exit from equity and business associations, sale of objects of the so-called social standard, reduction of funds for non-business purposes, sale and lease back of real estate, etc.) and intangible assets (employee dismissal, replacement and departure of experts, sale of patents or brands, loss of information resources, disintegration of business networks or evolved connections with customers, etc.). Because of these sacrifices, revolutionary change methods are not perceived as pleasant, but the cause of fear, uncertainty, distress and stress. As a rule, evolutionary change is achieved over a long period of time, as measured by a cross section of the situation at the beginning and at the end of a period in which the employees (and the external environment) do not perceive changes as drastic, dramatic or unpleasant, and the sacrifices are not noticeable or there are even none due to systematic work. Both types of changes affect all three levels: individual, group and organizational.

Regardless of the type of method for achieving change, the goal of both (evolutionary and revolutionary) is the same—the achievement of renewal (transformation, reorganization). *The renewal of a company* or an organization is based on new models, processes, systems, strategies, programmes, structures and culture, which enable the company as a whole to achieve a higher level of development based on improved efficiency and performance of the business.

In practice, it is often not possible to establish a precise demarcation nor between revolutionary and evolutionary methods, nor between the individual methods within one or the other group, since they are intertwined or followed by each other. Gradual and turning changes are not contradictions, but extremes in the extent of modes of change. Finding compromises between them—one more, the other less—is not successful, and they should be combined into a synthesis that allows more than unilateral grip to one or the other concept. The path to synthesis leads through the creative linking and upgrading of the features of both methods. Organizations need both evolution (improvements in products, services, quality) and the revolution (changes in vision, strategies and tactical approaches); otherwise, it is not possible to gain new competitive advantages. Evolutionary change methods may be revolutionary in some places, but this does not go the other way around, as a rule. For example, starting business operations under the ISO 9001 standards in one company will mean a radical transformation (revolution), while in another company, it will only be a more precise monitoring of the procedures which have already been implemented. This can, therefore, be the intertwined operation of the evolutionary and revolutionary methods, and the intertwined operation of the methods of restructuring and re-engineering.

Further below, we only deal with the restructuring method as a prototype (*mutatis mutandis*) of all kinds of major (revolutionary) changes in a company.

5.2 Company Restructuring Rules

The company has many internal structures, as well as those related to external participants (virtual company, outsourcing, business networks, etc.). The structure is generally a whole, which consists of interconnected and dependent elements (ingredients). Compared to the process, the structure is static, as it is a cross section of the elements and their connections at a given moment. Different areas (programmes, functions), activities or organizational units (sectors, departments, divisions, departments) in the company have a typical structure, whose combined effect, due to interconnection, forms the company structure. If the particular structure of the company or its individual components and the links between them does not correspond to the conditions required by the (changed) environment or a new vision and fundamental strategy, then the existing structure needs to be changed, and a new one has to be set up.

The method of revolutionary change, which means the transition from the existing structure to the new one, which enables greater efficiency and performance of the company's business, thus providing better opportunities for the survival and development of the company (organization), is often called *restructuring* (business practice has developed a number of different denominations for such radical and dramatic changes). Restructuring is, therefore, one of the methods of revolutionary changing and ways of achieving the company's renewal, so the above-mentioned general characteristics of revolutionary change apply here. In this method, we are not talking about minor changes, additions, refinements, adjustments, etc., but about extensive and radical turns.

The following important rules should be applied in the restructuring:

- It is done multidisciplinary (changing the structure in one area requires a change in structures in other areas);
- It originates from the already defined basic strategies of the company;
- It starts with programme-marketing structures (programme-marketing restructuring);
- It contains all the features of revolutionary change methods (previously mentioned).

Due to the extent, dramatic nature and the consequences of the major changes, it is understandable that, as a rule, restructuring is important due to its strategic role and content (=strategic restructuring), but in practice—similarly to crisis measures—it is often divided into financial and operational (all other areas), although such a division is not entirely appropriate, as one area (financial) may be placed in a privileged position and may unduly redirect resources and efforts.

As a rule, restructuring cannot be carried out only in a specific area (e.g. function), independently of others, but effects will only be visible with a coordinated change of several sectoral structures. The change in the programme portfolio (programme-marketing restructuring) may also require a change in the organization of the company (organizational restructuring), technologies (technological restructuring), financial resources (financial restructuring), employees (HR restructuring), information system (information restructuring), etc. At times, many changes are dependent on or initiated by ownership restructuring (change in ownership structure). Any change in leadership will bring new influential elements into the existing *organizational culture*. The particular emphasis is put on the need for a coordinated and simultaneous restructuring of the crisis management processes, which cannot, in any case, be managed solely by financial restructuring, leaving the remaining areas of business untouched. Research and business practice (e.g. Blatz and Haghani 2006, 19) repeatedly corroborate the correlation between comprehensive restructuring and the degree of success of such changes.

5.3 Suitability of Using the Restructuring Method

From the point of view of the threat or perspective of the situation in which the company is located, the restructuring may play the following roles:

- in eliminating the crisis;
- in preventing the crisis;
- in the accelerated development of a company;
- in strategic business or equity alliances;
- in insolvency proceedings.

The reversal of a crisis also requires a whole series of new sectoral structures (programme-marketing, HR, organizational, financial, production, etc.), which are primarily aimed at halting negative trends. Therefore, the setting up of new structures (and processes) at this stage is rapid, less extensive and incomplete, as short-term effects are observed. Only in the second phase, when it comes to setting the foundations for development with profitable operations, full and comprehensive restructuring projects with medium- and long-term effects are being implemented. Therefore, the role of restructuring in the period of the first phase of addressing the crisis (stopping negative trends) is less emphasized, and later on, it is a priority. Hence, the restructuring method is practically necessary after the stopping of negative trends, otherwise, the company will continue to do the same things that have led to the crisis.

An even more important role than the management of an acute crisis, when measures with short-term positive effects are at the forefront, is given to the restructuring in preventing crises and developing the company. Although the company's development involves activities which also mean the prevention of a crisis, different restructuring can occur only to build the company with significant changes (big steps) in order to keep up with the environmental situation, thereby preventing the emergence of a latent or acute crisis which would arise from stagnation in development (faster competition, changed demand or customer behaviour, etc.). The company can, through appropriate strategic planning, improve its competitive position and development potential by the regular restructuring of internal structures (small steps).

The restructuring plays a particularly important role in the after-integration processes of strategic business or equity alliances. Entry into strategic equity and business non-equity associations is a very demanding process, which involves not just the phase of executing a purchase (when taking over) or signing a cooperation agreement (in a strategic relationship), but comprises of a series of tasks and procedures that can be, given the course of the creation of a connection, classified into three periods: the period before the connection, the period of making the connection and the period after the conclusion of the connection. The third period is crucial when it comes to the realization of the objectives set in the first period and formally confirmed in the second period. Without a strategic and operational reciprocal adjustment of partners, which is, as a rule, radical and rapid, a synergistic effect $(2 + 2 = 5)$ will not be achieved, as the participants will retain only the sum of their resources and capabilities $(2 + 2 = 4$—costs). Integration in a connection can be: procedural (involves combining the systems and procedures of the participating companies at the operational, supervisory and strategic level); physical (resources and means—consolidation of programmes, production technologies, projects, business-production units, infrastructure); managerial and socio-cultural (the biggest issue—involves managers' transitions, changes in the organizational structure, the development of a consistent and corporate culture, models of strategic action, a system of motivation and the establishment of new management).

Restructuring is often a leading method of change in insolvency proceedings. If a company is unable to eliminate the state of acute crisis by extensive and radical changes in business operations and out-of-court agreements with creditors on the write-off, deferral or reduction of financial burdens, such companies are still able to decide for insolvency proceedings (bankruptcy, compulsory agreement and court liquidation procedure). In the event of a compulsory settlement, another large-scale sectoral restructuring will be required in addition to financial restructuring.

In all of these circumstances, it is almost impossible to avoid a *breakdown or disunion of a unified culture, or the occurrence of a temporary (intermediate) unhealthy (unproductive) culture*, which acts as an inhibitor on 1) the possibility of a complete renewal of the company and 2) the efficiency and success of further business. When a company finds itself in a state of acute crisis or a lagging development step and a step-down in competitiveness when large (revolutionary) changes are required, such a situation will always reflect also in the company's culture. The crisis has several dimensions (economic, social, traditional, psychological and legal), which also directly affect culture. For example, the social aspect includes changing the behaviour of the participants in the crisis, redistributing the position of an individual or certain groups in society, and increasing the proportion of individuals below the threshold of economic and social vulnerability, while the psychological aspect promotes the state of tensions and conflicts among participants in the organization, worries, stress and uncertainty, achieving the culmination of organizational problems, and there are only two options—failure or survival, which changes the "psychological profile" of the organization and its members, and more often the disease symptoms of the organization and its members occur. The crisis always causes psychosocial damage (Kovoor-Misra 2020, 192).

This said article *hypothesizes* that changing the culture due to its direct and indirect influence on ensuring the possibility of further existence and development is an integral part of a comprehensive renewal or restructuring of a company.

5.4 Organizational Culture, Ethics of Management and Restructuring of a Company

Culture can be defined as the set of the symbols of rituals, myths, the system of values, the diversity of the atmosphere, personality, etc. and last but not least as a system of commonly accepted and vivid images of values and attitudes. The corporate culture or *organizational culture* is an integral and corporate system of values, norms, rules, attitudes, beliefs, common attributes, ways of implementing processes and procedures, behaviour and work methods of employees, common goals and characteristics of the reciprocal process of influence, adaptation and interdependence of the organization and its environment. It represents how an organization solves problems to achieve the goals of the participants and the organization's own goals. The philosophy of the company as the mind-set of the company summarizes and creates a culture of the company that gives the desired foundations for the conduct of the participants in the company for the benefit of the company. There are several metaphors for conceptualizing organizational culture (Ehrhart et al. 2014, 128): culture as exchange-regulator, as compass, as social glue, as sacred cow, as affect-regulator, as disorder, as blinders, as world-closure.

The company's culture is integrated, diverse and fragmented by influential groups or individuals in the company, and these differences and contrasts are particularly evident in the period when a company finds itself in crisis when once a common (integral) culture is broken down into different parts. When the company is faced with a crisis, the behaviour of internal (employees, management, unions) and external participants (owners, creditors, suppliers, competitors, clients, state institutions) alters, and they react differently to the newly established conditions in the company. Such a disrupting organizational culture that adversely affects the efficiency and effectiveness of operations, especially when it comes to crisis management or challenging renewals to ensure the continued existence and development of the company, is a consequence of the disrupt balance between the initially harmonized interests of the participants in the company. Namely, in an acute crisis, the balance is disrupted since each participant takes all the measures necessary to protect his/her interests that can only be achieved by interfering within the area of interest of another participant. According to their role and position in the company, not all participants that share the same interests have the same power or influence. Since specific participants strive to achieve different advantages, their management of interests inside and outside the company also differs. The result of the crisis is usually the disintegration of a formerly inclusive organizational culture; therefore, the crisis management or transformation leader must also deal with the reintegration of disintegrated parts into a uniform culture of the company. Culture in the company is also referred to as a whole of the learned practice that employees share and transfer to new employees. In other words, culture is "the way things happen in a company" (Rock and Rock 1990, 239). Organizational culture allows individuals to learn and distinguish from appropriate and inappropriate behaviour. This can involve the questions of centralized or decentralized decision-making, slow or fast decision-making, short-term or long-term horizons, level of teamwork, degree of openness and confrontation, entrepreneurial behaviour and acceptance of risk, orientation towards processes or results, measurement and evaluation of outcomes, degrees of horizontal cooperation, focus on responsibility, way of communication, readiness to change, etc. The creation and formation of organizational culture are influenced by founders and managers at all levels of the organization, the joint learning of the participants in the organization over a longer period, the culture of the wider social environment and the activity in which the organization operates.

Ethics of management is directly linked to a personal and organizational culture as a particular aspect of culture, as a consolidated culture of a company can stimulate or distort ethical decision-making, which takes into account different social norms and rules of behaviour. The attitude of managers to ethics can be weak, moral, amoral or immoral. In his/her work, the manager inevitably encounters the values of the participants and inevitably experiences difficulties in deciding how to manage the organization in the event of incompatible or even opposing values of the participants, and last but not least, with his/her own values. Ethical are those decisions that take into account the interests of the participants and the moral action that implements these decisions. When deciding between different and opposing values, the decision-maker, manager, finds himself/herself in ethical distress, a dilemma. Regarding the power of culture and the appropriateness of the culture to implement an organization's policy, managers may face four basic options: ignore, exploit, use or change the culture. In one of the major surveys (Greve 2011, 242), 71% of 1224 respondents said that they would change their culture if that were possible. In a normally functioning organization, only 30% of employees are devoted to their work and aspire to the quality of their work, 50% of employees only spend their time at work, while 20% even perform unsatisfactory and counter-productive work (Gallup's survey, Kim and Mauborgne 2014). Therefore, there is always a possibility in this area to achieve changes with a positive outcome for the entire organization.

5.5 Changing the Organizational Culture

Every organization has a culture. It is entirely possible that the existing culture in the company is incompatible with the company's goals and strategies to achieve these goals, which reduces the organization's performance and causes problems in it. The symptoms of such an inhibiting culture are, for example, outdated guidelines, unwanted initiatives, de-motivation, bad atmosphere, uncertainty, distorted relationships, general distrust, accusation, victimization, narcissism, indifference to internal and external environmental actors, uncoordinated cultures of subsystems, closed subcultures that disable communication, the gap between words and actions leading to cynicism and mockery, obstruction of change, alienation among employees, etc.

Business practice and research suggest that culture is a factor in the success of the organization (Cameron and Quinn 2011, 6; Connors and Smith 2011, 16; Saleh 2016, 209), despite the fact that the relationship between culture and organizational performance would benefit from models that are more complex (Ehrhart et al. 2014, 294). Cultures that limit or inhibit success can be called: dysfunctional, tension-filled, paranoid, dramatic, depressive, schizoidal, destructive, unbalanced, toxic, etc. When an existing culture does not allow the long-term goals of the company to be achieved, it suppresses the possibility of further existence and development, or it may even be the potential cause of unethical decision-making or immoral action or even the emergence of a crisis, it is necessary to start changing the existing level of culture according to their ingredients, namely from the "toxic" culture to the healed one (re-inspired), in which the goals of the individual and the goals of the company go hand in hand. If culture fails, it needs to be changed (see Cameron and Quinn 2011, 13; Ehrhart et al. 2014, 193; Spiegel et al. 2017).

Changing culture in a company is an *extremely demanding task*, as it is:

- a long-lasting process (even over 10 years, often including even generational turnovers);
- a process faced by extremely strong resistance to change (it is about interfering with interests and values);
- a process that cannot be carried out radically and at one time, but constantly and gradually;
- a process that is most often possible only after the completion of other methods of revolutionary change.

Changing the culture contains both the characteristics of evolutionary change methods, since such changes cannot be carried out with one-time drastic and dramatic measures, but gradually and in the long run, as well as the revolutionary change methods, since at the same time such a change will be easier and more efficient, if it is going to *follow the performed revolutionary changes* in other areas, where the resistance to change is, as a rule, reduced. If the existence of a company is not compromised, the changing of a culture may be desirable (transactional); in the event of a need for an accelerated development step or an emerging or threatening crisis, it is necessary (transformational), which is why *changing culture should be an integral part of the company's overall restructuring*. It is cultural changes that can be the "differentiator" that brings competitive advantage and success in the changed rules of the game to every company (Connors and Smith 2011, 213).

Ehrhart et al. (2014, 131) cite the reasons why organizational culture is difficult to change: it is shared, stable, symbolic, expressive, subjective and unique, it has depth and breadth, it is grounded in history and tradition, it is transmitted to new members, it provides order and rules to organizational existence and it is a source of collective identity and commitment.

As this is about changing the consolidated ideology of individuals, it will often be easier to change culture when the departure (retirement) of individuals occurs, rather than having a long-lasting influence on their perceptions, values and behaviour, when exceptional resistance to change is expected (Michel 2013, 306). Therefore, the culture-changing process cannot be done at once, but gradually and slowly (Cameron and Quinn 2011, 121; Greve 2011, 242), although persistently and consistently. Organizational culture exists on two levels (Crandall et al. 2014, 100): on the surface level, which represents the typical behavioural patterns of the organization, and on the underlying level, which encompasses values and beliefs specific to the members of the organization. The latter is the most difficult to understand since it lies at the core of how members of the organization think about and interpret their work. Changing the culture is a changing of behaviour, the behaviour of people, where the expected resistance is the highest, and therefore the highest contributions are time, assets or capabilities. However, the culture of the company is becoming an increasingly important factor in exploiting the company's marketing and internal potential, and such contributions are, as a rule, justified. The personal example of managers is a prerequisite for effective nurturing and developing a company's culture; however, the management is not able to delegate the care of culture onto others. Leaders guide followers based on such an investment, thus preventing deviant behaviour, guiding in uncertainties, creating greater flexibility, promoting positive behaviour, and building trust and identifying with the goals of the organization.

Radical and dramatic changes can ruin the organization and its culture, and the new organization will have to build a new culture. Building an organizational culture requires the input of the manager's time, energy and resources, and such an investment is all the more necessary when it comes to global business operations in different social cultures when mixing cultures or acculturation occurs. Acculturation in the anthropological sense derives from the contact between two autonomous cultures and requires a change in one or another culture, including such a subjective organizational culture (shared patterns of values, beliefs, expectations of members of the organization) as well as an objective organizational culture (the specifics which they are developed by the organization), with a number of variants possible: cultural preservation, cultural assimilation, cultural integration and cultural transformation.

Literature offers various models, approaches and guidelines for changing cultures (e.g. Armenakis et al. 2011; Cameron and Quinn 2011; Connors and Smith 2011; Ehrhart et al. 2014); however, culture can be changed in steps that first starts with analysing the current situation, finding key conflicts, differences and deviations in internal relations, carrying out activities to eliminate them and reaching consensus on the desired organizational culture, and concluding with the integration of organizational culture with the objectives and policy of the organization.

Changing the culture, however, cannot, as a rule, be carried out when the existential goals of the company and the employees are at stake since in that case there are too stressful and risky situations. Therefore, it will be possible to begin changing the culture only when the foundations of continuity are provided (crisis management, restructuring, re-engineering). Changing culture can never begin with the intention of changing the culture, but by acting and changing the company itself (strategy, vision, information). Culture is the source (asset) of the company's power and legacy of past successes. Changing culture can be influenced by employee participation, communication, training and education, promotion of successes and awards, changes in structures and processes, changes in management, the arrival of new employees, new strategies. Often, culture is impossible to change a without change in governance, especially if culture is determined by those who run the company, so it should be started here (Armenakis et al. 2011; Moore 2016, 154; Connors and Smith 2011, 16).

The new culture will often be linked to the knowledge management when it comes to systematic search and use of knowledge in a particular organization when the organization optimally exploits available assets based on the knowledge of internal or external individuals, groups or communities (see Lussier 2017, 19).

5.6 Empirical Findings

The findings from the previous discussion were also verified in an empirical survey by analysing 40 cases of companies in Slovenia which attempted to solve an acute crisis with a compulsory agreement as a sort of insolvency proceedings in the period 2015–2017 (list: www.ajpes.si/eobjave), the integral part of which, in addition to financial restructuring, includes comprehensive business restructuring in all other areas (recent examples from the years 2018 and 2019 have not yet been covered since most of the restructuring procedures have not yet been fully completed, which does not alter the final findings). If bankruptcy is a mean of eliminating an uncontrollable crisis in a company, and its legal consequence is the formal winding-up of a company, the bankruptcy proceeds obtained from the sale of its assets are distributed among creditors in proportion to the amount and position of their claims, the compulsory agreement is primarily a rehabilitation process in which the company in the crisis, with the agreement of the creditors, undertakes financial restructuring on the one hand and prepares and adopts measures of business rehabilitation on the other hand, without which the sole financial restructuring, with which creditors are provided more favourable terms of payment of their claims in comparison to those if the company was in bankruptcy process, could not be successful. A key document to be submitted by a company in compulsory agreement proceeding is a publicly announced *financial restructuring plan* which, in addition to the terms of the financial restructuring, must include a description of other comprehensive restructuring measures to be undertaken by the company, and for each of these measures must have a timetable for the implementation, estimation of execution costs and assessment of the effects of the implementation of the measure on the elimination of the causes of insolvency, and short-term and long-term solvency.

If it has already been established that the changing culture due to direct and indirect impact on the success and efficiency of business is desirable, necessary or indispensable during the development period of the company, changing culture from inhibiting to encouraging and integrated is necessary especially when the company is threatened by crisis or is already facing one, but then changing the culture becomes part of a complete restructuring of the company. In order to implement a reversal strategy, culture often needs to be changed (Moore 2016, 154; Saleh 2016, 211).

In the analysis of 40 cases of Slovenian companies in the acute crisis, which, in the period 2015–2017, wanted to improve their position through the compulsory agreement procedure, it was shown that no change in culture as a direct measure was foreseen. In only five cases, traces of this kind of change can be detected indirectly in the context of changing the HR area, where plans for changing the number of employees or organizational measures are at the forefront. If a comprehensive restructuring in all areas is a condition for a successful renewal of the company, which ensures further existence and development, it was noticed in the analysed cases that in practice negligible attention was devoted to cultural change and rarely, and merely indirectly, is it mentioned as an integral part of a comprehensive restructuring. This may be one of the reasons (but not necessarily) why many procedures for remediation of the company's current state of affairs in an acute crisis have failed. The rehabilitation of a company denotes a process of recovery of a company in crisis with the goal to eliminate the existing unfavourable condition, which poses a threat to the future, to prevent further worsening within the management and to re-establish the conditions that will enable the company to continue to exist and develop (Dubrovski 2011, 117). The data show that formal insolvency procedures as a restructuring method are generally not successful (mostly 10% and less than 30%; Wood 2013, 113; Moore 2016, 1). The contribution to tackling such an issue is, therefore, the direction that, in addition to financial and business restructuring, the company is often required to change the culture, which has certain characteristics described, compared to the changing of other areas, as the new productive culture, as stated, directly and indirectly affects the efficiency and performance of operations, which is of crucial importance in the period of crisis management.

We are aware of the shortcomings of such qualitative research and the possibility that the financial restructuring plans from which the data were obtained are not necessarily the actual business plans, since the primary goal of these plans is to persuade creditors to accept the proposed financial settlement and therefore may not contain all the measures envisaged, or they are not described in detail, but this is a key and public document for creditors who decide on potential assistance to an insolvent company and support the proposed settlement. But even such a limited research clearly shows the *gap* between the declared need to change the culture in conditions of endangered further existence and development on the one hand, and the actual implementation of these changes in practice on the other.

5.7 Conclusion

If a company wishes to ensure its continued existence and development in today's competitive environment in the modern conditions of business operations, it must constantly implement changes, which are evolutionary or revolutionary, depending on the situation, whereas the changing of culture extends to both approaches and has some specifics in comparison with other areas of change. The article deals with the hypothesis that the change of culture due to its direct and indirect influence on ensuring the possibility of further existence and development is an integral part of a comprehensive renewal, restructuring of the company, when it is almost impossible to avoid a breakdown or disunion of a unified culture to that moment or the occurrence of a temporary (intermediate) unhealthy (unproductive) culture. When a company finds itself in a state of acute crisis or a lagging development step and a step-down in competitiveness when large (revolutionary) changes are required, such a situation will always reflect also in the company's culture. If the existence of a company is not compromised, the changing of a culture may be desirable (and the change transactional); in the event of a need for an accelerated development step or an emerging or threatening crisis it is necessary (and the change transformational), which is why changing culture should be an integral part of the company's overall restructuring.

Changing culture in a company is an extremely demanding task, as it is a lengthy process, a process faced with extremely strong resistance to change, a process that cannot be carried out radically and at one time, but constantly and gradually, and a process that is most often possible only after the completion of other methods of revolutionary change.

In the paper, the findings from the previous discussion were also verified in the empirical survey by analysing 40 cases of companies in Slovenia which attempted to deal with the acute crisis in the period of 2015–2017 through compulsory agreement insolvency proceedings. Its integral part, in addition to financial restructuring, is also a comprehensive business restructuring in all other areas. In the study of 40 cases of Slovenian companies in the acute crisis, which, in the period 2015–2017, wanted to improve their position through the compulsory agreement procedure, it was shown that no change in culture as a direct measure was foreseen. In only a few cases, traces of this kind of change can be detected indirectly in the context of the forecast of changing the personnel area, where other plans were at the forefront. In spite of the limitations, the mentioned research pointed out the gap between the declared need to change the culture in conditions of endangered further existence and development on the one hand, and the actual implementation of these changes in practice on the other.

References

Armenakis A, Brown S, Mehta A (2011) Organizational culture: assessment and transformation. J Chang Manag 11(3):305–328

Birkinshaw J, Goddard J (2009) What is your management model? MIT Sloan Manag Rev 50(2):81–90

Blatz M, Haghani S (2006) Innovative crisis management concepts—an up-to-date status evaluation. In: Blatz M, Kraus K-J, Haghani S (eds) Corporate restructuring. Springer, Berlin

Cameron KS, Quinn RE (2011) Diagnosing and changing organizational culture. Jossey-Bass, San Francisco

Christensen CM, Bartman T, van Bever D (2016) The hard truth about business model innovation. MIT Sloan Manag Rev 58(1):30–40

Connors R, Smith T (2011) Change the culture, change the game. Penguin, New York

Crandall WR, Parnell JA, Spillan JE (2014) Crisis management. Sage, Los Angeles

Dubrovski D (2016) Handling corporate crises based on the correct analysis of its causes. J Fin Risk Manage 5:264–280

Dubrovski, Drago. 2011. *Razsežnosti kriznega managementa.* Celje: Mednarodna fakulteta za družbene in poslovne študije

Ehrhart MG, Schneider B, Macey WH (2014) Organizational climate and culture: an introduction to theory, research and practice. Routledge, New York

Greve G (2011) Organizational burnout. Das versteckte Phänomen ausgebrannter Organisationen. Gabler Verlag, Wiesbaden

Kim WC, Mauborgne R (2014) Blue ocean leadership. Harv Bus Rev 92(3):60–72

Kovoor-Misra S (2020) Crisis management. Resilience & change. Los Angeles: Sage

Lussier RN (2017) Management fundamentals: concepts, applications, and skill development. Sage, Thousand Oaks

Michel L (2013) The performance triangle. LID Publishing, London

Moore H (2016) Business turnaround. How to do it. Longhirst Publishing, London

Rock ML, Rock RH (1990) Corporate restructuring. McGraw-Hill, New York

Saleh YD (2016) Crisis management. The art of success and failure. Mill City Press, Minneapolis

Spiegel M, Schmiedel T, vom Brocke J (2017) What makes change harder—or easier. MIT Sloan Manag Rev 58(3):88–89

Wood PR (2013) Principles of international insolvency (Part II). In: Fletcher IF (ed) A special collection celebrating 21 years. INSOL International & John Wiley & Sons, London

Zook C (2007) Unstoppable. Finding hidden assets to renew the core and fuel profitable growth. Harvard Business School Press, Boston

Chapter 6
Theoretical Background of Occupational Standards, Basic Concepts and Related Institutions

F. Pervin Bilir and Seyhan Bilir Güler

Abstract It is an important necessity to plan and evaluate the workforce, which is a driving force in the country's economy, in terms of quality and quantity, and to generate solutions oriented toward change and development. The efficiency and productivity of the labor market depend on scientific analysis of working conditions, making legislative regulations and executively applying these regulations. Occupational standards are also an important tool in this respect. Occupational standard is defined as the minimal norm indicating the required knowledge, skills, attitude and manner to successfully profess an occupation. In our today's world what we call informatics society; the countries restructure education and employment systems due to the positive correlation between education and development. Within this restructuring, particularly giving emphasize to occupational standards, occupational training standards, examination and certification systems, which will provide the coordination between education and employment, they endeavor to ensure the institutionalization also by implementing the active participation of government, labor and employers' organizations and non-governmental organizations. In this system, important concepts and institutions become prominent and need to be clarified. In this study, these prominent concepts are discussed and tried to be defined, and the functions of institutions that are established for occupational standards have been tried to be introduced.

Keywords Occupation · Occupational skill · Occupational standards · Vocational qualifications institution

F. Pervin Bilir
Faculty of Sports Sciences, Department of Sport Management, Çukurova University, Adana, Turkey
e-mail: pbilir@cu.edu.tr

S. B. Güler (✉)
Faculty of Economics and Administrative Sciences, Department of Business Administration, Trakya University, Edirne, Turkey
e-mail: seyhanguler@trakya.edu.tr

© The Author(s), under exclusive license to Springer Nature Singapore Pte Ltd. 2021   93
K. T. Çalıyurt (ed.), *New Approaches to CSR, Sustainability and Accountability,*
Volume II, Accounting, Finance, Sustainability, Governance & Fraud: Theory
and Application, https://doi.org/10.1007/978-981-33-6808-8_6

6.1 Introduction

In our era, the national and international policies are not aiming decades or the centuries but are aiming millenniums in line with development strategies. The business world of the countries focuses on realizing full and productive employment, including women and young. In the center of this focusing human takes place.

In organizations the resources that are not monetary or physical, can be controlled and contributing to the produced value is called as intellectual capital. Labor force is an intellectual capital (Kart 2015: 17). Qualifications of the intellectual capital and its employability are one of the most components of development. Certainly, the most important treasure of the manpower which is intellectual capital is knowledge. The labor force market of the time seeks for labor force having knowledge as a distinctive factor besides ability and education. The quality of the organizations significantly related to this labor force. Together with the quality of labor force, the product service quality and the quality of management, that is a total quality is an important indicator to determine the competitive capacity of organizations. The most important dimension of total quality is forming standards. The definition of quality lay emphasize on this. The target of education and employment processes gravitate to quality.

Despite the fact that technological developments bring into question of the changes in occupational structures, the qualified labor force always keeps its importance. In the changing and evolving business world, to be able to increase the employment and to be able to create a sustainable economy is possible by training qualified labor force needed by the local and sectoral labor markets. In general, the qualified labor force is educated and trained by formal and prevalent public and private education institutions in world countries. Due to the positive relationship between education and development, countries are restructuring the education and employment systems. Within this restructuring, particularly by giving importance to occupational standards, occupational training standards, examination and certification systems, which will provide the coordination between education and employment, they endeavor to ensure the institutionalization also by implementing the active participation of government, labor and employers. In this system, substantial concepts and institutions become prominent and need to be interpreted.

Turkey has already formed the required bodies with respect to the regulations intending to form the occupational standards; however, the standardization procedures for the occupations still continue. The concepts which are being used in occupations are not known by many people yet. In this study, these prominent concepts have been discussed and tried to be defined, besides the functions of institutions established for occupational standards have been tried to be introduced.

6.2 Theoretical Background of Occupational Standards

The journey of the concepts of division of labor, specialization and standardization which constitutes the fundamental background of occupational standards in historical process has started with industrial revolution. The technical, economic and social changes such as urbanization, industrialization, mechanization (mass production), specialization and standardization which have started with industrial revolution, created large and complex enterprises. In conjunction with the invention of steam engine in later of eighteenth century and at the beginning of nineteenth century, small-scale workplaces manufacturing with traditional methods gave place to factories making mass production (Mucuk 2014: 14). By 1900s, mainly Taylor but H. Fayol, L. Gilbert, H. Gantt et al. who were taking place in the system, started scientific studies with the purpose of overcoming the problems of traditional manufacturing system by means of scientific methods (Koçel 2020: 221). In all these processes, considering the basic qualifications related to occupational standards, it is seen that a theoretical background was formed and this is based on an extensive scope of application. Scientific Management Approach, Management Process Approach and Bureaucracy Approach point to determining the frequently accentuated tasks in scientific methods, their classification and assessment. For work and task description, and establishment of standards it is necessary to make arrangements like work study, job analysis and based on these to make job definitions and requirements. In line with this necessity, the first thing to be done is comprehending the definitions of these concepts. These definitions are given below.

Work study is a technique implementing to determine the standards relevant to the usage of production resources with methods and conditions developed by means of motion studies and work measurements (Akal 2005: 331). In scientific management approach it was denominated that business processes should be split into its components to standardize the work processes. To perform a job which motions should be done and how long each of those motions takes come into prominence as the determinative factors. Therefore, it is necessary to define the two concepts, motion study and time study, which constitute the job study. *Motion study* is the activity of determining the most suitable working methods and designs and also the standardization of production methods by paying attention to human-machinery relationship for doing a certain job (Yüksel 2007: 92). Time study is determining the required standard time for the job by means of methods such as chronometer, blackboard and filming (Yüksel 2007: 94). In another definition, it is a job measurement technique applied for recording time period and speed of performing the components of a certain job carried out under specified conditions and analyzing the data obtained for the purpose of calculating the required time to carry out the job being talked about at a predetermined performance level (Prokopenko 1995: 157).

Job Analysis is a technique that is examining the quality, quantity, requirements, responsibilities and working conditions of each of the works taking place in the organization separately and collecting information on the purpose of right, effective and healthy assessment of the works. The purpose of job analysis is to disintegrate the work to the smallest parts with respect to cognitive, affective and psycho-motor behavior areas and introduce meaningful wholes. Job analysis activities consist of the efforts devoted to determine the task, responsibility and working conditions involved in the works in organizations. In these efforts, in addition, it is also tried to determine the knowledge, skills and abilities that people who will perform the jobs should have (Tortop et al. 2006: 55).

With the contribution of all these techniques, now, the studies in regard to occupational standards have proceeded considerably. Occupational classifications and standards have been propounded, International Standard Classification of Occupations (ISCO), National Classification of Occupations as well as Vocational Qualifications Authority, National Qualifications Framework and Turkish Qualifications Framework (TYÇ–TQF) has been constituted. Below, these bodies were discussed and examined one by one.

6.3   Occupational Classifications and Standards

The changes experienced with the advancing technology enabled the emergence of new professions. Many works that people were doing are being done through computers and robots today. With globalization, the labor force also globalized. In light of these developments, the need for classification and standardization of the occupations arose. Presently many countries and organizations study on occupational classification systems. This is because the role of the employee in labor market is determined by occupational classification. To determine perceptively the behaviors that the occupation requires, it is necessary to classify the occupations existing in labor market, to define by the related parties of market and to be analyzed with respect to educational needs. By means of job analyses, the occupational behaviors that individual should have for performing the job are determined. In line with education and training needs determined by job analyses, occupational standards of the market are developed. Occupational standards can be expressed as; the minimum norms specified by authorized bodies to carry on an occupation successfully which pointing out what were those knowledge, skills, behaviors and attitudes concerning that occupation.

Occupational classifications overall classify the occupations exist in a country. It is an arrangement in groups of the tasks undertaken by the occupations in all businesses. It has two constituents; the classification system itself: This constituent provides instructions how jobs would be classified in detailed groups and how these detailed groups would be added into wider groups. It includes occupational titles and codes and also represents a value specified for the occupation (ILO, What is an Occupational Classification?).

- The Definitive Constituent: In general, this consists of elements of other jobs that belong to each of the defined groups, including tasks and goods and services produced by defining tasks, skill level and specialization, included and excluded occupations, entry restrictions, etc. It is possible to say that these explanations compose an occupational dictionary.

- An occupational classification can be compared to chart system of a country; here the top level corresponds to a small-scale road map for main highways and roads. The next level corresponds to a set of larger-scale maps for each of the main regions showing the provincial and local roads (ILO, What is an Occupational Classification?)

Occupational standards comprise elements such as the qualifications that people should have, and the working environment, the tools and equipment used and the minimum level of education/training should be received to be able to perform tasks related to a profession in the labor market to the minimum acceptable standards. Tuncer and Taşpınar (2004) express the function of occupational standards as follows:

> Occupational standard studies aim to make the employee more knowledgeable in technical terms in addition to make them more productive and more sensitive with regard to public health, social environment, etc. It is known that, the occupational standard determining studies will have serious effects on employment of the individuals leaving occupational system. Occupational standards, which will be the driving force for the establishment of a qualified vocational education/training system, will become more meaningful to the extent that graduates can use individual opportunities such as international agreements or free movement. (Tuncer and Taşpınar 2004: 1)

While occupational standards, examination and certification bodies are partly different from country to country, basically they serve the same purpose. The purpose on establishment of these institutions is to prepare or make prepared the occupational standards, to perform or make performed standard examinations and certifications in overall country. Furthermore, occupational standards are accepted as a dynamic process. In our country, the occupational standards and the lack of examination and certification system have been stated in II'nd and III'rd Five Year Development Plans (Demirezen 2002: 215–216). The content of the occupational standard prepared in our country is given at Fig. 6.1.

In the world, different occupational classification systems are being used. The national classifications in some countries are related to the classifications such as ILO (International Labour Organization), ISCO (International Standard Classification of Occupations), UNIDO (United Nations Industrial Development Organizations) and ISCI (International Standard Classification of Industry). Presently, the well-accepted occupational classification system in Europe is ISCO-08 (Tuncer and Taşpınar 2004: 2).

6.4 International Standard Classification of Occupations (ISCO)

International Standard Classification of Occupations (ISCO) is one of the principal international classifications that International Labor Organization ILO is responsible for. ISCO is an international member of economic and social classifications family. The development of International Standard Classification of Occupations (ISCO) goes back to decades. After the population census made in 1850 in America, the published tables constitutes the first de facto classification (Abraham 1999: 1). In

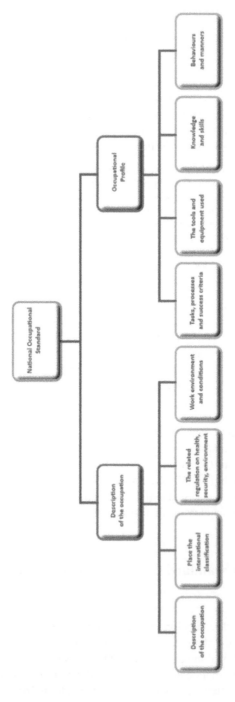

Fig. 6.1 Content of occupational standard. *Source* Taken from Vocational Qualifications Authority (MYK) web page

later continuum, despite the fact that the need for the classification of occupations according to international standards first started in 1923s, studies for the development of ISCO were initiated in 1947 at 6th International Conference of Labor Statisticians (ICLS), and the first positive step toward its establishment has been taken in 1949 by the 7th ICLS with the adoption of a temporary classification of the nine large groups.

In 1952, International Labor Organization—ILO published the international occupational classification. Based on eight industrialized countries' national classifications, detailed definitions of 1772 of the occupations were made.

Following the first ISCO published by ILO in 1958, therefore it is known as ISCO-58, it continued as ISCO-58, ISCO-68, and ISCO-88 with revisions. ISCO-88 is widely used since it has been adopted. Based on available evidences, ISCO-88 successfully exceeded ISCO-68 and became a model for national classification in many of the countries even if there were national classifications previously (Elias 1997). At the beginning of twenty-first century, it became necessary to update ISCO-88 for reflecting the changes in the occupational structure of labor force, for solving some of the defined problems, and the changes arising from the developments in information and communication technologies on labor force. The updated classification ISCO-08 has been adopted on December 2007.

ISCO-08 classification system is an updated system with structural changes parallel to the developments in business world, without changing the fundamental principles and bodywork of ISCO-88. Many of the countries are updating their national classification based on ISCO-08 or bring it into conformity with International Statistics Standard. ISCO-08 is an instrument for organizing the works by clearly defined groups in pursuant of assumed task at work and jobs. Three main purposes of ISCO-08 are these: To provide a basis for international reporting, comparison and sharing of statistical and administrative information about occupations,

- To be a useful model for the development of national and regional classification of occupations
- To provide an immediately available system in the countries which did not develop their national classifications.

The major occupational groups defined in International Standard Classification of Occupations ISCO are as follows: (1) Managers, (2) Professionals, (3) Technicians and Associate Professionals, (4) Clerical Support Workers, (5) Service and Sales Workers, (6) Skilled Agricultural, Forestry and Fishery Workers, (7) Crafts and Related Trades Workers, (8) Plant and Machine Operators and Assemblers, (9) Elementary occupations, (10) Armed Forces Occupations (ISCO-08 Part II).

In European Skills, Competences, Qualifications and Occupations (ESCO) 2942 occupations were defined. Each occupation, at the same time, is associated together with occupational profile. Occupational profiles explain the description, content and definition of the occupation. Furthermore, they list the knowledge and skill competences related to this occupational area according to European scale.

ISCO-08 is a four-level hierarchically structured classification that allows all jobs in the world to be divided into 436 unit groups. These groups constitute the most detailed level of the classification structure and based on their similarities in regard to skill level and skill competency required for jobs, they concentrate in 130 small groups, 43 sub-major-groups and 10 large groups. Thus, besides the international comparable data, it was provided to generate summary information for only 10 groups having highest concentration levels (ISCO-08 Part I).

The framework used to design and construct of ISCO-08 is based on two main concepts: Occupation concept and Skill concept. These concepts were explained below:

Occupation Concept

Since the words "job" and "occupation", which have different meanings, are used interchangeably both in terms of their theoretical and different languages, firstly, the concept of the occupation must be defined and its differences with the related concepts must be exposed.

Job is defined as a task and duties performed or meant to be performed by one person, including for an employer or in self-employment (ISCO-08 Part I). For most of the job owners, this task has been determined before they employed (Elias 1997: 6). Occupation on the other hand refers to the kind of work performed. It is also defined as the set of jobs that the fundamental tasks having high degree of similarity (ISCO-08 Part I). Occupation, being a Romanesque word passed down to Medieval French and then to English. The occupation word in English has been associated with acquiring a special knowledge and employment in areas where such knowledge is a prerequisite. Turkish Language Association (TDK–TLA) defines the concept of occupation as "A work which its rules designated and that is gained with a certain education/training, based on systematic knowledge and skills, is done to produce useful goods for people, to serve and to earn money in return. The concept of occupation has also been defined emphasizing the structural characteristics such as "traditional organization of labor", "consecution of institutionalized practices", "an activity form which is everlasting, institutionalized and having an expertise subject". Some other definitions that explain the content of the concept by driving forward the characteristics such as developed, complex, based on a special knowledge, presence of authority and autonomy in their field of work, relative boundedness of formal hierarchy comparing to other organizations, generates a permanent source of living in social division of labor, being "confined organizational society" (Karasu 2001: 39).

Some authors underline the entailment that, an engagement should have some characteristics in order to become an occupation. Goode (1996: 68) has listed the criteria for an engagement to be accepted as an occupation as follows:

- Occupation primarily is the activity area a person carries on principally and on a regular basis. The activities done once in a while as hobby or pleasure are not deemed occupation.
- Occupation should be performed as a fundamental form of source of living for an earning in return.
- A clear and standard definition of occupations should be made and they should base on systematic information.
- The occupation should have its own distinctive education/training practice or should be based on personal skills.

- Occupations should have professional behavior standards value the objectives of the occupation above the personal objectives of the people carry on that occupation
- Occupations should have professional principles and rules, occupational ethics and discipline unique to its own.

Yoder, on the other hand, addressed both ethic and technical dimensions of the issue (Tosun 1987: 406):

- Requirement of a certain knowledge, skill and experience for entering an occupation.
- Certain ethical standards to carry on the occupation.
- Commitment to occupation, ethical standards and the principles of serving to people.
- Having standard methods adopted in consent and understandable by all of the members of the area of occupation (profession).
- These methods and practices should be based on continuous research and specialist training.
- Professional publications related to occupational researches.
- A specialized terminology (This creates understanding and harmony among the members of the occupation and facilitate the development and teaching of science).

Today the meaning of the word of occupation is; what kind of work a person does as a general way of using time or it is the answer received when asked what kind of a work a person does. It is possible to express that the answer being talked about reflects a social status or a form of a classification (Elias 1997: 5). The tendency of occupational classifications reflect social strata today fell behind, and a general understanding about it is much more related to the characteristics of the work a worker does instead of the characteristics of the worker to be classified.

Occupational Skill

Skill is defined as the ability to carry out the tasks and duties of a certain job (ISCO-08 Part I). Skill means that the ability of practicing the knowledge, and to know how to complete the job and how to solve the problem. These include the cognitive and implementation dimensions. Cognitive dimensions comprise the logic, intuition and creative thinking, and the implementation dimensions comprise hand skill, the methods of job, the tools, materials and equipment to be used (ESCO). Skill and talent (ability) concepts usually confused with each other. Skill represents the use of the tools, materials and equipment related to the tasks given. Ability (talent), on the other hand, has got a wider content and it is the use and application of knowledge and skills in a unique way when faced with a new situation or unforeseen difficulty (ESCO). The skill level that for the first time was used in International Standard Classification of Occupations—ISCO-88 is a concept related to the amount of formal education or informal training, and work experience often associated with formal education and competent task performance (Elias 1997: 6).

In line with the objectives of ISCO-08 to arrange the occupations into groups, skill is considered in two dimensions. These are skill level and skill specialization (ISCO-8 Part I).

Skill level is defined as a function of the complexity and range of the tasks and duties to be performed in an occupation. Skill level is measured operationally by considering one or more of the following: (ISCO-8 Part I).

- The nature of the work performed in an occupation related to the tasks defined for each ISCO-08 skill level,
- The level of formal education defined in terms of the International Standard Classification of Education (ISCED-97) (UNESCO 1997) required competent performance of the tasks and duties involved,
- The amount of informal on-the-job training and/or previous experience in a related occupation required for competent performance of these tasks and duties.

Skill specialization defines the knowledge related to the tools-materials-equipment and services used for the produced good (Elias 1997: 6). In ISCO-08 four skill levels were determined. Each one of the skill levels comprises the typical tasks and required abilities of the occupation.

Skill Level 1: Occupations at this level typically involve the performance of simple and routine physical or manual tasks. Many of the occupations may require physical strength and endurance. For some jobs literacy and basic skills in arithmetic along with completion of primary education and basic education are required and on-the-job training may be required as well (ISCO-8 Part I). Some occupations classified at this level include office cleaners, carriers, garden workers and kitchen assistants.

Skill Level 2: The occupations at this level comprise the performance of the tasks such as operating machinery and electronic equipment. Many occupations at this skill level require relatively developed reading-writing and arithmetic skills and good interpersonal communication skills, also requires reading of information such as safety instructions and completion of written records of the job for all occupations. For the occupations at Skill Level 2, the knowledge and skills required for competence performance usually obtained by completing the first stage of secondary education (ISCED-97 Level 2). Some occupations require the completion of second stage of secondary education (ISCED-97 Level 3); these may involve one of the important components of specialized occupational education and on-the-job training. Some of the occupations require completion training special for that occupation after the graduation of secondary education (ISCED-97 Level 4). In some cases, experience and on-the-job training may substitute the formal education (ISCO-8 Part I). Some occupations defined at this level are butchers, bus drivers, secretaries, accountant clerks, sewing machinists, tailors, sales persons, police staff, hair dressers, electricians and mechanics.

Skill Level 3: The occupations at this level typically comprise of executing complicated technical and practical tasks that require technical and procedural knowledge in a specialized field. The occupations at this level usually require high level of literacy and arithmetic skills as well as well-developed interpersonal communication skills. These skills may include understanding of complex written materials, preparing factual reports and verbal communication under difficult conditions. The occupations at Skill Level 3, the knowledge and skills needed for competence performance usually obtained by means of studies in a higher education institution for 1–3 years after the graduation of secondary education (ISCED-97 level 5b). In some cases, inclusive education and long-term on-the-job training may substitute formal education. Some of the occupations defined at this level are shop managers, medical laboratory technicians, legal secretaries and commercial sales representatives.

Skill Level 4: The occupations at this level usually need to execute of tasks requiring complex problem-solving, decision making, and the tasks requiring creativity based on theoretical and factual knowledge in a specialized area. The occupations at this level require very high level literacy, digital and perfect communication skills. These skills in general include understanding of complex written materials and deliver complex opinions in media such as books, pictures, performances, reports and verbal presentations.

At Skill Level 4, the knowledge and skills required for needed performance of the occupations in general obtained as the result of study at a higher education institution for a time period of 3–6 years making a way for the award of a first degree or higher qualifications (ISCED-97 Level 5a or higher).

In some instances, there may be a comprehensive experience and on-the-job training are required in addition to the formal education. In most instances, appropriate formal qualifications are an indispensable requirement to enter into the occupation. Some of the occupations defined at this level comprise; sales and marketing managers, civil engineers, secondary school teachers, medical doctors, musicians, surgical nurses and computer system analysts.

In cases where formal education and training requirements are used as part of measuring the skill level of an occupation, these requirements are defined in terms of International Standard Classification of Education ISCED-97. ISCED-97 education levels can be used to help out defining that of the four skill levels. But, this does not mean that those skills needed to perform the tasks of a certain job could only be acquired through formal education. Skill can be acquired through informal training and experience as well.

6.5 National Occupational Classification and Vocational Qualifications Authority

As it was specified in ISCO-08, in cases where countries do not have required sources, capacities or have no time to develop a national occupational classification (NOC) designed to conform their realities and needs, at least in the short and medium run may adopt ISCO-08 with a minimum changes (ISCO-08 Part I). But, since the occupational structure and national policies differ by countries, they must create their own systems.

- To be a useful model for developing of the national and regional classifications of the occupations
- To provide an immediately available system in the countries which did not develop their national classifications.

The major occupational groups defined in International Standard Classification of Occupations ISCO are as follows: (1) Managers, (2) Professionals, (3) Technicians and Associate Professionals, (4) Clerical Support Workers, (5) Service and Sales Workers, (6) Skilled Agricultural, Forestry and Fishery Workers, (7) Craft and Related Trades Workers, (8) Plant and Machine Operators and Assemblers, (9) Elementary Occupations, (10) Armed Forces Occupations (ISCO-08 Part II).

On September 21, 2006, 5544 numbered Law has been accepted and published on 7/10/2006 dated and 26,312 numbered Official Gazette. With this Law, it was decided to establish Vocational Qualifications Authority to establish and operate the national competence system and working procedures and principles specified (MYK–VQA Law, 2006). After the Authority came into operation, some amendments have been done in MYK–VQA Law due to resolve the problems in practice and the needs for actualization of arrangements brought such as the European Qualifications Framework, National Employment Strategy, Life-long Learning Strategy, and Strengthening the Relationship of Employment and Occupational Education Action Plan. This amendment corresponded in 11.10.2011 dated and 665 Numbered Decree with Power of Law. Vocational Qualifications Authority has also undertaken very important responsibilities in work life with 04/04/2015 dated 6645 numbered Occupational Health and Safety Law and Law Regarding Make Amendments in Some laws and Decrees with Power of Law. Within this framework, it was made obligatory that the people who are working in high risk and very high risk occupations in our country have the VQA (MYK) Vocational Qualification Certificate, arrangements with regard to covering all the costs of exam and certification from unemployment insurance fund have already been made and also it was made obligatory that the aforementioned vocational education and trainings are conducted in accordance with the published national occupational standards published by Vocational Qualifications Authority (MYK). These arrangements transformed Vocational Qualifications Authority (MYK) into the Qualifications Authority of Turkey with respect to its duties and responsibilities. (Vocational Qualifications Authority (MYK) History, VQA (MYK) web).

The objective of 5544 Numbered Vocational Qualifications Authority (MYK) law has been specified as follows:

> The Objective of This Law is; to determine the principles of national qualifications in technical and professional fields, based on national and international occupational standards; the establishment of a Vocational Qualifications Authority to build and operate the necessary national qualifications systems to carry out activities related to audit, measurement and assessment, documentation and certification, determining its working principles and procedures, and to provide the arrangements for the issues related to Turkish Qualifications Framework. (Vocational Qualifications Authority (MYK) Law 2006)

It is an important approach for the Vocational Qualifications Authority to constitute the occupational standards and handle it at international level. Vocational Qualifications Authority aimed at fulfilling the needs of labor market with the studies and endeavors of national occupational standards prepared on the basis of business analyses and assessment and evaluation. Furthermore the occupational standards are generated by means of gathering the jobs under occupational definitions by systematically analyzing the jobs in labor market, and consolidation of positions and titles in a given sector. Therefore the occupational standards have the characteristics of an important source where the jobs relevant to a certain occupation systematically defined. Moreover, due to the changes in business world, the individuals' having some basic skills besides the occupational skills carries importance for the development of human resources and intensifying the relationships in-between education system and working life. These basic skills can be defined as; the information and communication technologies required by business life, foreign language, financial literacy, problem-solving, critical thinking, communication, leadership, career planning and looking for a job and besides these, artistic and sporting skills (Tenth Development Plan, p. 186).

6.6   National Qualifications Framework and Turkish Qualifications Framework (TYÇ–TQF)

National Qualifications Framework (UYÇ–NQF), is the body of principles and rules that are being used to define the qualifications present in a country, to classify and compare in specified criteria, and which consists of levels. NQF integrates the qualification systems available in a country and facilitates of the qualifications being more transparent and definable within the scope of the quality standards and horizontal and vertical movements of learners among the qualifications (TQF Communiqué 2015: 2). When the frameworks of European countries which formed their NQFs are reviewed, it is seen that their common targets are as follows (TQF Communiqué 2015: 3):

- To increase the international transparency in education and training, and to ensure compare and transfer the qualifications
- To increase the transparency of National Qualifications Systems
- To promote life-long learning
- To support and accelerate the tendency to use an approach based on learning outcomes in education and training
- To increase the permeability and flexibility of education and training systems to ensure transfer and progress
- To validate informal and free learning
- To increase the consistency among qualifications
- To provide a reference base for quality assurance
- To strengthen the cooperation among the stakeholders and to establish closer relationships with labor market.

Turkish Qualifications Framework (TQF–TYÇ) which takes place in the objective of Vocational Qualifications Authority (VQA) expresses the national qualifications system and in the 2nd Article of the same Law, the national qualifications system has been defined as follows:

It is the rules and activities related to develop and implement the technical and vocational education and training standards and the qualifications ground to these standards and authorization, auditing, measurement and assessment, documentation and certification in regard to these. (VQA Law 2006)

The decisions concerning to establish a policy aimed at preparing Turkish Qualifications Framework (TQF–TYÇ) have taken part in the priorities in many important policy documents such as Tenth Development Plan (2014–2018), National Employment Strategy (2014–2023), Turkey Life-Long Learning Strategy Document and Action Plan (2014–2018), Turkish Vocational and technical Education Strategy Document and Action Plan (2014–2018), Ninth Development Plan (2007–2013), 2011 national Youth Employment Action Plan, 2008 Turkish National Program and Life-Long Learning Strategy Document (2009–2013) (TQF Communiqué 2015: 7).

Turkish Qualifications Framework (TQF–TYÇ) prepared in line with European Qualifications Framework (EQF). TQF is the national qualifications framework showing all principles of qualifications gained by means of vocational, general and academic education and training programs including primary, secondary and higher education and other learning ways. TQF comprises all quality assured qualifications received in education and training system, in all learning environments and in several levels in our country (TQF Communiqué 2015: 4). In 5544 numbered Law the duties and responsibilities of Vocational Qualifications Authority (VQA) related to Turkish Qualifications Framework (TQF) stated as follows:

Procedures related to the establishment, development and keeping up-to-date of Turkish Qualifications Framework carried out by the Authority. All quality assured qualifications are incorporated into Turkish Qualifications Framework. The criteria related to ensuring the quality assurance of the qualifications specified by the Authority. For the establishment and carrying out of Turkish Qualifications Framework, decision and administration units such as board, commission and work groups constituted with the representatives of Ministry of National Education, Turkish Higher Education Council, Authority and the related parties can be formed. The procedures and principles related to forming and operating these units, the criteria of quality assurance, determining the institutions and organizations that will specify the quality assurance and administering Turkish Qualifications Framework shall be determined by the directive bring into force by Council of Ministers Decision. (VQA Law 2006)

The fundamental aims of Turkish Qualifications Framework (TQF) have been determined as follows (TQF Communiqué 2015: 3):

- To designate a clear and consistent method for defining, classifying and comparing the qualifications.
- To present an integrated framework comprising all quality assured qualifications (general, occupational, academic education and training programs as well as gained in other learning environments.
- Continuously improving the qualifications system in line with legitimizing the qualifications an individual gained in formal, informal and free learning environments.
- To contribute to the training of individuals who has got defined and measurable qualifications and equipped can be employed, and hence to decrease the unemployment.

- To improve the corporate cooperation of all the involved parties mainly the related institutions and organizations responsible with qualifications, the business world and the social stakeholders.
- To establish the fundamental criteria for acceptance of other countries' qualifications in Turkey and the qualifications of Turkey in abroad and hence to serve as comparison.

Many of the occupational qualifications presently exist in labor market in our country and those will be needed in future shall take part in Turkish Qualifications Framework (TQF). In Turkish Qualifications Framework (TQF), the qualifications systems of Ministry of National Education and Vocational Qualifications Authority (VQA) as well as High Education Board of Turkey Qualifications Framework (TYYÇ–HEBTQF) take place (TQF Communiqué 2015: 14).

Vocational Qualifications Authority (VQA) puts into practice all the procedures with regard to the development and implementing of Turkish Qualifications Framework (TQF) in cooperation with Ministry of National Education and High Education Board being in the first place, public bodies and institutions, workers and employers' unions, professional organizations and related non-governmental organizations (Turkish Qualifications Framework Structure, Vocational Qualifications Authority (VQA) web).

Turkish Qualifications Framework (TQF) has been designed in a structure consists of eight levels. Each level in Turkish Qualifications Framework (TQF) has been defined in accordance with the common learning outcomes which the qualifications at that level point in question have got. The cluster of definitions related to the learning outcomes, which defines each of the levels with respect to knowledge, skill and qualifications is named as level identifier and these level identifiers composes the kernel of Turkish Qualifications Framework (TQF). Level identifiers provide the basis for all other structures and tools in Turkish Qualifications Framework (TQF) (Designation of Turkish Qualifications Framework (TQF), (Vocational Qualifications Authority (VQA) web).

In Turkish Qualifications Framework (TQF), while the 1st Level qualifications define fulfilling the basic tasks, 8th Level qualifications define bring innovation into the working and learning area, the qualification of solving the new and complicated problems emerged by using the approaches and methods of different areas. Turkish Qualifications Framework (TQF) identifiers are presented below (TQF Communiqué 2015: 15) (Table 6.1).

6.7 Conclusion

The effectiveness and efficiency of the labor market depend on analyzing the working conditions scientifically, making legislative regularizations and their administrative implementations. Occupational standards are an important tool in this respect. Occupational standard is defined as the minimal norm specifying the required knowledge, skill, attitude and manner to carry out an occupation successfully. Establishment of occupational standards and qualifications are a matter of time.

Table 6.1 Major qualification types and their envisaged levels in TQF

TQF level	Name of qualification type	Responsible institution
1	Pre-school certificate of participation	MNE
2	Primary school certificate of education	MNE
	2nd Level vocational qualification certificate	VQA
3	Secondary school certificate of education[a]	MNE
	Journeyman's certificate	MNE
	3rd Level vocational qualification certificate	VQA
4	Certificate of proficiency	MNE
	Vocational and technical education and training high school diploma	MNE
	High school diploma	MNE
	4th Level vocational qualification certificate	VQA
5	Vocational school of higher education associate diploma (academic)[b]	CHE
	Vocational school of higher education associate diploma (vocational)[c]	CHE
	5th Level vocational qualification certificate	VQA
	Bachelor's degree	CHE
6	6th Level vocational qualification certificate	VQA
7	Postgraduate diploma (with thesis)	CHE
	Postgraduate diploma (non-thesis)	CHE
	7th Level vocational qualification certificate	VQA
8	Doctorate diploma (doctorate, proficiency in art/doctorate and specialty in medicine)	CHE
	8th Level vocational qualification certificate	VQA

TQF Qualification Types and their envisaged levels temporarily have been determined and in accordance with 20th Article of TQF Directive they will be revised based on TQF Board's proposal and TQF Coordination Board's approval
[a]Primary School diplomas given before 2012 shall be considered in this type
[b]They are the Vocational School of Higher Education Diplomas issued as the result of the successfully completing the first two years of Four-year license programs
[c]They are the associate degree diplomas issued by Vocational Schools of Higher Education
Source Taken from VQA web pages

Globalization of labor market increased for the internationally comparable knowledge. The importance of enhancing the quality of labor which takes place in the priority targets of Turkey stated in the Tenth Development Plan as follows:

> The importance of the global level qualified labor force gradually increases. The increase of the level of education and the qualifications of labor force will continue to affect the economic development of countries and individuals. Along with the level of education, the qualification of the labor force is expected to be a determining factor in labor force

movements. It is predicted that the demand for qualified labor force will increase in all countries. (Tenth Development Plan p. 11).

Since the outputs of education system are the inputs of labor market, it is necessary that the qualifications of education system should be in quality of responding the requirements of labor market. Therefore, it is necessary that the labor force all over the world should have a valid occupation and certification to prove their skill levels (Demirezen 2002: 214). In Turkey, the occupational certification is made by means of in formal vocational and technical education institutions with diploma, in apprenticeship training with journeyman's certificate and proficiency certificate, in informal education institutions with completion certificate. Mısırlı (2002), expresses that, labor force and vocational education and training look like the links of a chain; the first link is the standard of the occupation that the training will be provided, other links on the other hand consist of education programs which will be prepared based on the standards of the occupation, the education environment, materials and tools and also the practice of the profession, and the last link is receiving the certificate of competency (qualification certificate).

It is a requirement to plan and evaluate the labor force, which is a driving force in the country's economy, in terms of quality and quantity, and to generate solutions for change and development. In this respect, the studies and endeavors for increasing the efficiency and the quality of labor force take place in the targets of developed and developing countries. Due to the inadequacies in planning of labor force and education in Turkey, employability of the graduates fail and in many fields the university graduates could not be employed. Particularly today in an environment where there are employees who should work without having chance for a choice of profession, and who do not know why and how to do the job they are practicing (those who could not or unable to receive education related to their jobs), it is inevitable that the occupational accidents are high, job satisfaction is low. In this context, performing job analysis and job descriptions by scientific methods by the related bodies and the establishment and implementation of standards appropriate for occupational groups in different sectors will solve these problems in the labor market to a certain extent. Concordantly, it is necessary to complete the links of the chain. The factors composing the fundamental qualifications of occupational standards can be listed as follows:

• Comprise the issues to be possessed with regard to the occupation.
• Reflect the levels of occupational qualification.
• Involve the requirements in the subjects of health, safety and environment protection related to the occupational area.
• It is provided the active participation of the social parties into the preparation process.
• Written clearly and understandable.
• Promote life-long learning of the individual.
• Do not involve discrimination issues.
• Is based on job analysis.

The answer of the question of how the above mentioned occupational standards provide benefits in practice may become the following items:

- Increasing the qualification/proficiency in labor force will lead the worker/employee to know the job they practice, know why and how they do that job, and undertake the required authorities and responsibilities, and increase of their work motivation.
- Improving the effectiveness and quality of the products; the increase of occupational qualification of the employee will ensure the higher quality of the product and service provided.
- To increase the active circulation of ability and knowledge among works and workplaces, and with the establishment of a system based on occupational standards and occupational qualifications, free movement of the labor force in international arena with respect to quality will be ensured (Acar 2016: 294).

In the world and Turkey, the occupational classifications have been made, the required institutions have been established; the occupational standards have been published and still continue to be published. As of the moment, in Turkey the numbers of national occupational standards published on the Official Gazette reached to 853 (Vocational Qualifications Authority (VQA) Statistics, VQA web). On the other hand, in order for these published occupational standards to be known by the employees, informative meetings and new publications are needed. In Turkey, some studies have been conducted about the occupational standards directed some occupational groups (Mısırlı 2002; Tuncer and Taşpınar 2004; Erdoğan and Dinç 2009; Güven 2010). The studies will be conducted devoted to some occupational groups may provide contribution to preparing the occupational standards and a better understanding of occupational standards.

References

Abraham KG (1999) Revising the standard occupational classification system. U.S. Department of Labor, Report 929. https://www.bls.gov/soc/2000/socrpt929.pdf Accessed on 02 Mar 2020

Acar OK (2016) Mesleki Yeterlilik Kurumunun çalışma hayatında iş tanımlama açısından önemi: örnek olarak insan kaynakları yönetimi alanında yaptığı çalışmalar. Süleyman Demirel Üniversitesi Sosyal Bilimler Enstitüsü Dergisi, Özel Sayısı: 286–303

Akal Z (2005) İşletmelerde performans ölçüm ve denetimi: çok yönlü performans göstergeleri. 6. Baskı, Ankara: Milli Prodüktive Merkezi Yayınları

Demirezen M (2002) Piyasa meslek standartları. Planlama Dergisi-Özel Sayı (DPT'nin kuruluşunun 42. Yılı): 213–218

Elias P (1997) Occupational classification (ISCO-88) concepts, methods, reliability, validity and cross-national comparability. OECD Labour Market and Social Policy Occasional Papers, Paris, OECD Publishing, No 20. https://doi.org/10.1787/304441717388. Accessed on: 29 May 2019

Erdoğan M, Dinç E (2009) Türkiye muhasebe standartları ve muhasebe meslek mensuplarının bilgi düzeylerinin incelenmesi. Muhasebe Ve Finansman Dergisi 43:154–169

ESCO, European skills/competences qualifications and occupations. https://ec.europa.eu/esco/por tal/escopedia/Skill. Accessed on: 29 Aug 2017

Goode W (1996) Topluluk içinde topluluk; meslekler, meslekler ve sosyoloji, (Der. ve Çev. Z. Cirhinlioğlu). Gündoğan Yayınları, Ankara. Accessed on: 02 May 2020

Güven D (2010) Profesyonel bir meslek olarak Türkiye'de öğretmenlik. Boğaziçi Üniversitesi Eğitim Dergisi 27(2):13–21

ILO. What is an Occupational Classification? http://www.ilo.org/public/english/bureau/stat/isco/docs/intro1.htm. Accessed on: 01 Sept 2019

ISCED-97 International Standard Classification of Education. https://ec.europa.eu/eurostat/cache/metadata/Annexes/educ_uoe_h_esms_an2.htm. Accessed on: 16 June 2019

ISCED (1997) International Standard Classification of Education. United Nations Educational, Scientific and Cultural Organization (UNESCO). http://www.unesco.org/education/information/nfsunesco/doc/isced_1997.htm. Accessed on: 01 Sept 2019

ISCO-08 Part I Introductory and Methodological Notes. http://www.ilo.org/public/english/bureau/stat/isco/isco08/index.htm. Accessed on: 30 Aug 2019

ISCO-08 Part II Structure of the International Standard Classification of Occupations. http://www.ilo.org/public/english/bureau/stat/isco/isco08/index.htm. Accessed on: 30 Aug 2019

ISCO-08, International Standard Classification of Occupations, vol 1. http://www.ilo.org/public/english/bureau/stat/isco/docs/publication08.pdf. Accessed on: 30 Aug 2019

Karasu K (2001) Profesyonelleşme olgusu ve kamu yönetimi. Mülkiyeliler Birliği Yayınları, Ankara

Kart EM (2015) Örgütsel Sinizm, 2. Baskı, Ankara, Nobel Akademik Yayıncılık Eğitim Danışmanlık TİC.LTD.ŞTİ

Koçel T (2020) İşletme Yöneticiliği, Yönetici Geliştirme, Organizasyon ve Davranış. 18. Baskı, Istanbul: Beta Yayınevi

Mısırlı I (2002) Turizm sektöründe meslek standartları ve mesleki belgelendirme sistemi (Sertifikasyon). Anatolia: Turizm Araştırmaları Dergisi 13(1):39–55

Mucuk I (2014) Modern İşletmecilik. 19. Baskı, İstanbul: Türkmen Kitabevi

MYK İstatistikler, MYK web. https://portal.myk.gov.tr/index.php?option=com_meslek_std_tas lak&view=taslak_listesi_yeni&msd=2&Itemid=432. Accessed on: 02 May 2020

MYK Kanunu (2006) https://www.resmigazete.gov.tr/eskiler/2006/10/20061007-1.htm. Accessed on: 03 Sept 2019

MYK, Tarihçe, MYK web. http://www.myk.gov.tr/index.php/tr/kurumsal/tarihce. Accessed on: 03 Sept 2019

Onuncu Kalkınma Planı (2014–2018). http://www.kalkinma.gov.tr/Lists/Kalknma%20Planlar/Att achments/12/Onuncu%20Kalk%C4%B1nma%20Plan%C4%B1.pdf. Accessed on: 31 Aug 2019

Prokopenko J (1995) Verimlilik Yönetimi Uygulamalı El Kitabı, (Çev. Olcay Baykal ve diğerleri) Milli Prodüktivite Merkezi Yayınları, Ankara

Tortop N, Aykaç B, Yayman H, Özer MA (2006) İnsan kaynakları yönetimi. Human resources management.). Nobel Yaygın Dağıtım, Ankara

Tosun K (1987) İşletme Yönetimi. 4. Baskı, İstanbul: İstanbul Üniversitesi Yayını, Yayın. No: 3462

Tuncer M, Taşpınar M (2004) Meslek Standartları ve Çeşitli Mesleki Sınıflama Sistemleri. Fırat Üniversitesi Doğu Anadolu Bölgesi Araştırmaları 2(3):1–10

Türk Dil Kurumu, Büyük Sözlük, Accessed: http://tdk.gov.tr/. Accessed on: 28 Feb 2020

TYÇ Tasarımı, MYK web. http://www.myk.gov.tr/index.php/en/tycnin-tasarm. Accessed on: 03 Jan 2020

TYÇ Tebliğ (2015) Türkiye Yeterlilikler Çerçevesine Dair Tebliğ. Tebliğ No: 2015/1. http://myk.gov.tr/images/articles/editor/130116/TYC_teblig_2.pdf. Accessed on: 03 Jan 2020

TYÇ Yönetmeliği. MYK web. http://myk.gov.tr/images/articles/TYC/TYC_Yonetmeligi_v2.pdf. Accessed on: 03 Jan 2020

TYÇ Yönetim Yapısı, MYK web. Accessed on: 03 Sept 2019

Yüksel Ö (2007) İnsan kaynakları yönetimi. 6. Baskı. Gazi Kitabevi, Ankara

Chapter 7
Do the Companies Benefit from Improved Disclosure Performance? Evidence from the Airport Industry

İsmail Çağrı Özcan

Abstract In a world of rising concerns regarding sustainability, social responsibility, and corporate governance, environmental, social, and governance (ESG) metrics become a critical performance indicator for almost all major stakeholders of the companies ranging from shareholders, lenders, and managers to consumers and institutional investors. This chapter aims to contribute to the ESG literature by testing if the ESG disclosure performance affects the profitability and market valuation of the publicly traded airport companies. Based on a sample of 20 airports from 13 countries over the 2007–2017 period, the findings of the ordinary least squares, random-effect, and fixed-effect regressions reveal that higher ESG disclosure scores lead to both higher profitability and market valuation.

Keywords ESG disclosure · Financial performance · Airport industry · ROA · Tobin's Q · Corporate governance

7.1 Introduction

There is a growing interest in the environmental, social, and governance (ESG) in the business world. As a result of famous scandals such as those of Lehman Brothers, Enron, and Arthur Andersen, creditors now reward firms with better governance practices and transparency through charging lower interest rates (Bhojraj and Sengupta 2003) and such firms can achieve lower cost of equity (Chen et al. 2009). Besides, social and sustainability issues are also becoming a major determinant of business success since consumers tend to buy the products and services more of the firms having improved environmental and social performance. Regarding the cost of equity, previous research documents that improved social responsibility performance is associated with a lower cost of equity (El Ghoul et al. 2011; Dhaliwal et al. 2014). Likewise, Plumlee et al. (2015) reveal the positive linkage between voluntary environmental disclosure performance and higher market valuation.

İ. Ç. Özcan (✉)
Department of Aviation Management, Ankara Yıldırım Beyazıt University, Ankara, Turkey
e-mail: icozcan@ybu.edu.tr

© The Author(s), under exclusive license to Springer Nature Singapore Pte Ltd. 2021   113
K. T. Çalıyurt (ed.), *New Approaches to CSR, Sustainability and Accountability,*
Volume II, Accounting, Finance, Sustainability, Governance & Fraud: Theory
and Application, https://doi.org/10.1007/978-981-33-6808-8_7

The airport industry, where there exists a large group of private operators following the deregulation and privatization waves, is not free from the tendency regarding the ESG issues. Unlike the days of government ownership, publicly listed airport companies are now under the pressure of capital markets. Therefore, among others, they have to comply with governance standards. In addition, they should improve their public image through social and environmental responsibility actions in a more commercially-oriented airport business where the passengers are becoming the real customers of the airports rather than the airlines. For all these reasons, it becomes more crucial for airport companies to pay more attention to their ESG efforts.

The goal of this chapter is to examine the association between the ESG disclosure performance of the publicly traded airport companies and their accounting prof-itability and market valuation. We use a dataset coming from 20 airport companies and spanning from 2007 to 2017. Our results reveal that airport companies with higher ESG disclosure scores tend to be more profitable and their stocks tend to appreciate in value. The second part of this chapter consists of a literature review and an explanation of both data and methodology. The second part presents the empirical findings, and Part 5 outlines the conclusion and policy implications.

7.2 Literature Review, Methodology, and Data

When we look at comparable ESG research on the transport industry, we observe that they tend to concentrate on the aviation industry because of its high number of companies to examine. Skouloudis et al. (2012) go over the airport activity reports to figure out what they have done regarding corporate social responsibility. Rotondo and Marinò (2016) search for the factors affecting the financial and general disclosure performance of the airports in Italy. The findings of Özcan (2019a, BA) reveal that larger boards, higher number of independent directors, increased sales, profitability, financial leverage, tangibility, and being established in a country with a common law system can increase the ESG disclosure scores of the airport companies. Concerning the airlines, Wang et al. (2015) report that Chinese airlines with state control tend to have better CSR performance.

In addition to the ESG disclosure activities in the aviation industry, there is a smaller group of research focusing on other transport modes. With respect to the rail industry, Özcan (2020a) reports, in his former study, that government ownership has a positive association with the ESG disclosure performance. In the latter study, Özcan (2020b) reveals that rail companies with higher ESG disclosure performance tend to have higher ROA.

This chapter aims at addressing the research gap regarding ESG activities in the transport industry. More particularly, it focuses on testing if improved ESG disclosure performance has a positive effect on the profitability and market valuation of the airport companies. The estimation adopted to test these linkages is as follows:

$$Y = f \text{ (ESG Disclosure, Leverage, Size, Tangibility, Growth, Lagged } Y) \quad (7.1)$$

Using the model above, this chapter runs ordinary least squares (OLS), random effects (RE) and fixed effects (FE) regressions. To measure how ESG disclosure performance affects the profitability and market valuation, this study adopts return on assets (ROA), return on equity (ROE), and Tobin's Q as the dependent variable. To deal with changing tax practices among nations, we use the pretax income for both ROA and ROE, which are equal to the ratio of pretax income to the total assets and the ratio of pretax income to the equity, respectively. Among several formulas to calculate Tobin's Q, we pick the one which corresponds to the sum of the market capitalization of equity and total debt divided by total assets.

The focus of this study is the association between the ESG disclosure performance and the financial performance of the airport companies. To measure the ESG disclosure performance, we adopt the ESG disclosure scores of the companies published by Bloomberg. When calculating these ESG disclosure scores, Bloomberg goes over individual environmental (like pollution, carbon emissions, and renewable energy), social (like human rights and diversity), and governance (like executive compensation and independent directors) indicators.

As discussed earlier in the literature, firms with improved ESG performance should get many financial benefits such as lower cost of both debt and equity and higher market valuation. One group of research employs aggregate ESG performance (which incorporates environmental, social, and governance indicators at the same time) when analyzing its impact on financial performance. Weber (2014), for example, reports that the stocks of the Chinese firms disclosing their ESG reports are more likely to outperform those of the firms without ESG reports. Based on a sample of 403 US companies, the findings of Fatemi et al. (2017) suggest that improved ESG disclosure leads to lower Tobin's Q but the stocks of the firms with higher ESG strength tend to appreciate in value.

A larger body of studies, on the other hand, focuses on a single dimension of ESG. The most widely used dimension is social responsibility. The findings of both Waddock and Graves (1997) and McWilliams and Siegel (2000) reveal a positive association between corporate social responsibility performance and firm profitability. Apart from accounting profitability, improved corporate social responsibility performance can also lead to higher market valuation. Edmans (2011), for example, documents that the rank of the companies in the "100 Best Companies to Work for in America" has a positive effect on their stock returns. Similarly, the findings of Fatemi et al. (2015) and Harjoto and Jo (2015) suggest that firm valuation can be improved through higher corporate social responsibility expenditures and corporate social responsibility, respectively. Despite such studies reporting the positive effect of corporate social responsibility efforts on firm financial performance, we should note Renneboog et al. (2008) underline that the direction of the causation is not certain.

Against the literature on the positive linkage between corporate social responsibility and firm financial performance, several studies document counter-evidence. Boyle et al. (1997) report that the stock performance of the firms participating in an ethical initiative does not differ from those of the firms not participating. Likewise, Alexander and Bucholz (1978) fail to provide evidence on the positive effect of corporate social responsibility on stock performance. More strikingly, Brammer et al. (2006) show that the stock performance of the firms is more likely to worsen when their corporate social performance increase. In this study, in line with the majority of the relevant literature, we anticipate a positive association between ESG disclosure performance and the financial performance of the airport companies.

We include five control variables into our analyses apart from our policy variable (ESG disclosure performance). The comparable studies come to a consensus on the positive association between financial performance and firm growth. Using profitability ratios, Zeitun and Tian (2007), Memon et al. (2012), and Le and Phan (2017) report the positive effect of firm growth on ROA, and Abor (2005) and Le and Phan (2017) document a similar impact on ROE. Le and Phan (2017), on the other hand, indicate a positive association between firm growth and Tobin's Q from a valuation perspective. The related studies differ in measuring growth. Memon et al. (2012), for example, use asset growth to take the growth of the firms into consideration. On the other hand, a larger body of research, including Abor (2005), Margaritis and Psillaki (2010), Fosu (2013), Zeitun and Tian (2007), and Le and Phan (2017) measure the growth by the sale growth. In this study, we pick sales growth, which corresponds to the ratio of current sales to the last year's sales figure, in line with the majority of the prior literature to measure the growth of the airport companies. Our expectation is that our growth variable will get a positive coefficient.

The size of the airport companies is a significant determinant of their financial performance. The size can be a strong factor in financial performance for two reasons. The first reason is that it is more likely for larger airports to serve a higher number and percentage of international flights, which are the major source of commercial revenues especially because of their duty-free sales potential. Secondly, a minimum level of service must be achieved for some airport services like fire-fighting and air traffic control and a minimum level of infrastructure investment, like runways, must be done regardless of the level of air traffic. Therefore, larger airports have a relative advantage to recover such fixed expenses. For all these reasons, one can anticipate observing a positive association between size and financial performance of the airport companies. There exist several different ways to measure the size of the firms. One group of studies, including Kyereboah-Coleman (2007), El-Sayed Ebaid (2009), Khan (2012), Zeitun and Tian (2007), Hasan et al. (2014), Fosu (2013), and Bandyopadhyay and Barua (2016) adopt total assets. Another major body of research like Majumdar and Chhibber (1999), Abor (2005), Margaritis and Psillaki (2007), Margaritis and Psillaki (2010), and Memon et al. (2012) employ sales. In the analyses, we decide to calculate the size of the airport companies by the natural logarithm of their net sales, and we anticipate that it will get a positive coefficient.

We also adopt the leverage of the airport companies as another control variable. The literature does not come to a consensus on the possible effect of leverage on financial performance. Free cash flow theory suggests that debt can prevent the firms' managers from misusing the firms' money for unprofitable investments. Therefore, higher leverage should contribute to profitability pursuant to this theory. Contrarily, pecking order theory opts for equity in place of debt. Accordingly, firms with lower leverage are more likely to improve their financial performance if the pecking order theory is valid. Against these two theories, the theory of capital structure irrelevance coined by Modigliani and Miller (1958) denies the effect of debt levels on the firm value.

The relevant literature consists of studies providing supporting evidence for all these contradicting theories. Regarding the positive linkage, Memon et al. (2012) and Fosu (2013) report that firms with higher leverage tend to increase their ROA, whereas the findings of Margaritis and Psillaki (2007) and Margaritis and Psillaki (2010) suggest the positive effect of leverage on the firm efficiency. Contrarily, Majumdar and Chhibber (1999), Khan (2012), Pouraghajan et al. (2012), and Le and Phan (2017) document how higher leverage leads to lower financial performance indicators such as RAO, ROE, and Tobin's Q. In this study, we measure the financial leverage by dividing the total liabilities by the total assets. We expect that the leverage variable will get a negative coefficient.

We include the tangibility as another control variable. This variable is important in that the tangibility of the airports, which are capital extensive by their nature because of high levels of infrastructure spending on the runways and passenger terminals, is very probably a strong determinant of their financial performance. During times of economic growth, higher tangibility can lead to improved performance. The findings of Margaritis and Psillaki (2007) and Margaritis and Psillaki (2010) provide evidence on this positive effect of tangibility on firm efficiency. Oppositely, firms heavily investing in fixed assets cannot make flexible financial decisions during economic recessions Memon et al. (2012) report how a higher tangibility ratio leads to lower ROA using a dataset coming from Pakistani textile firms. The tangibility ratio we use in this study is the ratio f fixed assets to the total assets. We anticipate that the coefficient of the tangibility ratio will be positive.

Finally, we also add the one-year lagged values of the response variables. Several studies examining the financial performance adopted the one-year lagged values. Examples include Fosu (2013), Bandyopadhyay and Barua (2016), Le and Phan (2017), and Özcan (2019a, BB). Our anticipation is to find a strong and positive association between the response variables and their lagged values.

We use the Bloomberg database to collect the financial statistics we adopt. Table 7.1 shows the descriptive statistics of the sample, and Table 7.2 depicts the correlation matrix of the variables. The mean–variance inflation factor of 1.57 reveals that the level of multicollinearity is within acceptable limits.

7.3 Empirical Results

The results of the OLS and panel data estimations are presented in Table 7.3. For each individual dependent variable (ROA, ROE, and Tobin's Q), we run separate OLS, FE, and RE estimations. Columns 1, 2, and 3 outline the results of the OLS, FE, and RE models where we employ ROA as the dependent variable. The coefficient of the ESG variable, which is the focus of this study, is statistically significant at the 1% level for OLS and RE models and at the 5% level for FE estimation. Our findings suggest

Table 7.1 Descriptive statistics

Variable	Definition	Expected sign	Mean	Std. Dev	Minimum	Maximum
ROA	The ratio of pretax income to total assets		0.0822	0.0447	−0.0052	0.1977
ROE	The ratio of pretax income to equity		0.1516	0.0959	−0.0128	0.5642
Tobin's Q	The sum of the market capitalization of equity and total debt divided by total assets		1.6787	0.7809	0.6911	5.0697
ESG Disclosure	ESG scores published by Bloomberg Database	+	27.2076	14.7714	7.85	57.85
Sales growth	The ratio of net sales to its last year figure	+	1.0924	0.1402	0.3701	1.6785
Size	The natural logarithm of net sales of each airport company (adjusted for inflation)	+	5.9238	0.9897	3.2355	7.8825
Financial leverage	The ratio of total liabilities to total assets	−	0.4232	0.2035	0.0600	0.9118
Tangibility	The share of long term assets in the total assets	+	0.8126	0.1142	0.4544	0.9907

that a 1-point increase in the ESG disclosure performance of an airport company is likely to increase its ROA by 0.0006, 0.0007, and 0.0008 according to OLS, FE, and RE models, respectively (holding other independent variables constant). Our findings also reveal that Table 7.3 indicates ROA is negatively associated with both the financial leverage and tangibility, whereas higher growth rates and lagged ROA are expected to contribute to ROA. In addition, we document that there is a positive linkage between size and ROA, but we should note that this finding is only suggested by the FE model.

The second three columns of Table 7.3 depict the results of the regressions when we regress ROE on the independent variables. Similar to the association between ROA and ESG disclosure, we report that higher ESG disclosure scores tend to increase the ROE of the publicly traded airport companies. Regarding adopted control variables, we document a positive effect of growth and a negative effect of tangibility on ROE. Expectedly, we also find a strong linkage between ROE and its one-year lagged value.

In the first six columns of Table 7.3, we use profitability measures (ROA and ROE) as the dependent variables. In the remaining three columns, on the other hand, we employ Tobin's Q to measure financial performance. Regarding our policy variable, our findings indicate that airport companies with better ESG disclosure performance are more likely to have a higher market valuation. More concretely, we expect that a 1-point increase in the ESG disclosure performance of an airport company should lead

Table 7.2 Correlation matrix of the variables

	ROA	ROE	Tobin's Q	ESG disclosure	Financial leverage	Size	Tangibility	Growth	Lagged ROA	Lagged ROE	Lagged Tobin's Q
ROA	1.00										
ROE	0.66	1.00									
Tobin's Q	0.56	0.54	1.00								
ESG Disclosure	−0.02	0.40	0.07	1.00							
Financial leverage	−0.47	0.27	−0.12	0.56	1.00						
Size	−0.31	0.05	−0.09	0.52	0.57	1.00					
Tangibility	−0.35	−0.04	−0.08	0.28	0.33	0.16	1.00				
Growth	0.22	−0.01	0.07	−0.23	−0.30	−0.21	−0.17	1.00			
Lagged ROA	0.81	0.49	0.47	−0.09	−0.42	−0.37	−0.29	0.11	1.00		
Lagged ROE	0.53	0.84	0.46	0.34	0.26	−0.01	−0.00	−0.17	0.68	1.00	
Lagged Tobin's Q	0.46	0.44	0.60	0.01	−0.09	−0.10	−0.02	0.19	0.55	0.47	1.00

Table 7.3 Regression results

	ROA			ROE			Tobin's Q		
	OLS (1)	FE (2)	RE (3)	OLS (4)	FE (5)	RE (6)	OLS (7)	FE (8)	RE (9)
ESG disclosure	0.0006*** (3.74)	0.0007** (2.47)	0.0008*** (4.04)	0.0009** (2.51)	0.0022*** (3.79)	0.0014*** (3.45)	0.0071** (2.06)	0.0172* (1.96)	0.0092** (2.19)
Leverage	−0.0548*** (4.31)	−0.1030*** (4.82)	−0.0744*** (4.73)	0.0297 (1.14)	0.0267 (0.5)	0.0328 (1.14)	−0.4650* (1.79)	0.0110 (0.02)	−0.5484* (1.69)
Size	−0.0002 (0.06)	0.0231*** (2.85)	0.0018 (0.49)	−0.0036 (0.70)	0.0099 (0.56)	−0.0041 (0.68)	−0.0066 (0.13)	−0.5940** (2.38)	−0.0318 (0.51)
Tangibility	−0.0373** (2.13)	−0.0899*** (3.63)	−0.0707*** (3.39)	−0.0425 (1.17)	−0.1462*** (2.74)	−0.0778* (1.96)	−0.2384 (0.65)	−1.9961*** (2.68)	−0.4982 (1.10)
Growth	0.0362** (2.30)	0.0296** (2.41)	0.0315** (2.49)	0.1158*** (3.46)	0.0885*** (3.27)	0.1041*** (3.68)	0.0287 (0.08)	−0.1595 (0.41)	−0.3697 (1.00)
Lagged ROA	0.6857*** (13.98)	0.3585*** (6.12)	0.5228*** (9.66)	–	–	–	–	–	–
Lagged ROE	–	–	–	0.8560*** (17.34)	0.4870*** (7.23)	0.7872*** (14.62)	–	–	–
Lagged Tobin's Q	–	–	–	–	–	–	0.7230*** (11.35)	0.4544*** (5.67)	0.6627*** (9.43)
Constant	0.0326 (0.95)	−0.0177 (0.34)	0.0622* (1.95)	−0.0986 (1.39)	−0.0270 (0.24)	−0.0383 (0.65)	1.0620 (1.38)	5.7886*** (3.62)	1.5885** (2.41)
R^2	0.76	0.39	0.71	0.77	0.61	0.74	0.65	0.17	0.40
F-value	27.97	25.39	–	29.33	19.39	–	15.78	9.69	–
Prob > F	0.0000	0.0000	–	0.0000	0.0000	–	0.0000	0.0000	–

(continued)

Table 7.3 (continued)

	ROA			ROE			Tobin's Q		
	OLS (1)	FE (2)	RE (3)	OLS (4)	FE (5)	RE (6)	OLS (7)	FE (8)	RE (9)
Wald Test	–	–	248.58	–	–	337.27	–	–	103.74
Prob > χ^2		–	0.0000		–	0.0000		–	0.0000
Number of groups	–	20	20	–	20	20	–	20	20
Number of observations	168	168	168	168	168	168	165	165	165

Notes (1) Sale figures (to measure size) in natural logs. (2) t-statistics in parenthesis. (3) ***, **, and * stand for significance levels at 1%, 5%, and 10%, respectively. (4) Year dummies not shown for OLS regression to an increase in Tobin's Q in the range of 0.0071–0.0172. The coefficient of the ESG variable is statically significant at the 5% level in the OLS and RE estimations and at the 10% level in the FE estimation. Apart from the policy variable, our regressions document that higher leverage tends to decrease Tobin's Q according to OLS and RE regressions. In addition, the findings of the FE estimation revealed that higher sales and tangibility ratios are associated with a lower market valuation of the airport companies. However, we should note that these results are only supported by FE regression.

7.4 Conclusion

The rise of the ESG phenomenon brings new challenges to the companies. Apart from their classical focus on profitability and stock market performance, they now need to perform well with respect to social responsibility, sustainability, and corporate governance. Using a sample of 20 airport companies over the 2007–2017 period, this chapter aims at investigating if airport companies with improved ESG disclosure performance can transform this achievement into traditional performance measures like profitability and market returns. Our analyses reveal that the efforts of the airport companies regarding ESG disclosure pay off in terms of higher ROA, ROE, and stock returns.

The findings of this study suggest practical implications for the airport industry. Taking the positive effect of ESG reporting performance on the profitability and market valuation, the managers of the airport companies should take necessary actions to improve their ESG disclosure performance. A complementary future research might use survey methodology to evaluate the attitudes of the airport managers toward ESG disclosure activities.

References

Abor J (2005) The effect of capital structure on profitability: an empirical analysis of listed firms in Ghana. J Risk Fin 6(5):438–445
Alexander GJ, Buchholz RA (1978) Corporate social responsibility and stock market performance. Acad Manag J 21(3):479–486
Bandyopadhyay A, Barua NM (2016) Factors determining capital structure and corporate performance in India: Studying the business cycle effects. Q Rev Econ Finance 61:160–172
Bhojraj S, Sengupta P (2003) Effect of corporate governance on bond ratings and yields: the role of institutional investors and outside directors. J Bus 76(3):455–475
Boyle EJ, Higgins MM, Rhee GS (1997) Stock market reaction to ethical initiatives of defense contractors: theory and evidence. Crit Perspect Account 8(6):541–561
Brammer S, Brooks C, Pavelin S (2006) Corporate social performance and stock returns: UK evidence from disaggregate measures. Financ Manage 35(3):97–116
Chen KC, Chen Z, Wei KJ (2009) Legal protection of investors, corporate governance, and the cost of equity capital. J Corp Finan 15(3):273–289

Dhaliwal D, Li OZ, Tsang A, Yang YG (2014) Corporate social responsibility disclosure and the cost of equity capital: the roles of stakeholder orientation and financial transparency. J Account Public Policy 33(4):328–355

Edmans A (2011) Does the stock market fully value intangibles? Employee satisfaction and equity prices. J Fin Econ 101(3):621–640

El Ghoul S, Guedhami O, Kwok CC, Mishra DR (2011) Does corporate social responsibility affect the cost of capital? J Bank Finance 35(9):2388–2406

El-Sayed Ebaid I (2009) The impact of capital-structure choice on firm performance: empirical evidence from Egypt. J Risk Fin 10(5):477–487

Fatemi A, Fooladi I, Tehranian H (2015) Valuation effects of corporate social responsibility. J Bank Fin 59:182–192

Fatemi A, Glaum M, Kaiser S (2017) ESG performance and firm value: the moderating role of disclosure. Glob Fin J 38(45):64

Fosu S (2013) Capital structure, product market competition and firm performance: evidence from South Africa. Q Rev Econ Fin 53(2):140–151. https://doi.org/10.1016/j.qref.2013.02.004

Harjoto MA, Jo H (2015) Legal vs. normative CSR: differential impact on analyst dispersion, stock return volatility, cost of capital, and firm value. J Bus Ethics 128(1):1–20

Hasan MB, Ahsan AM, Rahaman MA, Alam MN (2014) Influence of capital structure on firm performance: evidence from Bangladesh. Int J Bus Manage 9(5):184–194

Khan AG (2012) The relationship of capital structure decisions with firm performance: a study of the engineering sector of Pakistan. Int J Account Fin Report 2(1):245–262

Kyereboah-Coleman A (2007) The impact of capital structure on the performance of microfinance institutions. J Risk Fin 8(1):56–71

Le TPV, Phan TBN (2017) Capital structure and firm performance: empirical evidence from a small transition country. Res Int Bus Fin 42:710–726

Majumdar SK, Chhibber P (1999) Capital structure and performance: evidence from a transition economy on an aspect of corporate governance. Public Choice 98(3–4):287–305

Margaritis D, Psillaki M (2007) Capital structure and firm efficiency. J Bus Fin Acc 34(9–10):1447–1469

Margaritis D, Psillaki M (2010) Capital structure, equity ownership and firm performance. J Bank Fin 34(3):621–632

McWilliams A, Siegel D (2000) Corporate social responsibility and financial performance: correlation or misspecification? Strateg Manag J 21(5):603–609

Memon F, Bhutto NA, Abbass G (2012) Capital structure and firm performance: a case of textile sector of Pakistan. Asian J Bus Manage Sci 1(9):9–15

Modigliani F, Miller MH (1958) The cost of capital, corporation finance and the theory of investment. Am Econ Rev 48(3):261–297

Özcan İÇ (2019a) Determinants of environmental, social, and governance disclosure performance of publicly traded airports. Int J Transp Econ 46(3):77–92

Özcan İÇ (2019b) Capital structure and firm performance. Eur J Transp Infrastruct Res 19(3):177–195

Özcan İÇ (2020a) Determinants of environmental, social, and governance reporting of rail companies: does state ownership matter? In: New trends in public sector reporting. Palgrave Macmillan, Cham, pp 153–173

Özcan İÇ (2020b) Environmental, social, and governance disclosure and financial performance: evidence from the rail industry. In: Sustainability reporting, ethics, and strategic management strategies for modern organizations. IGI Global, pp 244–253

Plumlee M, Brown D, Hayes RM, Marshall RS (2015) Voluntary environmental disclosure quality and firm value: further evidence. J Account Public Policy 34(4):336–361

Pouraghajan A, Malekian E, Emamgholipour M, Lotfollahpur V, Bagheri MM (2012) The relationship between capital structure and firm performance evaluation measures: evidence from the Tehran Stock Exchange. Int J Bus Commerce 1(9):166–181

Renneboog L, Ter Horst J, Zhang C (2008) Socially responsible investments: institutional aspects, performance, and investor behavior. J Bank Fin 32(9):1723–1742

Rotondo F, Marinò L (2016) Extent and determinants of voluntary disclosure for regulatory purposes in the Italian airport industry. Int J Discl Gov 13(2):157–177

Skouloudis A, Evangelinos K, Moraitis S (2012) Accountability and stakeholder engagement in the airport industry: an assessment of airports' CSR reports. J Air Transp Manag 18(1):16–20

Waddock SA, Graves SB (1997) The corporate social performance–financial performance link. Strateg Manag J 18(4):303–319

Wang Q, Wu C, Sun Y (2015) Evaluating corporate social responsibility of airlines using entropy weight and grey relation analysis. J Air Transp Manag 42:55–62

Weber O (2014) Environmental, social and governance reporting in China. Bus Strateg Environ 23(5):303–317

Zeitun R, Tian G (2007) Capital structure and corporate performance: evidence from Jordan. Australas Account Bus Fin J 1(4):40–61

Part III
New Approaches in CSR, Climate Change, Sustainability Reporting

Chapter 8
Corporate Social Responsibility Report: Examination of Glass Manufacturing Companies on Istanbul Chamber of Industry 500

İlknur Eskin

Abstract Corporate social responsibility reporting is the presentation of economic, environmental and social performance of enterprises in annual reports or in different reports. The corporate social responsibility report enables the business to communicate with stakeholders and is effective in their learning and decision-making processes. In this study, primarily corporate social responsibility reporting is explained theoretically. Subsequently, corporate social responsibility reports of glass manufacturing companies in Istanbul Chamber of Industry 500 and web pages of non-reporting companies were examined according to content analysis method. As a result of the research, it was determined that the companies of SISECAM Group, the global brand of the glass sector, disclosed their economic, social, environmental indicators and policies in both sustainability reports and annual reports and on the official Web site.

Keywords Social responsibility · Corporate social responsibility report · Glass manufacturing companies

8.1 Introduction

Corporate Social Responsibility (CSR) requires companies that provide information to the environment, society, investors and other stakeholders. In order to achieve their economic objectives, enterprises should take sustainability as a basis in their activities and explain the content and development of these activities. According to researches on this subject, the number of companies reporting on CSR social responsibility has increased in recent years. Because nowadays, stakeholders want to know which activities they are in contact with in order to ensure economic, social and environmental sustainability. For this reason, companies provide information on CSR in their official web pages, annual reports and sustainability reports.

İ. Eskin (✉)
Department of Accounting, Uzunkopru School of Applied Sciences, Trakya University, Edirne, Turkey

© The Author(s), under exclusive license to Springer Nature Singapore Pte Ltd. 2021   127
K. T. Çalıyurt (ed.), *New Approaches to CSR, Sustainability and Accountability,*
Volume II, Accounting, Finance, Sustainability, Governance & Fraud: Theory
and Application, https://doi.org/10.1007/978-981-33-6808-8_8

In the study, after giving place to the theoretical explanation of CSR, ISO (Istanbul Chamber of Industry) 2017 in Turkey in research set by the 500 industrial establishments located within the glass manufacturing company in the context of CSR reports they publish, the information announced by the official Web site of the company making the reporting content analyzed by analysis method. In the conclusion part, the general evaluation of the research was made.

8.2 Corporate Social Responsibility Reporting

According to the definition of the European Commission; CSR is a concept in which businesses voluntarily integrate social and environmental issues in their interactions with business activities and stakeholders (EU Green Paper 2001). According to another definition, social responsibility is the policies and practices of the company, which voluntarily conduct its activities with economic interests, as well as respect for the individual, society and the environment, including relations with all stakeholders. The Company discloses its policies and practices in the annual report, CSR report, sustainability report and information document on the Web sites (Leitoniene et al. 2015: 334). The concept of CSR consists of four elements (Sert 2012: 34):

- Businesses have responsibilities beyond producing goods and services for profit.
- Businesses contribute to the solution of social problems.
- Businesses are responsible to not only shareholders, also to the environment which is social stakeholder.
- Businesses not only focus on economic values, but in extended sense, it serves to humanistic values.

CSR is increasingly important because it is effective in business and public decisions. The change periods of the corporate social responsibility report are given in image 1 below. The first period that began in the 1970s was when accountability and company promotion came to the forefront, focusing on environmental issues, but not these problems associated with the company's activities. The second period, which began in 1980, is the stage in which companies evaluate the interests of the public, customers, suppliers and investors by evaluating their activities in CSR fields. The third period, which began in 1990, is the period in which companies evaluate social and environmental issues, have certified standards related to processes and report them in an integrated manner (Juscius et al. 2014: 89) (Fig. 8.1).

In a 1998 research, it was found that 98% of the Fortune 500 companies had Web sites and 89% of these companies provided information about CSR. In a global survey of senior executives and board members in 2002, the idea that CSR came to the forefront as an important agenda item in many board meetings and became increasingly important in the coming years. In the "International Corporate Responsibility Reporting" survey conducted by KPMG in 2005, it was found that 52% of the 250 companies in the region published social responsibility reports in addition to the annual reports (Montiel 2008: 245). KPMG's "Corporate Social Responsibility

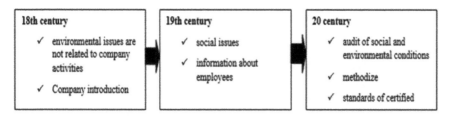

18th century	19th century	20 century
✓ environmental issues are not related to company activities ✓ Company introduction	✓ social issues ✓ information about employees	✓ audit of social and environmental conditions ✓ methodize ✓ standards of certified

Fig. 8.1 Development of corporate social responsibility report. *Source* Juscius et al. (2014)

Reporting" survey, published in 2017, analyzed CSR and sustainability reports of companies in two sample groups. The first group represents a total of 4,900 companies from the top 100 companies from each of the 49 countries, while the second group represents the 250 companies with the highest revenues in the Fortune 500 in 2016. In the research, it was found that 78% of the companies included their financial and non-financial data in the financial reports, when analyzed by sector, it is found that each sector reports 60% or more has been determined that the reporting rate. Also in research, it was determined that GRI reporting standard is the most preferred report in CSR reporting and two-thirds of the companies surveyed use GRI G4 guidelines and standards (KPMG 2017: 5–6). These researches show the development of CSR at global level over the years.

In today's global business world, executives see CSR practices not only as a ethical obligation, but also as an economic necessity. From the 2000s onwards, we are also exhibiting an awareness that businesses cannot survive in the market in the long run simply by producing products or services (Gürel 2010: 114).

8.3   Literature Review

With the increasing importance of CSR in recent years, the number of researches has increased. The literature focuses on the relationship between financial performance and CSR and different results were reached in these studies. Some studies have found a negative relationship between CSR and firm performance. Crisostomo et al. (2011) examined 78 companies in Brazil during 2001–2006 and found a negative relationship between CSR and financial performance of these companies. Selçuk and Kıymaz (2017) examined the annual reports and web pages of the companies registered in the stock exchange İstanbul index for the years 2009–2011 by using content analysis method. In this study they found a negative relationship between CSR and financial performance of companies. In addition, no significant relationship was found between research and development expenses and firm performance. In some studies, a positive correlation was found between CSR and company performance. Bernal-Conesa et al. (2017) found that Spanish technology companies had a positive impact on the reputation and economic performance of CSR practices. Sıla and Cek (2017) examined the 2010–2016 periods of the Australian companies they took as samples and tested the impact of their economic, social and governance performance on their economic performance. In this study, it was determined that social performance of companies made the most important contribution to economic performance, there was a positive relationship between environmental performance and economic performance, and governance performance had no significant effect on economic performance. Maqbooln and Zameer (2018) examined 28 commercial banks registered in the Indian stock exchange in the years 2007–2016 and stated that the banks' CSR performances had a positive effect on their financial performance.

Studies have focused on the analysis of the sector of CSR practices in Turkey. İcigen et al. (2016) 13 international hotel chains operating in Turkey's CSR activities were examined by Web sites and social media pages of content analysis method. In this study, it was determined that the most common CSR applications of hotel establishments are environment, disaster and poverty, education, and local issues and health. Büyüksalvarcı et al. (2016) examined the CSR activities of Dedeman Konya Hotel. Gucenme and Aytac (2016) analyzed the annual activity reports of the companies included in the BIST Sustainability Index and analyzed the practices of these companies on environmental and social sustainability. In the study, it was determined that companies have included social sustainability information in their annual reports since 2012. Fidan and Acar (2017) evaluated CSR activities of Akbank, Garanti Bank and İş Bank based on cooperation. In this study, it was stated that banks cooperate nationally and internationally. Karadeniz and Unlubulduk (2018) evaluated the CSR activities of the five companies with the highest brand value in the world and the airlines traded on stock exchange Istanbul. In the study, it was determined that the most frequently reported activities of the companies are environmental practices.

8.4   Standards of Corporate Social Responsibility Reporting

This section examines the global standards for CSR. These standards are summarized below. Sustainability reports, which started with CSR and environmental reporting first in the 1980s and nowadays adhere to standards, gain importance due to frequent economic crises due to economic, social and climatic conditions. Sustainability reports have been met with strict standards and metrics by the Global Reporting Initiative (GRI), based in the Netherlands. The Sustainability Reporting Guidelines, which has been continuously developed since 1999, has been updated for the fourth time in 2015 and has become G4 standards (Gucenme and Aytac 2016: 53). This standard helps businesses set goals, measure their performance and manage change to make their operations more sustainable. The sustainability report, reports on the positive or negative impact of an enterprise on the environment, society and economy. Thereby, sustainability reporting helps to understand and manage the impact of sustainability developments on the organization's activities and strategy by making abstract issues tangible and concrete (GRI G4 2013: 5).

The insufficiency of the information presented in the sustainability reports in the business model and strategy of the company makes it difficult for investors to understand the relationship between the sustainability performance and financial performance of companies and how sustainability creates value in the company. This discrepancy between the information provided prevents investors from seeing the entire picture and making the right decision about the company's current and future performance (TUSİAD 2015: 37). Therefore, the concept of integrated reporting, which goes beyond the merger of financial and sustainability reports, aims to establish the connections between financial and non-financial information and to demonstrate the impact of the presented information on the value creation capacity of the company (Altınay 2016: 57). With the establishment of IIRC in 2010, global studies on integrated reporting have gained an institutional structure. IIRC published in December 2013 International Framework (Jhunjhunwala 2014:75).

Founded in 1946 the International Organization for Standardization (ISO) ensures that products, services and processes are reliable and of high quality with internationally recognized standards. ISO also publishes standards for social responsibility. These are: ISO 9001 Quality Management System Standard, ISO 14001 Environmental Management Standard, ISO 50001 Energy Management System, ISO 26000 Social Responsibility Management System, OHSAS 18001 Occupational Health and Safety Management System (www.iso.org).

8.5 Corporate Social Responsibility Activities in Turkey

The first regulations regarding CSR Capital Markets Board of Turkey (CMB) published in 2003, "Corporate Governance Principles. These principles were revised in 2005 and 2011. In 2007, Istanbul Stock Exchange (ISE) established the "Corporate Governance Index, and required the CMB "Corporate Governance Compliance Report". The "Corporate Governance Principles, which were published in the Official Gazette No. 28871 on 2014 and which came into force with the "Corporate Governance Report", were revised. This organization aims to evaluate publicly held companies in accordance with the principles of transparency, accountability, responsibility and fairness. To this end, the rating agencies determined by the CMB evaluate the statements of publicly held companies regarding their compliance with corporate governance principles. As a result of the evaluation, the company which scores at least 7 out of 10 points is included in the BIST Corporate Governance Index. This index aims to measure the price and return performance of the companies with a valid grade (www.spk.gov.tr; www.borsaistanbul.com). Another important development in this respect is the calculation and publication of Borsa İstanbul's BIST Sustainability Index since 2014. This index is calculated on the basis of the performance of publicly held companies in environmental, social and corporate governance issues and subject to valuation according to international sustainability criteria. BIST Sustainability Index includes 62 companies in 2019 (www.borsaistanbul.com).

Widespread in the private sector in order to ensure international standards of CSR concept in Turkey, civil society with the participation of leading public and the academic world peace social responsibility Corporate Social Responsibility Association was established (www.kssd.org.tr). The association "Corporate Social Responsibility Report in Turkey" was published in 2010. In the report, Turkey, where voluntary corporate social responsibility, but multinational companies as a result of positive pressure applications and extensions on local suppliers for other Turkish companies also stated that creates a driving force. In addition, the report states that the "Corporate Governance Principles" declared by the Capital Markets Board have created awareness and understanding of the reporting of stakeholder policies and thus CSR practices (Türkiye'de Kurumsal Sosyal Sorumluluk Değerlendirme Raporu 2008: 3–11).

8.6 A Research on Corporate Social Responsibility Reports of Glass Production Companies in ISO 500

In this part of the study, the purpose and importance of the research, scope and data, methodology of the research are explained and the findings of the research are determined.

8.6.1 Purpose and Importance of Research

Research in Turkey in 2017, ISO (Istanbul Chamber of Industry) set by the 500 industrial establishments located within the glass manufacturing company of CSR within the scope of the reports they publish, the information disclosed in the official web page if the companies do not make reporting was analyzed by content analysis method. It is aimed to draw conclusions about the CSR applications of these companies.

The reason why the glass sector has been chosen is that applications are an important issue in terms of sustainability of natural resources during glass production and glass recycling. For this reason, it is important to examine and evaluate the practices of glass production enterprises in order to ensure economic, environmental and social sustainability.

8.6.2 Data

The companies included in the research consist of 6 glass manufacturing companies within 500 industrial enterprises determined by ISO in 2017. The reports published by CSR companies within the scope of CSR were obtained from the official web pages.

The statements of companies that do not report CSR are taken from the official web pages.

8.6.3 Methodology

It has been determined which reporting type the companies that are included in our research have chosen primarily within the scope of CSR. Afterward, CSR reports and official web pages of companies were evaluated according to content analysis method according to determined economic, environmental and social indicators. In the determination of these indicators, approaches of Gucenme and Aytac (2016), Karadeniz and Unlubulduk (2018) and GRI G4 Guide were used.

8.6.4 Findings

As a result of the research conducted on the corporate web pages of the companies included in our research, the informations made by companies within the scope of CSR are given in Table 8.1. When the chart is examined, Trakya glass, Paşabahçe glass, Anadolu glass and Trakya Yenişehir glass companies report their CSR reports in their annual reports. It is seen that the Corporate Governance Principles Compliance Statement is reported under the heading of "social responsibility and sustainability reports published on the official web pages. Since Trakya Yenişehir glass company is a subsidiary of Trakya glass company, financial and non-financial information of the company is included in the reports of main company. Park glass and Duzce glass companies provide information about CSR on their official web pages.

8.6.4.1 Corporate Social Responsibility Reporting Approaches of Glass Production Companies

CSR approaches of the companies covered by the research are as follows:
Trakya Glass Company Turkey Bottle and Glass Factory, Inc. is an organization affiliated with the ("Sisecam Holding"). The Company has announced its environment and energy, quality, human policies and systems in line with its sustainability approach on its official Web site. Since 2017, the Company has been publishing a sustainability report in accordance with GRI standards. This report covers all businesses and affiliates of the company. Established in 2015, Trakya Yenişehir Glass Company is a subsidiary of Trakya Glass Company CSR approaches are included in the sustainability reports published by Trakya Glass Company. Pasabahce and Anadolu Glass companies are belong to Sisecam Group. These companies have announced CSR policies on their official Web sites. Since 2014, they prepare and publish a sustainability report in compliance with GRI Standards every year.

Table 8.1 ISO top 500 companies internal glass production companies (2017)

Row number	Row number of first 500 companies	Company name	Net sales (TL)	Reporting type	Information on the corporate web page	Field of activity
1	111	Trakya Glass company	1.921.747.117	Sustainability reporting, annual report of the group, Group corporate governance principles compliance statement	CSR approaches are explained	Flat glass production and sales
2	92	Paşabahçe glass company	1.280.254.409	Sustainability reporting, annual report of the group, Group corporate governance principles compliance statement	The topics focused on CSR were explained	Production and sale of glassware
3	473	Anadolu glass company	1.436.271.719	Sustainability reporting, annual report of the group, Group corporate governance principles compliance statement	CSR approaches are explained	Production and sale of glass packaging
4	282	Park glass company	440.029.739	Inaccessible	CSR policies are explained	Production and sale of glass packaging
5	–	Duzce glass company	441.165.540	Inaccessible	CSR approaches are explained	Flat glass production and sales

(continued)

Table 8.1 (continued)

Row number	Row number of first 500 companies	Company name	Net sales (TL)	Reporting type	Information on the corporate web page	Field of activity
1	98	111	Trakya Glass company	1.921.747.117	Sustainability reporting, annual report of the group, Group corporate governance principles compliance statement	CSR approaches are explained	Flat glass production and sales
6	473	286	Trakya Yenişehir glass company	333.477.775	Sustainability reporting (subsidiary of Takya glass company) group corporate governance principles compliance statement	Disclosed within the main company (subsidiary of Trakya glass company)	Flat glass production and sales

The document on CSR reporting could not be found on the official Web site of Park Glass company. However, the company has announced CSR approaches on its Web site. Here, quality, occupational health and safety, food safety, environment, energy and information security issues come to the fore. The Company has also announced its policies for recycling, energy saving, emission reduction and optimum use of water resources within the framework of sustainability approach. After all, there is no information on when this information was posted on the Web site and how long it was updated.

The document related to CSR reporting could not be found on the official Web site of Duzce Glass Company. Yet, the company has announced its practices on quality, environment and energy, information security and research issues within the framework of sustainability approach on its Web site. Nevertheless, it is not known when this information was written to the Web site and how long it was updated.

8.6.4.2 Indications of Economic Sustainability

The sustainability reports of the companies included in our research and the official web pages of non-reporting companies were examined. Sisecam Group disclosed economic performance indicators such as tax paid, production, net profit, sales revenues, number of employees and capacity in its sustainability reports. Park Glass Company explained its production capacity and number of employees in its corporate information. Düzce Glass Company explained the production capacity amount and product range in its corporate information. However, there is no information as to the date on which this information appeared on the official Web site or how long it was updated.

8.6.5 Indications of Environmental Sustainability

The studies carried out by the companies involved in the research on environmental sustainability are given in Table 8.2. In the chart, it is seen that the companies in Sisecam Group have taken the necessary actions and used international standards in order to ensure environmental sustainability. Although Park Glass and Duzce Glass companies provide information on environmental sustainability on their official web pages, they did not disclose indicators of their environmental performance (energy consumption rates, water use amount, greenhouse gas emissions, etc.).

8.6.5.1 Indications Related to Social Sustainability

Table 8.3 shows the social sustainability activities of the companies covered by the research. In the chart, it is seen that the companies of Sisecam Group are doing the necessary works to ensure social sustainability. Park glass and Duzce glass companies

Table 8.2 Indications of environmental sustainability

Year 2017	Trakya Glass Company	Paşabahçe Sisecam	Anadolu Glass Company	Park Glass Company	Duzce Glass Company
Environmental penalty	No penalty	No penalty	No penalty	No information provided	No information provided
Information on environmental sustainability	+	+	+	+	+
ISO 9001 Quality Management System	+	+	+	+	+
ISO 14001 Environmental Management System	+	+	+	+	+
ISO 50001 Energy Management System	+	+	+	No information provided	No information provided
ISO/TS 16949 Automotive Quality Management System	+	No information provided	No information provided	No information provided	No information provided
Fighting with Climate change	+	+	+	No information provided	No information provided
Greenhouse gas emissions reduction studies	+	+	+	No information provided	+
Usage of Energy efficiency projects	+	+	+	No information provided	+
Waste management and recycling projects	+	+	+	No information provided	+

have not provided enough information on the official Web site. Park Glass Company explained social responsibility and ethical work policies. However, it is not possible to reach a conclusion about the company's practices from this information. On the official Web site of Duzce Glass Company, they explained their activities on occupational safety and health under the heading of sustainability. But this information is

Table 8.3 Indications related to social sustainability

Year 2017	Trakya Glass Company	Paşabahçe Sisecam	Anadolu Glass Company	Park Glass Company	Duzce Glass Company
Information on social sustainability	+	+	+	+	+
Information about social projects	+	+	+	No information provided	No information provided
Education and training and culture and sports a support activities	+	+	+	No information provided	No information provided
Explanation of the existence of the code of ethics	+	+	+	No information provided	No information provided
Explanation about human resources policies	+	+	+	No information provided	No information provided
Efforts to increase customer satisfaction	+	+	+	No information provided	+
OHSAS 18001: occupational health and safety management system	+	+	+	No information provided	+
Explanations on occupational health and safety	+	+	+	No information provided	+
Donations and charities and sponsorships	+	+	+	No information provided	No information provided

insufficient to evaluate the company's studies on social sustainability. Park Glass and Duzce Glass companies did not disclose the indicators of their social performance (gender, age, number of employees by year, average number of employees per year, diversity and equal opportunity, Labor and Social Security data, etc.).

8.7   Conclusions and Evaluations

CSR is a concept that adopts the ethical principles and responsibility awareness toward all areas of responsibility in the internal and external environment of the enterprise and adopts the decision making and implementation accordingly. Nowadays, businesses have to consider social and environmental factors while realizing their economic goals. CSR also shares its activities with stakeholders in line with the principle of transparency. Companies can provide information about CSR on their official web pages, annual reports, sustainability or integrated reporting. Since there is no legal regulation as to what kind of reporting should be provided, different practices are used by businesses.

In the research, the sustainability reports and official web pages of the companies producing glass in ISO 500 within the scope of CSR in 2017 were examined. In the investigation, the examination of the data of only the companies producing glass in ISO 500 is a limitation. The evaluation of the findings obtained in the research is as follows:

- Sisecam Group, the most important representative of the glass sector, preferred sustainability reporting as a CSR reporting type. Group companies have prepared the reports in accordance with GRI G4 reporting framework. The reports include practices and performance indicators related to economic, social and environmental sustainability of companies. Climate change, scarcity of resources, digitalization, economic balances and innovation have come to the fore in the Group's operations. Reports are as voluminous as annual reports (about 55 pages). Sisecam Group also provided information on CSR in its annual reports under the "social responsibility in heading of the Corporate Governance Compliance Statement.
- Park Glass and Duzce Glass companies, which do not report CSR, have announced their CSR policies on their official web pages. Yet, when this information was written to the web page and how long it was updated was not specified. There is no information provided about economic, social and environmental performance indicators of companies.

References

Altınay A (2016) Entegre Raporlama ve Sürdürülebilirlik Muhasebesi. Süleyman Demirel Üniversitesi Sosyal Bilimler Enstitüsü Dergisi 25:7

Bernal-Conesa J, Briones-Peñalverb A, DeNieves-Nieto C (2017) The integration of CSR management systems and their influence on the performance of technology companies. Euro J Manag Bus Econ 25:121–132

BIST sürdürülebilirlik endeksi. http://www.borsaistanbul.com/endeksler/bist-pay-endeksleri/surdurulebilirlik-endeksi. 17 June 2019

Büyükşalvarcı A, Şapçılar M, Uyaroğlu A (2016) Kurumsal Oteller ve Sosyal Sorumluluk Projelerinin Değerlendirilmesi. Selçuk Üniversitesi Sosyal Ve Teknik Araştırmalar Dergisi 12:187–194

Crisostomo V, Freire F, Vasconcellos F (2011) Corporate social responsibility, firm value and financial performance in Brazil. Soc Respons J 7:295–309

EU Green Paper. https://ec.europa.eu/transparency/regdoc/rep/1/2001/EN/1-2001-366-EN-1-0.Pdf. 11 Mar 2019

Fidan Z, Acar Z (2017) Kurumsal Sosyal Sorumluluk Çalışmalarında İşbirliği: Akbank Garanti Bankası Ve Türkiye İş Bankası Üzerine Bir Değerlendirme. Selçuk İletişim 9:40–63

GRI G4 Sustainability Reporting Guidelines. https://www.globalreporting.org/resourcelibrary/GRIG4-Part1-Reporting-Principles-and-Standard-Disclosures.pdf. 11 Mar 2019

Gürel T (2010) Kurumsal Sosyal Sorumlulukta Yeni Yaklaşımlar ve Tartışılan Konular. Selçuk Üniversitesi İletişim Fakültesi Akademik Dergisi. Cilt:6, Sayı:3, 114

Gücenme Gençoğlu Ü, Aytaç A (2016) Kurumsal Sürdürülebilirlik Açısından Entegre Raporlamanın Önemi ve BIST Uygulamaları. Muhasebe ve Finansman Dergisi 72:51–65

https://www.parkcam.com.tr. 17 Mar 2019

https://www.duzcecam.com.tr. 17 Mar 2019

https://www.sisecam.com.tr. 17 Mar 2019

İçigen E, Çevik B, Doğan O (2016) Türkiye'de Faaliyet Gösteren Uluslararası Konaklama İşletmelerinin Sosyal Sorumluluk Uygulamalarının İncelenmesi. Mediterranean J Human VI:299–310

ISO Standards. https://www.iso.org/standards.html. 03 Mar 2019

Jhunjhunwala S (2014) Beyond financial reporting-international integrated reporting framework. Ind J Corporate Gov 7(1):73–80

Juscius V, Sneideriene A, Griauslyte J (2014) Assessment of the benefits of corporate social responsibility reports as one of the marketing tools. Reg Form Dev Stud 11(3):89

Karadeniz E, Ünlübulduk S (2018) Dünyada Marka Değeri En Yüksek Havayolu İşletmeleri İle Borsa İstanbul Havayolu İşletmelerinde Kurumsal Sosyal Sorumluluk Faaliyetlerinin Analizi. Seyahat Ve Otel İşletmeciliği Dergisi 15:370–385

Leitoniene S, Sapkauskiene A, Dagiliene L (2015).Theoretical issues and practical implications of corporate social accounting and reporting in Lithuania. Proc Econ Fin 32:334

Maqbooln S, Zameer M (2018) Corporate social responsibility and financial performance: an empirical analysis of Indian Banks. Future Bus J 4:84–93

Montiel I (2008) Corporate social responsibility and corporate sustainability separate pasts, common futures. Organ Environ 21(3):245

Sert N (2012) Türkiye'de Özel Sektörün Kurumsal Sosyal Sorumluk Anlayışına İlişkin Yarar Algısı: Kurumsal Sosyal Sorumluluk Faaliyetlerinin Duyurulmasında Web Sitelerinin Kullanılması. Online Acad J Inform Technol 9:34

Selçuk E, Kiymaz H (2017) Corporate social responsibility and firm performance: evidence from an emerging market. Account Fin Res 6(4):42–50

SPK Kurumsal Yönetim. https://www.spk.gov.tr/Sayfa/Index/10. 17 Feb 2019

Sıla I, Cek K (2017) The impact of environmental, social and governance dimensions of corporate social responsibility on economic performance: Australian evidence. Pro Comput Sci 120:797–804

The KPMG Survey of Corporate Responsibility Reporting 2017. https://assets.kpmg/content/dam/kpmg/xx/pdf/2017/10/kpmg-survey-of-corporate-responsibility-reporting-2017.pdf. 08 June 2019

Türkiye'de Kurumsal Sosyal Sorumluluk Değerlendirme Raporu 2008. http://www.iye.org.tr/wp-content/uploads/2012/12/KSS_Degerlendirme_Raporu_2008.pdf. 02 Apr 2019

Türkiye Kurumsal Sosyal Sorumluluk Derneği. https://www.kssd.org. 05 Mar 2019

TÜSİAD (2015) Kurumsal Raporlamada Yeni Dönem: Entegre Raporlama, Yayın No: T/201510-567, ISBN 978-605-165-012-8

Chapter 9
Talent Management or Human Capital? An Analysis of Corporate Communication Strategies with Integrated Reports

Stéphane Trébucq and Anne Goujon Belghit

Abstract Different issues are identified in literature regarding talent management and human capital such as risk management, the need to be innovative, or attractiveness in the labor market in order to develop a competitive advantage. In this research, we mainly wonder why and how listed companies report and disclose information about their talent management programs. Indeed, social performance has become a major issue for Socially Responsible Investors, and other pragmatic shareholders want to understand how companies use their talent in order to create value. Our sample has been built with IIRC examples database composed of 116 reports, in May 2015. We have selected reports signaled for their remarkable disclosures about intangible capitals. A total of 11 listed companies were found. Then, we built a liked-peer sample, with 11 similar listed companies. Our findings highlight that the quality of reports remains disappointing. Most companies fail to document how they manage their human capital, and which practices are actually implemented in order to manage talents. The efficiency, or performance, of such programs is not disclosed, and one can also wonder if they are truly being properly assessed.

Keywords Talent management · Human capital · Integrated reports · Communication strategies

9.1 Introduction

Talent management and human capital are becoming popular topics for practitioners but also for academics over the last years. In a highly competitive environment, companies direct more of their strategy on their human resources management in order to stand out and improve overall performance (Gavino et al. 2012). Similar issues are identified and associated to these two concepts such as risk management, the need to be innovative, or attractiveness in the labor market. The latter is central

S. Trébucq (✉) · A. G. Belghit
University of Bordeaux, Bordeaux, France
e-mail: stephane.trebucq@u-bordeaux.fr

© The Author(s), under exclusive license to Springer Nature Singapore Pte Ltd. 2021   141
K. T. Çalıyurt (ed.), *New Approaches to CSR, Sustainability and Accountability,*
Volume II, Accounting, Finance, Sustainability, Governance & Fraud: Theory
and Application, https://doi.org/10.1007/978-981-33-6808-8_9

because it will capture future talent who are not yet working in the company, which helps enhance the employer brand (Viot and Benraiss-Noailles 2014) and sends a positive signal perceived by potential future candidates (Ewerlin 2013). Ewerlin (2013) underlines that companies pay attention to their communication strategy through their Web sites, job advertisements, or in their personnel reports because they want to position themselves as attractive employers (Schuler et al. 2011); they are well aware of the interconnection between their intangibles. The originality of this research relies on considering human capital and talent management while at the same time identifying how companies communicate to shareholders on these matters. However, these concepts still need to be more clearly defined. In this research, we mainly wonder why and how listed companies report and disclose information about their talent management programs and about their human capital management practices. Indeed, social performance has become a major issue for Socially Responsible Investors, and other pragmatic shareholders want to understand how companies create value in order to secure their investment. Knowing more about the way human capital and talents are managed can then become key information, seeing it as a major driver for future performance. Since the Enron scandal (2001), there has been a growing need for a better understanding of business models, corporate strategies, and governance system in order to evaluate risks and opportunities. Even if there are official international social-related accountability standards like the financial reports which are regulated by the IASB (International Accounting Standard Board), or the sustainability report regulated by the GRI (Global Reporting Initiative), there is still the issue of how efficient companies communicate above their global performance. In response to this situation, the IIRC (International Integrated Reporting Council) has emerged on the international scene of independent authorities and standard setters of corporate reporting. This international organization suggests the publication of a new report, entitled "integrated reporting" or <IR>, in order to better explain the value creation processes in comparison to classical reports, with new information requirements. Thereby, listed companies are asked to describe their contribution to social performance, their intangible capitals, as well as their interconnections. The IIRC's framework clearly indicates "human capital" but quite strangely, the words "talent" or "talent management' are absent. We then first wonder and question if and how "talent management" and "human capital" should be considered differently and separately, and how companies actually report about them. Another central question is about integrated reports, in order to determine why companies adopt this new standard and to what extent such publications bring us new insights about the way "talent management" is conducted and/or "human capital" is managed. In order to answer to these questions, we will first question literature on human capital as well as on talent management in order to demonstrate that these two concepts are linked and should be used by companies in their communication. Then, we try to understand reporting strategies of listed companies on these subjects. Our empirical study is then based on the small sample of companies which have started to apply the <IR> framework. We analyze their content within the NVivo software, in comparison with their previous disclosures before the integrated reporting adoption or test, and with a liked-peer sample of companies with similar sizes and sector ships.

9.2   Literature Review

9.2.1   Definition of Key Concepts of "Talent Management" and "Human Capital"

Since the previous study of McKinsey in 1997 regarding the "war of talent" and the necessity for companies to improve their human resources practices in order to develop a competitive advantage, there is still no clear definition of the concept. In fact, it is a multilevel concept that can be explained from an individual perspective, a group level or from an organizational approach (Wilska 2014) and more recently from a societal level (Claus 2019).

First, a talented person can be seen as a "creative, resourceful" individual (Borkowska 2005; Wilska 2014) who has "outstanding potential" (Listwan 2010; Wilska 2014) with a high level of motivation and knowledge (Ingram 2011) as well as specific skills, experience, behaviors (Cheese et al. 2008; Wilska 2014) and innate gifts, intelligence, judgments, and character (Michaels et al. 2001).

Then, from a unit level, talent management can be defined as a set of collective attributes (Armstrong 2011) restricted to a small group of individuals who inspire their colleagues because they attain outstanding performance (Berger 2004).

From an organizational perspective, talent management is a hot topic that can be identified from an inclusive or an exclusive approach. The inclusive one refers to strategic human resources management whose aims are to increase the organizational productivity through better recruitment processes or through the identification of the right person for the right job (Claus 2019; Scullion et al. 2010; Downs and Swailes 2013; Hejase et al. 2016; Lewis and Heckman 2006; Lockwood 2006). In order to cope with the competitive environment, organizations need to "acquire, retain, and develop" their human resources (Wilska 2014) in order to "give both the employees and the employing organization tools to better match what the employee needs and what the organization requires in terms of performance" (Schein and Van Maanen 2016). Then, the exclusive approach has been promoted by Collings and Mellahi (2009) because "if talent management is applied to all of an organization's employees (i.e., including poor performers as well as top performing employees), it is difficult to differentiate talent management from conventional human resource management." These authors then propose a conceptual and performance model for "talent management," based on the constitution of a talent pool and its assignment to pivotal positions, in order to improve work motivation, organizational commitment, extra-role behavior, and finally financial and economic performance. Talking about "pivotal positions" or "strategic roles" also means that talent management is only designed and dedicated to the "happy few" or an *elite* of top-ranked executives and managers (Mellahi and Collings 2010) and that the departure of a talent person would cause severe problems for the business (Stewart 1997; Huang and Tansley 2012). Issues for organizations are very important because talent management is clearly connected to competitive advantage and shareholder value. According to Lewis and Heckman (2006), this talent management also has to be complemented by a clear strategic analysis, looking forward for market opportunities and right competencies needs, and an organization of an enterprise-wide data system, in order to simulate future lack of competencies and better organize promotions, successions, and knowledge management (Vaiman et al. 2012). Lewis and Heckman (2006), on the basis of Zuboff's work (1988), suggest to develop a strategic talent management based on two modalities: the difficulty to replace a talented employee and his or her added value. Middle managers can be considered as key talent employees within organizations while they have the responsibility to lead change. Their talent depends on their prompting ability to face new situations (Whysall et al. 2019).

The talent management approach is closed to the "human capital" concept even if the latter notion is more theoretically and economically routed in the work of Schultz (1961) and Becker (1975, 2002). There is no consensus regarding the definition of human capital as it is a multilevel concept, just like the talent management approach.

First, on the individual level, human capital can be defined as an individual's knowledge, ideas, skills, and health (Becker 2002) or as a set of KSA meaning knowledge, skills, and abilities (Coff 2002; Coff and Kryscynski 2011; Crook et al. 2011; Nyberg et al. 2014, Ployhart et al. 2014).

Then, on a unit level, human capital can be defined as "the aggregate accumulation of individual human capital that can be combined in a way that creates value for the unit" (Wrigt and McMahan 2011) or as the combination of individuals' KSAOs, meaning knowledge, skills, abilities, and other characteristics (Ployhart and Moliterno 2011; Ployhart et al. 2014).

Finally, from the organizational perspective, Gamerschlag and Moeller (2011) link "human capital reporting" to benefits in terms of motivation and commitment, innovation, attractiveness and reputation, and finally financial performance, which refer more broadly to human resources management. Strategic human capital management is necessary in order to achieve to a sustaining competitive advantage (Campbell et al. 2012), thanks to competencies that are valuable, rare, inimitable, and nontransferable (Barney 1991; Prahalad and Hamel 1990; Wernerfelt 1984; Lepak and Snell 1999, 2002). Lepak and Snell (1999) also suggest developing a strategic human resources management based on two modalities: uniqueness and the value of human capital.

As can be seen, "talent management" and "human capital" are close and interconnected notions, conceptualized as multilevel approaches that mobilize human resources management practices and tools. Each individual talent and high potential employee has also his or her own human capital, which can be more or less useful for the strategic goals of the organizations. It certainly depends on managerial decisions, but also on external circumstances that cannot be fully under managerial control. Both concepts seem to be compatible with a resource-based view. Talent or specific human capital can in both cases help to build inimitable resources, at least for a while. However, we still know little about the acceptability of such concepts, and how companies use them in practice.

9.2.2 Integrated Reporting: Key Characteristics and Challenges

Human capital or talent management reporting can then be useful, if there is a possible link with financial performance or with social and environmental performance (Gilbert and Rasche 2008; Rasche 2009; Gilbert et al. 2011). Integrated reporting has also recently emerged as a new reporting standard and system, in order to better inform investors about the key value drivers. Standards define rules, procedures, and methods in order to evaluate organizational actions (Crane and Matten 2007), they are identified as soft law as they are not transposed into legal obligations (Gilbert et al. 2011). This refers to the problem of the real force of constraints and its efficiency on organizational governance or shareholders as there is no hierarchical authority, no agreement on standard methodology or sanctions. This is why Gilbert et al. (2011) recommend giving more opportunities to stakeholders in order to "meaningfully participate both in the governance and implementation of standards." Some have been skeptical about its success (Flower 2015; Verschoor 2011) and have noticed that different economic and institutional environments might impact its use (Frías-Aceituno et al. 2013). This new standard also raises questions about its usefulness, or the reliability and quality of information it will provide to investors (Cheng et al. 2014; Knauer and Serafeim 2014; Rensburg and Botha 2014).

The IIRC launched its framework in December, 2013. <IR> includes also some key content elements such as organizational overview and a description of the external environment, corporate governance, business model, risks and opportunities, strategy and resource allocation, performance, outlook, and materiality of issues reported. It also provides a clear definition of human capital, as follows: "people's competencies, capabilities, and experience, and their motivation to innovate, including their (1) alignment with and support for an organization's governance framework, risk management approach, and ethical values, (2) ability to understand, develop, and implement an organization's strategy, (3) loyalties and motivations for improving processes, goods, and services, including their ability to lead, manage, and collaborate." Social capital and intellectual capital are also defined and distinguished from human capital. Social capital includes abilities to share information with others, especially stakeholders, and protect interests of communities and the society as a whole. Intellectual capital corresponds to organizational, knowledge-based intangibles, including intellectual property and "organizational capital," such as tacit knowledge, systems, procedures, and protocols. In fact, the IIRC definition of human capital does not fully fit with the academic one, which includes knowledge components, and social or relational abilities.

Quite interestingly, one can also observe that talent is not used in the framework. It is somewhat surprising if we refer to Benito-Osorio et al. (2014) findings because they point out that "introducing work–life balance practices benefits the company with respect to talent retention and higher employee engagement, as well as achieving a positive impact on productivity, costs and business results." These elements are not taken into consideration in the formal integrated report framework.

It then raises questions about how companies will in practice apply this definition and document their actions in terms of human capital and talent management. Moreover, if we refer to El Abboubi and Nicolopoulou's (2012) findings, based on the idea that "the strength and the sustainability of the network established between the company and its stakeholders are subsequently dependent on the way the corporation translates its own interests and those of the stakeholders into common goals," then we can suggest that companies are willing to communicate through the integrated report on their global performance.

This is why another challenge is also to better understand communication strategies (search of legitimacy, search of attractiveness for future employees), and the level of transparency of such disclosures.

9.3 Methodology

9.3.1 Sample of Corporate Reports and Methodology

Our sample has been built with IIRC examples database composed of 116 reports, in May 2015. We selected reports signaled for their remarkable disclosures about intangible capitals. In the end, 11 listed companies were found. These corporate reports were published in 2013 or 2014, and in some cases, remained officially an "annual report," and in other cases an "integrated report."

For each on these companies, we then downloaded their external reports from two years prior (coded as year N-1, and year N-2), in order to assess if their use of the IIRC framework had effectively changed something. We also built a liked-peer sample, with 11 similar listed companies, using SIC sector codes (3 digits) and market capitalizations as benchmark criteria (information taken from the infinancials database) (Table 9.1).

Each Web site of these companies was checked, and all reports that could disclose information about social performance, human capital, or talent management were downloaded. Some companies did not have any sustainability reports like Atlantia, DBS, Itau Unibanco, Companhia Brasileira de Distribuicao, Vienna Insurance, and Citigroup. The final database of reports is composed of 107 reports (see Appendix Table 9.5). A total of 55 of them are annual reports, 39 are sustainability reports, and 9 are presented and entitled as integrated reports. Among these last reports, 5 of them come from the IIRC database of samples, but some companies like Atlantia and Sasol had integrated reports before the year taken as an example and model by the IIRC. In our sub-sample 2, used as a control group, we found only one company with one integrated report, not referenced by the IIRC: UniCredit for the year 2014. For this last company, the integrated report replaced the previous sustainability reports, but many other cases might exist and are possible. Iberdrola and Sasol, in sub-sample 1, have maintained their sustainability report with the edition of their integrated report. Others, like Lawson or Itau Unibanco, have fully merged or replaced their

Table 9.1   Description of the sample

SIC code	Sector	Listed companies with reports given as examples by the IIRC (sub-sample 1)		Listed companies with similar size and activities, not being taken as examples by the IIRC (sub-sample 2)	
161	Highway and street construction	Atlantia SpA	1	Abertis Infraestructuras S.A.	12
291	Petroleum refining	Eni SpA	2	Statoil ASA	13
491	Electric services	Iberdrola SA	3	American Electric Power Company	14
734	Building cleaning and maintenance services	Interserve Plc	4	Mitie Group PLC	15
508	Machinery and equipment-wheeler	Itochu Corp	5	Mitsui & Co Ltd.	16
541	Grocery stores	Lawson Inc.	6	Comp. Brasileira de Distribuicao Grupo Pao de	17
138	Oil and gas field services	NK Rosneft' OAO	7	Ecopetrol S.A.	18
630	Insurance carriers	RSA Insurance Group PLC	8	Vienna Insurance Group	19
131	Crude petroleum & natural gas	Sasol Ltd.	9	Ptt Pcl	20
602	Commercial banks	DBS Group Holdings Ltd.	10	UniCredit SpA	21
602	Commercial banks	Itau Unibanco Holding SA	11	Citigroup Inc	22

previous reports now using the integrated report. Finally, some companies, like Eni, Interserve, Itochu, Rosneft, RSA Insurance or DBS, started to only partially adopt the IIRC standard within their annual report. Three marginal reports have also been found, with a statutory report for Statoil in 2011, a society report for Interserve in 2013, and an integrated management report for Ecopetrol in 2012 and 2013. These two last forms of reports have been classified separately, even if they are, respectively, close to sustainability reports or integrated reports.

9.3.2   Qualitative Analysis

As previously exposed, our main research question is about what and how companies report concerning their management approaches. One can wonder if integrated reports, considering the framework content, develop better interest and information on talent management or human capital practices. This can be tested from different perspectives. First, one can compare reports according to their reporting format, and then according to their evolution in a recent period of time. It is then possible to better characterize examples of reports used by the IIRC with a comparison of similar companies. These comparisons can help to understand if companies that use or that are inspired by the integrated reporting standard have a different way of communicating about their human capital or talent management.

NVivo, a qualitative research software, was used in order to conduct a systematic analysis of qualitative data (Richards 1999; Bazeley and Jackson 2013). One function of the software is to view segments of the analyzed corpus which generates a visual overview of the content. NVivo is a powerful tool used for finding all paragraphs including some key words within reports. Our approach is focus on "human capital" and "talent management." First, we identified the occurrence of these two concepts in three different report supports found on the Internet: the integrated report, the annual report and the sustainability report. The same approach was used to see how often "human capital" and "talent management" were mobilized during the past years. Then, we checked the proximity between each of them, which allowed us to identify any potential relationship between emergent concepts. Finally, coding stripes provided us with a valuable exploratory tool that facilitated finding the main information associated with our key concepts. The software highlights how human capital and talent management are used in practice.

9.4 Results and Discussion

9.4.1 Empirical Results

We first tried to compare reports according to their format and their evolution in time. Our first two sets of requests can help to determine the number of paragraphs including the expressions "human capital" and "talent management" (Table 9.2).

Table 9.2 Comparison between different types of reports

	"Human capital"			"Talent management"		
	All sample	Sub-sample 1	Sub-sample 2	All Sample	Sub-sample 1	Sub-sample 2
Integrated report	**68 (7, 56)**	56 (7, 00)	12 (12, 00)	**13 (1, 44)**	9 (1, 13)	4 (4, 00)
Annual report	**22 (0, 40)**	15 (0, 52)	7 (0, 23)	**19 (0, 35)**	13 (0, 52)	6 (0, 20)
Sustainability report	**20 (0, 51)**	10 (0, 33)	10 (0, 56)	**14 (0, 36)**	7 (0, 33)	7 (0, 39)

Number of paragraphs or references (divided by the number of reports)
(All sample and sub-samples; by main reporting types)

The number of paragraphs using "human capital" seems to be significantly higher for integrated reports compared to the other reporting forms (68 vs. 22 or 20). This phenomenon is also observed for "talent management" (13 vs. 19 or 14). These results seem to show that companies just apply the IIRC standard, which asks for better information about "human capital" with no specific demand about "talent management." The application of the IIRC standard tends to multiply the number references to this concept of intangible capital. Results by sub-samples clearly show that a large amount of these references to "human capital" are achieved by companies belonging to sub-sample 1 (45% of them have an integrated report). In the sub-sample 2, only one company gets an integrated reporting, which represents only 9%. The other figures showing the number of references divided by the number of reports in our database is also interesting. It shows that "talent management" is used more often in integrated reports than in other kind of reports (1.44 vs. 0.35 or 0.36). Again, this result is due to the companies found in sub-sample 1.

As can be seen in Table 9.3, the use of the concept of "human capital" has highly changed in recent years, in our sample. The IIRC standard has certainly influenced the preparers of reports on the topic "human capital," even if it has had no particular influence on "talent management" information and transparency. Results show that the references to "human capital" have increased in sub-sample 1, and reached their highest number during the year of report selected by the IIRC. Such a phenomenon is not observed on our control group, sub-sample 2. One can also notice a slight increase of the "talent management" quotes within sub-sample 1, showing that this group might have a higher interest for this concept and practice, than in sub-sample 2.

Our next empirical findings try to check how "human capital" and "talent management" are used in similar contexts, with some same concepts. Using the list of the 31 concepts used by Vergauwen and al. (2007) in order to assess the disclosure and information about "human capital" within corporate reports, we are able to check the proximities. NVivo provides the opportunity to compare contents of each node, according to its content. These nodes have been obtained through SQL requests in order to find the words or expressions, and then get paragraphs including them. One

Table 9.3 Effects of the new IIRC standard on reports

	"Human capital"			"Talent management"		
	All sample	Sub-sample 1	Sub-sample 2	All Sample	Sub-sample 1	Sub-sample 2
Reports of year N	**62 (1, 68)**	48 (2, 53)	14 (0, 78)	**18 (0, 49)**	13 (0, 68)	5 (0, 28)
Reports of year N-1	**44 (1, 26)**	29 (1, 61)	15 (0, 88)	**16 (0, 46)**	9 (0, 50)	7 (0, 41)
Reports of year N-2	**9 (0, 11)**	4 (0, 22)	5 (0, 29)	**12 (0, 34)**	7 (0, 39)	5 (0, 29)

Number of paragraphs or references (divided by the number of reports)
(All sample and sub-samples; by years N, N-1, N-2)

node has been created for "talent management," and another one for paragraphs using only the word "talent."

The obtained classification tree shows a first cluster with a high proximity between "human capital" and "talent management," which are close to "career development," "training program," "empowerment," "employee benefits," and "intelligence." This cluster is close to another separate one, including "education," "expertise," "knowledge," "competence," and "know-how." A third cluster seems to be more distant, with notions such as "employee retention," "employee satisfaction," "employee skill," "employee value," "expert team," and "human asset." After the first results, we only retained 19 concepts out of the initial list. Other concepts were either not used or absent.

We then coded these concepts for each sub-sample, in order to observe and check any differences.

Figures 9.1 and 9.2 show differences between sub-sample 1 and 2.

For companies taken as an example by the IIRC, the word "talent" is often used with "human capital," but this is not the case for "talent management." This means that one needs to differentiate people of "talent" and the action of "management." Thus, on one hand, for companies of sub-sample 1, "human capital" appears to be conceived as a quality of employees. It is used with words "competence," "expertise," "knowledge," "know-how," and "education." On the other hand, "talent management" is seen more as a process and practice, and is used next to other notions such as "career development" or "employee retention." "Human capital" can be used for all employees, and "talent management" can be targeted for individuals with high potential. As a consequence, "employee satisfaction," in this case, is connected to "talent management."

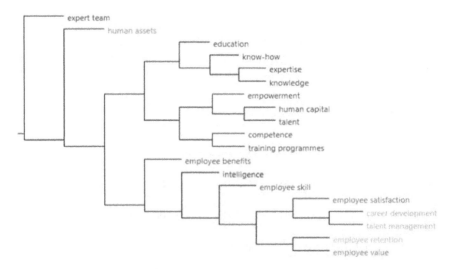

Fig. 9.1 Classification of nodes for sub-sample 1 according to their content (NVivo)

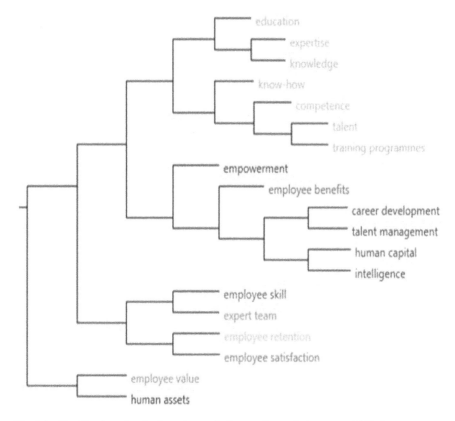

Fig. 9.2 Classification of nodes for sub-sample 2 according to their content (NVivo)

Companies from the second sub-sample have a more classical way of reporting, and use exceptionally integrated reports. They certainly have a different view from sub-sample 1 (see graph 2, about sub-sample 2). For these companies, "human capital" and "talent management" are closer concepts. Their approach seems also to be more abstract and limited, with notions such as "intelligence," "empowerment," or "career development" close to "human capital" and "talent management." Other qualities, such as "talent," "competence," "knowledge," "expertise," and "know-how" belong to a close, but different, cluster. Therefore, these companies seem to be more process-oriented, but fail to connect such processes to "employee satisfaction." For this reason, it might also be possible that their practices could be less efficient, but such hypothesis would need further investigation and will be discussed later in this article.

We have then explored what is really said about "human capital" and "talent management." Our first observations show very general comments about "talent management," which are unable to allow an external analyst to truly understand the quality of practices and the logic underlying such programs. Companies might also use more corporate reports in order to signal the existence of such programs than to explain them in detail.

As the empty spaces in Table 9.4 suggest, some companies fail to fully communicate about their "human capital" or "talent management." Such concepts do not exist in their reports. This is the case for only one company in sub-sample 1 (companies n°4: Interserve), but three companies in sub-sample 2 (companies n°14: Statoil, n°14 American Electric Power, n°19 Vienna Insurance). The number of companies talking about their "human capital" and about their "talent management" program is also higher in sub-sample 1, with six companies. Only two companies do so in sub-sample 2, where it is more common that one concept or the other is used exclusively. Our conclusion is that companies which have adopted the integrated report as a new standard of communication have a higher probability of using both concepts (66%) than with other formats (25% in case of annual or sustainability reports).

Companies from sub-sample 1 talk more about their "human capital" and "talent management," which suggests that their selection as examples by the IIRC is meaningful. However, companies do not publish quantitative or more detailed information. Atlantia (company n°1 in our sample) is the only exception. It is an early adopter of the integrated reporting standard and has a special section in its report about "human capital" (priorities, resources with employees and labor cost, training hours, turnover, reasons of termination, health and safety, diversity, age, seniority and parental leave) and "investments in human capital" (search, selection, and retention of talents, relations with the academic world, horizontal and vertical mobility, special training projects, evaluation and performance management, long-term incentives, non-cash incentives, health and safety initiatives, risk management and control activities, and employee engagement).

9.5 Discussion

Our qualitative research shows that the "human capital" has become increasingly popular with the recent IIRC framework. Companies attracted by such a new standard of reporting probably have a more strategic conception of human capital, viewed as a general and global strategic resource. "Talent management" thus becomes a complementary practice for them, designed for an *elite*, with the greatest impact on value creation.

Looking at reporting formats, companies adopting an integrated report might communicate their interest for future employees and talents more clearly. Some of them might also try to catch up with their main competitors. For example, Atlantia, DBS or Itau Unibanco had no sustainability reports before their adoption of the integrated reporting. This situation is more exceptional in our control group, with only one company in this case (Comp. Brasileira de Distribuicao Grupo Pao de). Some companies also seem to react when their competitor adopts an integrated report. For example, we have found in our sub-sample 2, Ecopetrol with an "integrated management report" for 2012 and 2013, and Unicredit with an "integrated report"

Table 9.4 Extract of main paragraphs when concepts of "human capital" or "talent management" are employed

Sample Ref. number	Company	Examples when «human capital» is employed	Examples when «talent management» is employed
1	Atlantia SpA	«Human capital: attract talent, development, and know-how enhancement, meritocratic organization, protection of labor as an asset, ongoing improvement of safety and health conditions in the workspace, activity internationalization (…) investments in human capital (…) Analytical figures human capital» (integrated report 2012)	«implement talent management processes» (integrated report 2012)
2	Eni SpA	"The main capitals used by Eni (…) human capital …" (annual report 2013)	
3	Iberdrola SA	"Human capital is without doubt Iberdrola's main asset and the focus of its strategy" (integrated report 2014)	"Talent management: (…) - drive staff qualifications, preparing employees to work in a multicultural environment and making continual efforts to improve their employability—develop alternatives to compensate for factors stemming from the aging of the workforce—define a framework to develop a global quality management system (…) (integrated report 2014)

(continued)

Table 9.4 (continued)

Sample Ref. number	Company	Examples when «human capital» is employed	Examples when «talent management» is employed
4	Interserve Plc	"(…) we will continue our aggressive investment in diverse human capital" (sustainability report 2014)	
5	Itochu Corp		"Develop a talent management process, which encourages the preparation of individual development plans by talented personnel who will play key roles in growing revenues and earnings overseas" (annual report 2014)
6	Lawson Inc.	"Since I became president, we have invested considerable time and expense on in-house training and education programs, such a Lawson University, to nurture this type of corporate culture and its human capital" (annual report 2012)	
7	NK Rosneft' OAO	"(…) significant increase in development index of human capital in Primorsky Territory" (sustainability report 2011)	
8	RSA Insurance Group PLC		"Rigorous performance and talent management processes are in place across the Group to ensure an ongoing focus on high performance and the development and acquisition of talent. (…)" (annual report 2014)

(continued)

Table 9.4 (continued)

Sample Ref. number	Company	Examples when «human capital» is employed	Examples when «talent management» is employed
9	Sasol Ltd.	"To ensure we have sufficient and appropriate financial and human capital to deliver to our aspirations, we have prioritized and focused our growth portfolio (…)" (integrated report 2013)	"We meet our transformation requirements in South Africa through talent management and succession planning, employment equity, (…)" (integrated report 2014)
10	DBS Group Holdings Ltd.	«The quality and commitment of our human capital is fundamental to our success» (annual report 2013)	«Ensure alignment between reward and the Group Talent Management initiatives with particular focus on attraction and retention of talent including current and future leaders of the Group» (annual report 2014)
11	Itau Unibanco Holding SA	«Our human capital is our greatest assets we have» (integrated report 2013)	«All our employees undergo some type of performance appraisal (…) The goals are to provide a mapping of skills and to support an individual development plans and decisions regarding promotions" (annual report 2012)
12	Abertis Infraestructuras S.A.		«Managing talent and professional development» (sustainability report 2011)
13	Statoil ASA		

(continued)

Table 9.4 (continued)

Sample Ref. number	Company	Examples when «human capital» is employed	Examples when «talent management» is employed
14	American Electric Power Comp.		
15	Mitie Group PLC		«We continue to implement our talent management program and have succession plans in place for key management» (sustainability report 2013)
16	Mitsui & Co Ltd.	«Human capital: expertise specialized in a diverse range of industries, regional expertise, business development opportunities, managerial excellence, versatility, and flexibility to act globally" (annual repot 2014)	
17	Comp. Brasileira de Distribuicao Grupo Pao de	«Human capital GPA's management model (…) seeks to attract, develop, and retain talent» (annual report 2012)	
18	Ecopetrol S.A.	«Corporate risk map: human capital deficit» (integrated management report 2013)	«Ecopetrol (…) has included an explicit guiding principal on human talent management, aimed at generating value for the organization (…)" (integrated management report 2013)
19	Vienna Insurance Group		

(continued)

Table 9.4 (continued)

Sample Ref. number	Company	Examples when «human capital» is employed	Examples when «talent management» is employed
20	Ptt Pcl	«PTT invests in human capital development by promoting systematic knowledge management and continuing education, as well as investing in innovation» (sustainability report 2013)	
21	Unicredit SpA	«Human capital: our colleagues' competencies, capabilities, experience, and motivation to innovate» (integrated report 2013)	«We understand that our colleagues are our most valuable assets (…) The UniCredit CIB Talent Management Review identifies, develops, and supports the division's most promising staff members to facilitate their professional success. The program, which is structured over three years, provides valuable training experiences, mentoring opportunities, meaningful exchanges with senior management and exposure to challenging business scenarios" (integrated report 2014)
22	Citigroup Inc.		

Comment: if table cells are left blank, this means that no significant paragraph has been found for the year 2014. Such companies have not directly collaborated with the IIRC, but do not want to lose their reputation and advance in terms of reporting.

Despite such modifications, improvements in the quality of reports remain disappointing. Most companies fail to document how they manage their human capital, and which practices are actually implemented in order to manage talents. The efficiency, or performance, of such programs is not disclosed, and one can also wonder if are actually being assessed and well assessed. It then becomes difficult to estimate the real level of maturity and excellence of such practices. However, some companies try to assess their social performance through surveys. Some of them only mention the existence of climate surveys (Atlantia), but others disclose the obtained results or conclusions in more detail, like Eni and Interserve.

Finally, our results underline the complexity of the relationships between organizations, international social-related accountability, shareholders, and external stakeholders as shown in Fig. 9.3.

The complexity of the relationships explains the lack of relevant information regarding the human capital practices and talent management diffused in the official communication accountability reports. Indeed, even if companies create competitive advantages thanks to these approaches, the international social-related accountability relies on soft law, and there is very much information regarding relevant identified standards. That is why organizations opt for prudence and prefer not to publish key information unless they have been asked by a specific framework as our results show with the integrated report. These findings are similar to those of Liu et al. (2014) as it highlights that even if human capital or talent management create a sustainable competitive advantage, firm investments in intangible assets differ. They point out that new types of investors have emerged these last years, and they notice their impact on strategic decisions as it reduces the degree of freedom of human resources

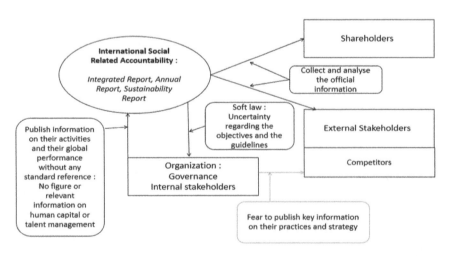

Fig. 9.3 Relationship between organizations, International social related accountability, shareholders and external stakeholders

officers. Information regarding talent management or human capital practices is not relevant as performance is mainly due to a complex system of complementariness that cannot be translated by figures. So why are these firms reluctant to communicate on these matters? Scholars underline that human capital and talent management are mainly tacit and difficult to evaluate, which is why stakeholders lack information. Moreover, as these intangible assets are difficult to identify clearly by figures, firms cannot estimate their level of contribution to their performance and there is a mistrust regarding the diffusion of key information.

9.6 Conclusion

This study's aim was to investigate the influence of reporting standards on corporate disclosures about "human capital" and "talent management." As expected, the IIRC standard appears to be related to a higher level of interest for "human capital" and "talent management." Companies whose reports have been taken as examples by the IIRC also have a more clear distinction between concepts and practices. "Human capital" remains a general argument, where "talent management" can be transposed into more precise human resources practices. Companies that are similar in size and sector and which have not been extracted in the IIRC database sample develop different behaviors. Firstly, they are less focused on "human capital." Secondly, they rarely use both concepts at the same time. Unfortunately, all reports, whatever the standard used, remain at a very general and strategic level. The IIRC standard only provides an explicit definition of "human capital," without any clear guidance to measure it. As empirically observed, some companies still do not communicate about human capital or talent management. Disclosing narrative information then remains enough to distinguish oneself and send a positive signal to financial markets. "Talent management" is almost as popular as "human capital" as a concept, but might have different effects on performance. It might depend on its complementarity with a broader strategic view of "human capital," its methodology of assessment and the way it is communicated and made transparent for employees and other stakeholders. A standard that could help to compare "talent management" from one company to another, and help analysts to achieve sectorial benchmarking would also be welcome. Our results show that organizations are not engaged in turning the accountability standards supports into an opportunity as suggested by Rasche (2010). Several questions remain unanswered such as the agreement on the standard definition, the real efficiency of these reporting standards, their goal, the willingness of organizational governance and stakeholders, or the quality of their relationship.

Appendix

See Appendix Table 9.5.

Table 9.5 Our database of reports

Sample	Sample Ref. number	Company	2011	2012	2013	2014
Sub-sample 1	1	Atlantia SpA	ar	ar, ir	ar, **ir**	
	2	Eni SpA	ar, sr	ar, sr	**ar**, sr	
	3	Iberdrola S.A.		sr	sr	sr, **ir**
	4	Interserve Plc	ar, sr	ar	sr2, **ar**	
	5	Itochu Corp.		ar, sr	ar, sr	**ar**, sr
	6	Lawson Inc.	ar, sr	ar, sr	**ir**	
	7	NK Rosneft' OAO	ar, sr	ar, sr	**ar**, sr	
	8	RSA Insurance Group PLC		ar, sr	ar, sr	**ar**, sr
	9	Sasol Ltd.		sr, ir	sr, ir	sr, **ir**
	10	DBS Group Holdings Ltd.		ar	ar	**ar**
	11	Itau Unibanco Holding S.A.	ar	ar	**ir**	
Sub-sample 2	12	Abertis Infraestructuras S.A.	ar, sr	ar, sr	ar, sr	
	13	Statoil ASA	ar, ar2	ar	ar, sr	
	14	American Electric Power Company		ar, sr	ar, sr	ar, sr
	15	Mitie Group PLC	ar, sr	ar, sr	ar, sr	
	16	Mitsui & Co Ltd.		ar, sr	ar, sr	ar, sr
	17	Comp. Brasileira de Distribuicao Grupo Pao de	asr	asr	asr	
	18	Ecopetrol S.A.		imr	imr	
	19	Vienna Insurance Group	ar	ar	ar	
	20	Ptt Pcl		ar, sr	ar, sr	ar, sr
	21	Unicredit SpA		ar, sr	ar, sr	ar, ir
	22	Citigroup Inc.	ar	ar	ar	

Comments: for sub-sample 1, letters are in bold and underlined when the report has been selected by the IIRC

ar: annual report

sr: sustainability report

ir: integrated report

imr: integrated management report

asr: annual and sustainability report

ar2: statutory report

sr2: society report

References

Armstrong M (2011) Armstrong's handbook of strategic human resource management. Kogan Page, London

Barney JB (1991) Firm resources and sustained competitive advantage. J Manag 17:99–120

Bazeley P, Jackson K (2013) Qualitative data analysis with NVivo. Sage, Los Angeles/London/New Delhi/Singapore/Washington

Becker G (1975) Human capital. National Bureau of Economic Research

Becker G (2002) The age of human capital. In Lazear EP (ed) Education in the twenty-first century. Hoover Institution Press, Stanford, CA, pp 3–8

Benito-Osorio D, Muño-Aguado L, Willar C (2014) The impact of family and work-life balance on the performance of Spanish listed companies. Management 17(4):214–236

Berger LA (2004) Creating a talent management system for organization excellence: connecting the dots. In: Berger LA, Berger RB (eds) The talent management handbook. Creating organizational excellence by identifying, developing, and promoting your best people. McGraw-Hill, New York, pp 3–21

Borkowska S (2005) Kilka refl eksji tytułem wstępu. In: Borkowska S (ed) Zarządzanie talentami. Wydawnictwo IPiSS, Warszawa, pp 11–13

Campbell BA, Coff R, Kryscynski D (2012) Rethinking sustained competitive advantage from human capital. Acad Manag Rev 37:376–395

Cheese P, Thomas RJ, Craig E (2008) The talent powered organization: strategies for globalization, talent management and high performance. Kogan Page, London

Cheng M, Green W, Conradie P, Konishi N, Romi A (2014) The international integrated reporting framework: key issues and future research opportunities. J Int Fin Manag Acc 25:90–119

Claus L (2019) HR disruption—time already to reinvent talent management. BRQ Bus Res Q 22(3):207–215

Coff RW (2002) Human capital, shared expertise, and the likelihood of impasse in corporate acquisitions. J Manag 28:107–128

Coff RW, Kryscynski D (2011) Drilling for micro-foundations of human capital–based competitive advantages. J Manag 37:1429–1443

Collings DG, Mellahi K (2009) Strategic talent management: a review and research agenda. Hum Resour Manag Rev 19:304–313

Crane A, Matten D (2007) Business ethics, 2nd edn. Oxford University Press, Oxford

Crook TR, Todd SY, Combs JG, Woehr DJ, Ketchen DJ Jr (2011) Does human capital matter? A meta-analysis of the relationship between human capital and firm performance. J Appl Psychol 96:443–456

Downs Y, Swailes S (2013) A capability approach to organizational talent management. Hum Resour Dev Int 16:267–281

El Abboubi M, Nicolopoulou K (2012) International social-related accountability standards: using ANT towards a multi-stakeholders analysis. Management 15:391–414

Ewerlin D (2013) The influence of global talent management on employer attractiveness. Z Pers 27(3):279–304

Flower J (2015) The international integrated reporting council: a story of failure. Crit Perspect Acc 27:1–17

Frías-Aceituno JV, Rodríguez-Ariza L, García-Sánchez IM (2013) Is integrated reporting determined by a country's legal system? An exploratory study. J Clean Prod 44:45–55

Gamerschlag R, Moeller K (2011) The positive effects of human capital reporting. Corp Reput Rev 14:145–155

Gavino MC, Wayne SJ, Erdogan B (2012) Discretionary and transactional human resource practices and employee outcomes: the role of perceived organizational support. Hum Resour Manag 51(5):665–686

Gilbert DU, Rasche A (2008) Opportunities and problems of standardized ethics initiatives—a stakeholder theory perspective. J Bus Ethics 82:755–773

Gilbert DU, Rasche A, Waddock S (2011) Accountability in a global economy: the emergence of international accountability standards. Bus Ethics Q 21(1):23–44

Hejase HJ, Hejase AJ, Mikdashi G, Bazeih ZF (2016) Talent management challenges: an exploratory assessment from Lebanon. Int J Bus Manage Econ Res 7(1):504–520

Huang J, Tansley C (2012) Sneaking through the minefield of talent management: the notion of rhetorical obfuscation. Int J Hum Resour Manag 23:3673–3691

Knauer A, Serafeim G (2014) Attracting long-term investors through integrated thinking and reporting: a clinical study of a biopharmaceutical company. J Appl Corp Fin 26:57–64

Lepak DP, Snell SA (1999) The human resource architecture: toward a theory of human capital allocation and development. Acad Manage Rev 24:31–48

Lepak DP, Snell SA (2002) Examining the human resource architecture: the relationships among human capital employment, and human resource configurations. J Manag 28:517–543

Lewis RE, Heckman RJ (2006) Talent management: a critical review. Hum Resour Manag Rev 16:139–154

Listwan T (2010) Zarządzanie talentami – nowy nurt zarządzania kadrami w organizacjach. In: Jagoda H, Lichtarski J (eds) Kierunki i dylematy rozwoju naukii praktyki zarządzania przedsiębiorstwem. Wydawnictwo Uniwersytetu Ekonomicznego we Wrocławiu, Wrocław, pp 20–27

Liu X, Van Jaarsveld DD, Batt R, Frost AC (2014) The influence of capital structure on strategic human capital: evidence from U.S and Canadian firms. J Manag 40:422–448

Lockwood NR (2006) Talent management: driver for organizational success. SHRM Research Report

Mellahi K, Collings DG (2010) The barriers to effective global talent management: the example of corporate élites in MNEs. J World Bus 45:143–149

Michaels E, Handfield-Jones H, Axelrod B (2001) The war for talent. Harvard Business School Press, Boston

Nyberg AJ, Moliterno TP, Hale D, Lepak DP (2014) Resource-based perspectives on unit-level human capital: a review and integration. J Manag 40:316–346

Ployhart RE, Moliterno TP (2011) Emergence of the human capital resource: a multilevel model. Acad Manag Rev 36(1):127–150

Ployhart RE, Nyberg AJ, Reilly G, Maltarich MA (2014) Human capital is dead; long live human capital resources! J Manag 40:371–398

Prahalad CK, Hamel G (1990) The core competence of the corporation. Harvard Bus Rev 68:79–91

Rasche A (2009) 'A necessary supplement': what the United Nations global compact is and is not. Bus Soc 48:511–537

Rasche A (2010) Collaborative governance 2.0. Corporate Governance: Int J Bus Soc 10:500–511

Rensburg R, Botha E (2014) Is integrated reporting the silver bullet of financial communication? A stakeholder perspective from South Africa. Pub Relat Rev 40:144–152

Richards L (1999) Using NVivo in qualitative research. Sage , London/Thousand Oaks/New Delhi

Schein EH, Van Maanen J (2016) Career anchors and job/role planning: tools for career and talent management. Organ Dyn 45:165–173

Schuler RS, Jackson SE, Tarique I (2011) Global talent management and global talent challenges: strategic opportunities for IHRM. J World Bus 46(4):506–516

Schultz TW (1961) Investment in human capital. Am Econ Rev 51:P1-17

Scullion H, Collings DG, Caligiuri P (2010) Global talent management. J World Bus 45(2):105–108. https://doi.org/10.1016/j.jwb.2009.09.011

Stewart TA (1997) Intellectual capital: the new wealth of organizations. Doubleday/Currency, New York

Vaiman V, Scullion H, Collings D (2012) Talent management decision making. Manag Decis 50:925–941

Vergauwen P, Bollen L, Oirbans E (2007) Intellectual capital disclosure and intangible value drivers: an empirical study. Manag Decis 45(7):1163–1180

Verschoor CC (2011) Should sustainability reporting be integrated? Strateg Fin 93:12–14

Viot C, Benraiss-Noailles L (2014) Employeurs démarquez-vous! La marque employeur, un gisement de valeur inexploité ? Manag Int 18(3):60–81

Whysall Z, Owtram M, Brittain S (2019) The new talent management challenges of Industry 4.0. J Manag Dev 38(2):118–129

Wernerfelt B (1984) A resource-based view of the firm. Strateg Manag J 5:171–180

Wilska E (2014) Determinants of effective talent management. J Pos Manag 5(4):77–88

Wright PM, McMahan GC (2011) Exploring human capital: putting human back into strategic human resource management. Hum Resour Manag J 21:93–104

Zuboff S (1988) In the age of the smart machine: the future of work and power. Basic Books, New York

Chapter 10
Social Discount Rate and the Cost of Climate Change Risk in Turkey

M. Kenan Terzioğlu

Abstract The cost of climate change risk should be analyzed not only from an economic perspective but also based on policies formulated, using climate science forecasts, the allocation of rights, and crucial or behavioral assumptions. The discount rate (pure rate of time preference, growth in per capita consumption, and relative risk-aversion), an indicator of the severity of climate change and desirable climate policy-level, is vital in estimating the social cost of carbon. Moreover, changes in temperature, precipitation, increase in sea level, and the sensitivity to emissions affect the vulnerability of the sectors within climate models. This study identifies social discount rate and cost of carbon within key factors of climate change adaptation and focuses on the range of uncertainty since the uncertainty is often skewed, and the damage function is often nonlinear.

Keywords Discount rate · Social cost of carbon · Climate change risk · Valuation

10.1 Introduction

Temperature affects the dynamics of chemical, biological and ecological mechanism (Burke et al. 2015). The mechanism interactions and aggregate poses make difficult and complex to determine the effects of the potential temperature changes that influence economic outcomes (Dell et al. 2012) and the response of the future economy to a changing climate. Future emission assumptions, climate sensitivity, discount rate and time is important in examining climate policy benefits and determining SCC values.

Social discount rate (SDR), an economic evaluation method, measures the use of cost–benefit analysis in allocating public resources, subject to specified constraints. When the EU started financing investment projects, it became essential to calculate SDR recommended-levels, a heavy fiscal burden may be emerged within high-SDR

M. K. Terzioğlu (✉)
Economics and Administrative Sciences Faculty, Econometrics Department, Trakya University, Edirne, Turkey
e-mail: kenanterzioglu@trakya.edu.tr

© The Author(s), under exclusive license to Springer Nature Singapore Pte Ltd. 2021   165
K. T. Çalıyurt (ed.), *New Approaches to CSR, Sustainability and Accountability,*
Volume II, Accounting, Finance, Sustainability, Governance & Fraud: Theory
and Application, https://doi.org/10.1007/978-981-33-6808-8_10

and unfeasible project may be processed within low SDR, since the EU presented SDR as cost–benefit analysis guide for investment projects. SDR can be calculated using the social opportunity cost of capital or social time preference rate (STPR). While the former is more common in developing countries and the US, the latter is mostly applied in developed countries (Shelunstsova 2009). SDR calculated with STPR reflects the primary purpose of public investment projects better, which is enhancing social benefits (Kazlauskienė 2015). SDR depends on the approach and data range. Although countries where SDR is legally confirmed calculate it periodically, they rarely change the method in determining the rate. In other countries, each institution determines the rate to use. Within the framework of efficient allocation of resources, it is vital to have a generally accepted (non-institutional) SDR for the country. The SDR should apply to the investments in the country because of differences in economic and capital structure, financial development and efficiency of instruments, presence in the international capital market and STP (Zhuang et al. 2007). An accurate SDR, which is vital in uncovering the economic effects of extracting exhaustible resources, affects the benefits and costs of policies (Slade 1982).

STPR is related to a country's utility discount rate (UDR), average growth rate (g), and elasticity of marginal utility of consumption (e). Value judgments and clarity over what is being measured affects the quantitative significance of the UDR. Although based on pure time preference (PTP) alone, the parameter is zero (Ramsey 1928; Pigou 1932; Broome 1992), when additional part in the UDR as survival-risk (life-chance) is considered, PTP rate is between 0 and 0.5% (Pearce and Ulph 1999). Moreover, as Newbery (1992) suggested, based on mortality rate, it is appropriate to use a rate that is close to 1%. Kula (1985) proposed a UDR close to 2%, following Stern (1977). Kula (2004) and Evans and Sezer (2005) used p, a mortality-based measure, in determining results that are approximately 1%; it was considered inappropriate to factor in the PTP of individuals. The rate of 1% is acceptable in most developed countries. HM Treasury (1997) settled on a p-value of 1%, whereas HM Treasury (2003) selected 1.5%, 0.5% PTP element and the 1% life-chance element, which was referred to as catastrophe risk rather than life-chance (HM Treasury 2003). There are few studies on developing countries' crude mortality rates; therefore, the rates used for developed countries were also used for developing countries. This study determines the rates in Turkey.

Although the effectiveness of investment evaluations is vital, it has been used by just a few studies to determine the SDRs of developing countries. They used different methods in estimating (e). Based on observed consumption behaviors, Kula (1984, 1987), Evans and Sezer (2002), Evans (2004), Percoco (2008), and Schad and John (2012) used the Ramsey formula to estimate SDR of developed countries. Based on government tax policies, Evans (2004, 2005), Evans and Sezer (2005), Percoco (2008), and Schad and John (2012) estimated SDR of developed countries. Based on observed consumption behaviors, Sharma et al. (1991), Kula (2012), and Kazlauskiene and Stundziene (2016) estimated SDR of developing countries. Based on government tax policies, Lopez (2008) estimated SDR of developing countries. Zhuang et al. (2007) determined that the developing countries SDRs higher than developed countries SDRs. Florio and Sirtori (2013) stated that the rate fluctuates differently among cohesion fund countries and others. Moreover, based on the general demand of food, Evans (2005), Sezer (2006), Halıcıoglu and Karatas (2011), Uzunkaya and Uzunkaya (2012), Halıcıoglu and Karatas (2013), Kaplan (2014), and Akbulut and Seçilmiş (2019) estimated the SDR for Turkey. Personal taxation and other methods rarely have limitations. This study determines the rates in Turkey using taxation methods within average production wage (APW).

A discount rate is an essential indicator of the relative magnitude of social cost of carbon (SCC). SCC is an estimation of the present value of the potential economic damage due to emitting an additional ton of greenhouse gases into the atmosphere. Since the costs of emission reduction are beneficial, the discounted value of climate change damage can be prevented with marginal reductions. Anthoff et al. (2009) examined the changes resulting from differentiating the parameters of SCC. The estimation of SCC varies depending on assumptions about social preferences specifications (sophisticated), climate system (tipping points), technologies, optimal mitigation policy modeling under uncertainty, etc. and feed-backs among them (Greenstone et al. 2013; Jensen and Traeger 2014; Dietz and Stern 2015; Berger et al. 2017; Lemoine and Rudik 2017; Hänsel and Quaas 2018; Cai and Lontzek 2019, Okullo 2020 and Ploeg 2020). Ricke et al. (2018) estimated, quantifying uncertainties, country-base and aggregate SCC. This paper aims to contribute to the literature since there is limited study based on the SDR and almostly none study in SCC for Turkey. After general information is given about the paper, the models used in SDR and SCC is examined in the second part. SDR components and magnitude of SCC are re-computed for Turkey in the third part and the last part is reserved for the results.

10.2   Country Perspective

Turkeys' expanding energy demand, middle-income country with low emissions history, is met by fossil-fuels and its' emissions growth begin to rise and become high emitting countries even though constrain promises. While Turkey is the member of Organization for Economic Co-operation and Development (OECD), leading in tackling climate change, since 1992, it is listed in the "Annex I-II" groups of countries and has not been participated in formal negotiating blocs in the United Nations Framework Convention on Climate Change (UNFCCC). Turkey is removed from Annex II, meaning not obliged to contribute to climate finance, and special circumstances is recognized by the parties in 2001 and joined the UNFCCC in 2004. The renewable energy law and Act targeting to increase geothermal energy enacted in 2005 and 2007, respectively. Turkey, the only party with no-emissions reduction commitment, joined the Kyoto Protocol in 2009. Climate change strategy up to 2020 is published to set out policies in transition to a low carbon economy and to tackle climate change in short-/mid-/long-term plans is announced with climate change action plan in 2011. Turkey, operating in voluntary carbon markets, accepted regulatory framework for mandatory emissions reporting system, paving the way for the emissions trading system, in 2012. Tax deductions for renewables up to 2030 is introduced with electricity market law in 2013. According to Potsdam Institute for Climate Impact Research (PIK), emissions raised faster compared with Annex I countries between 1990 and 2013 period in Turkey. In 2015, Turkey submitted a pledge to the UNFCCC to prepare for Paris Agreement and had not promised any action before 2020. After energy efficiency laws entered into force in 2007 and 2012, energy efficiency action plan passed in 2018. Turkey's Paris pledge evaluated as critically insufficient by Climate Action Tracker. Access to the Green Climate Fund (GCF) has been stipulated for the Paris Agreement. Not only climate but also for technology and capacity improving is provided by channels such as multilateral development banks, financial institutions, and funds.

Turkey, locating at the eastern-end of the Mediterranean-basin expected to be affected by drought due to human-induced climate change, has vulnerability to increase in water stress levels, forest fires, rise in sea level where population density is high and health problems (heat waves, vector-borne diseases, etc.). Turkey is criticized for the business as usual level/method and the determination in reduction levels seems not transparent. There are high uncertainties in the emissions data in land use, land use changes, and forestry (LULUCF) of Turkey because of the accounting methods. Since market-based instruments are important in climate policies, to achieve 2030 mitigation target, using carbon credits from international mechanisms can lead to emission exporting to other developing countries from Turkey.

10.3   Model Structure

STPR, based on Ramsey equation, reacts to changes in UDR with PTP rate (p) based on survival-risk, the elasticity of marginal utility of consumption(e), and average rate of growth of per capita real consumption (g).

$$STPR = p + eg \qquad (10.1)$$

UDR in Eq. (10.1), consisting of PTP rate (∂; depending on value judgments) and life chances ($\mathcal{L}$) calculated, using crude-death rate, considers both the average lifetime and relative importance of the utility of generations (Pearce and Ulph 1999). Although the p-value of the countries is uncertain, the value is not based on the data that consists of the characteristics of the countries. The p-value can be included in the analysis based on some common set of values. The appropriate value for ∂ is a value that is almost zero. The likelihood of survival and mortality-based measures of $\mathcal{L}$ is estimated for various countries.

The mortality-based approach is used to estimate the UDR in this paper. The p values are based on mortality rates ($\partial = 0$). Crude mortality rates do not fit on a smooth curve, so graduation methods were used in modeling the fluctuations in the mortality rates (Renshaw 1991). Although the risk factors are assumed to be homogeneous for individuals in the mortality models, heterogeneity should be considered in the crude mortality rates because random fluctuations affect the results. Moreover, frailty models can be used since they consider the effects of explanatory variables (Duchateau and Janssen 2008). The life-span varies depending on genetic makeup, living conditions, and environmental factors. Since the assumption of the frailty parameter affects the underlying mortality rate, Gompertz-Makeham models are used in the underlying mortality rate. In the Gompertz-Makeham model, which was used in the distribution to model the life-span of humans and mortality, death rates were modeled with an exponential rate. Thus, the force of mortality is given as:

$$\mu(t) = \alpha + \beta e^{\gamma t}, \quad \alpha, \beta \geq 0 \tag{10.2}$$

where, α represents a constant for age-related mortality rates and the $\beta e^{\gamma t}$ represents the mortality of all age-related deaths. The survival function is given as:

$$S(t) = e^{-\int_0^t (\alpha + \beta e^{st})ds} = e^{\frac{-\alpha t + \beta(e^{\gamma t} - 1)}{\gamma}} \tag{10.3}$$

When $\beta > 0$ and $\gamma > 0$, then $\mu(t)$ is an increasing function of time (Norberg 2002). This paper uses the survival function and mortality rates to determine the UDR based on the Gompertz-Makeham model parameters that were determined by Terzioğlu and Sucu (2015) for Turkey.

Due to the differences in policy implementation approaches of various countries and different socioeconomic groups, (e) in Eq. 10.1 is vital in estimating the country-base SDRs. Since different results can be emerged in estimation of (e) using revealed social values, government spending or tax policies, indirect behavioral evidence and survey method, it is a complex issue. The advantages of using the tax-based method are that the theory is understandable and easy to use, and the data are consistently available and allows for comparison between countries. Income is not taxed on subsistence wage; diminishing marginal utility applies to income that exceeds the subsistence level.

The tax-based approach, where taxable income (Y), total income tax-liability or income tax function $(T(Y))$, average income tax rate $(T(Y)/Y)$, and marginal tax rate (t), is given as

$$U(Y) - U(Y - T(Y)) = k \tag{10.4}$$

where the tax structure based on equal absolute sacrifice of satisfaction (EASS-sacrifice of utility (k) for all tax payers is same) rather than the more complex tax structure theories (Stern 1977).

$$U(Y) = \left(Y^{1-e} - 1\right)/(1 - e) \tag{10.5}$$

the individuals' utility functions are iso-elastic and the elasticity of marginal utility
of substitution can be shown as

$$\frac{(Y^{(1-e)} - 1)}{(1 - e)} - \frac{[(Y - T(Y))^{(1-e)} - 1]}{(1 - e)} = k$$

$$Y^{-e} - [Y - T(Y)]^{-e}(1 - t) = 0$$

$$e = \log(1 - t)/\log(1 - T(Y)/Y) \tag{10.6}$$

In this paper, in Eq. 10.5, taxable income, after deducting standard tax allowances
is appropriate for calculating the average tax rate, is used to prevent strong upward
bias in e values at relatively low levels of income While marginal tax rates change
lead to average tax rates changes, but not vice versa (Evans 2005). In this paper,
income tax rates are examined, where "income tax only" model is more consistent
in the underlying theory of EASS.

The elasticity of the marginal utility with the concepts of smoothing consumption
and risk aversion; and consumption growth rate as one of the major variable in emissions becomes more important in uncertainties. While the discount rate in Ramsey
equation is constant, due to the uncertainty about economic growth rates, with a long-
time horizon, discount rate is handled hyperbolic in Monte-Carlo analysis (Guo et al.
2006; Weitzman 2013).

STPR can also be used for the optimal discount rate in climate change when
the elasticity of the marginal utility, uncertainties and asymmetric impacts, and the
growth rate are considered within the scope of climate change and its effects. The
definition of SCC (using (ρ), (e), (g), monetized impacts, emissions/additional emissions in metric-tons of carbon) proposed by Anthoff et al. (2009) is considered, with
a little difference in the equation-pattern, in US dollars per ton of carbon, on a
country basis but not on a regional or global basis. The price of carbon, SCC, estimations can be obtained using Integrated Assessment Models (IAMs), consolidating
interdisciplinary climate research inputs (Bijgaart et al. 2016). IAM are utilized to
reveal climate-economy interactions and to form policy-making/recommendations
on emissions (Dell et al. 2012). The SCC, measured in $/TtCO_2$, formula is expressed
as

$$\text{SCC}(t) = \Delta\theta(c)Y(t)W(\sigma, \gamma) \tag{10.7}$$

where the economic relevant measure for climate sensitivity $(\theta(c))$, the damage time
indicator $(W(.))$, the discount rate (σ), and climate system parameters (γ). $\Delta\theta(c)Y(t)$
is an economic loss related to one unit increase in CO_2 and $W(\sigma, \gamma)$, measuring
within number of (effective) years, converts the future income losses to a present
value. $W(.)$, measuring mean lifetime of income for $\sigma = 0$ and economic lifetime of
losses for $\sigma > 0$, plays important role both in emissions and damages connections
and in prediction power of the IAM. Dynamic Integrated Climate-Economy (DICE)
model (Nordhaus 2007), Policy Analysis of the Greenhouse Effect (PAGE) model
(Hope 2006) and Framework for Uncertainty, Negotiation and Distribution (FUND)

model (Anthoff and Tol 2009) are models of climate economics (Ackerman and Stanton 2012).

The SCC, in dollars per ton of carbon, is estimated with the monetized impact of climate change by calculating differences in impacts, discounting to the current year, and normalizing the difference in emissions between 2000 and 2019. Regarding uncertainty, the expected value of the SCC ($E(SCC)$) is shown as

$$E(SCC) = \frac{1}{k} \sum_{i=1}^{k} SCC(\theta_i) \tag{10.8}$$

using uncertain input parameters vector (θ) and Monte-Carlo runs-number (k) (Anthoff et al. 2009).

10.4 Discounting the Social Cost of Carbon

The long-term impacts of PTP rate and uncertainties on climate change are diversified; they depend on the country's status and income groups. Based on life chances, the likelihood of survival (Acar and Tutkun, 2020) and mortality-based measures of L have been estimated for Turkey, within the framework of positive UDR. The regulatory authority indicates in the relevant legislation that insurance companies may use tables CSO 1953 and CSO 1980 to ensure accurate calculations since they reflect mortality in Turkey. Although life tables should be based on the characteristics of each country, in developing countries such as Turkey, life tables cannot be created because of the difficulties in obtaining data. Although the tables that insurance companies create can be used in actuarial calculations, they do not give accurate results since they reflect their portfolios rather than the whole. However, indirect methods such as the Orphanhood-approach-based that provides adult mortality estimates at a significant level in developing countries can be employed. The Orphanhood-approach-based life tables are explanatory for country-related probabilities. Compared with CSO-1980 life table, the Orphanhood-approach-based life tables provide accurate mortality rates. The Gompertz-Makeham law was adopted in modeling life-span. The Gompertz–Makeham parameters ($\alpha = 0.0007$, $\beta = 0.0006$, and $\gamma = 0.0831$), determined by Terzioğlu and Sucu (2015), with the life table created by Kırkbeşoğlu (2006) for Turkey, was used to determine the suitable value of (p) to discount future utility in Turkey. The PTP and death rates are used to calculate the UDR. Based on relevant literature, the PTP rates used in this study are 0, which makes the UDR equivalent to the life chances obtained from mortality rates, and 0.5%; the p-values of the PTP rates are 0.96% (approximately 1%) and 1.46% (approximately 1.5%), respectively.

In this study, a tax-model based on the EASS principle was applied. (e) was estimated using not only income tax but also all-in tax (including employees' social security contributions) effective marginal and average tax rates for Turkey obtained from the OECD tax database. Compared with the results of only income tax-based approach, the results of the all-in tax rates show lower values for Turkey.

The (e) value for Turkey is measured at wage distribution points to provide plausible/consistent results. Tax rate change, within the wage level, may occur above (low (e)-values) or below (high (e)-values). Also, as a precaution, an average (e) value is taken to reduce distortions after the (e) values are measured at different wage levels. While the e values vary between 1.24 and 1.46 for 2019 and an average value is 1.23 in 2000–2019 periods for all-in tax in Table 10.1, the e values vary between 1.40 and 1.94 for 2019 and an average value is 1.47 in 2000–2019 periods for income tax. Table 10.1 shows that the highest (e) value of 1.33 and 1.75 at lowest wage level (0.67 APW) is not proportional to the values of the other levels, all of which are close to 1.23 and 1.47, respectively; thus, the (e) value of 1.33 and 1.75 is an outlier and excluded in the average measure calculations. The representative e value for Turkey is taken as 1.47, approximately 1.5. Annual growth rate of per capita real consumption data that STPR focuses, measured consistently and based on accounting approach, is taken from the OECD national accounts database. The social discount rate for Turkey is presented in Table 10.2.

Intergovernmental Panel on Climate Change (IPCC) data distribution center, Hadley Centre/Climatic Research Unit Temperature (HadCRUT) dataset, Shared Socioeconomic Pathways (SSPs) database of International Institute for Applied System Analysis, OECD database, climate data archive in Willmott, Matsuura and Collaborators' Global Climate Resource pages is used for the country-base data and projections. Growth rates and temperature increases are from 2020 to 2100. Due to the limitations on the availability of Turkey-base inputs, when data at the country-level is not available, regional-level data is taken into account. Similarly, when data on the region cannot be reached, global data is taken as basis. Within the scope of this paper, Anthoff and Tol et al. (2013) paper was followed (the assumptions can be found in http://www.fund.model.org).

Carbon cycle uncertainties (Falkowski et al. 2000), climate sensitivity uncertainties (Knutti and Hegerl 2008) and thermal inertia uncertainties (Winton et al. 2010) are some factors in the amount of projected temperatures and uncertainties in the timing (Huntingford et al. 2009; Ricke and Calderia 2014). The climate sensitivity, measuring warming-speed, long-term increase in temperature due to the expectation of doubling of the CO_2 concentration in the atmosphere, remains significantly uncertain (Roe and Baker 2007).

The results are reported within the concept of with and/or without climate change uncertainty. The uncertainties within economic and population growth, emissions and energy usage are taken as a multimodal and all scenarios are treated with equal probability.

In this paper, re-analysis of the SCC; examination the effects of climate sensitivity and other uncertainties, considering scenarios, in Monte-Carlo model, is done on country-based using FUND (Guo et al. 2006; Tol 1997, 1999, 2006) model, the integrated assessment model. One of the regions of FUND is Middle East (MDE) that

Table 10.1 Social discount rate

	All-in tax				Income tax			
	0.67APW	APW	1.33APW	1.67APW	0.67APW	APW	1.33APW	1.67APW
2019	1.41	1.46	1.32	1.24	1.94	1.87	1.55	1.40
Average (2000–2019)	1.33	1.24	1.24	1.21	1.75	1.48	1.47	1.49
	Social Discount Rate = 2.29				Social Discount Rate = 2.79			

GDP growth (annual %): 0.88
p-value (%) 0.96 for ∂ = 0, approx. 1%
e(%):Average Income tax = 1.47

GDP growth (annual %): 0.88
p-value (%) 0.96 for ∂ = 0.5, approx. 1.5%
e(%):Average Income tax = 1.47

Table 10.2 Social cost of carbon

	Without uncertainty		With uncertainty	
	$p = 1; e = 1.5$	$p = 1.5; e = 1.5$	$p = 1; e = 1.5$	$p = 1.5; e = 1.5$
RCP4.5	2.11	0.81	16.27	9.42
RCP6.0	1.89	0.61	17.11	8.66
RCP8.5	4.38	1.28	34.88	13.96

includes the group of countries including Turkey. The impact of warming is determined using nonlinear response function with Representative Concentration Pathway (RCP) of future warming, within the scope that future responses to temperature changes is similar to today's economies (Burke et al. 2015).

Determining the SCC, expected economic damages from emissions, with country-based approach reveals the heterogeneity effect of climate damage and helps in formulating relevant policies and reviewing country-specific uncertainties. Although the magnitude of SCC varies due to the scenarios and discount rates, in Table 10.2 as a function of the (ρ) and (e), SCC for Turkey with and without uncertainty is found positive. The scenarios are defined by the rates of population growth, economic growth, and changes in temperature. While the E(SCC) decreases with the discount rate, the E(SCC) increases apparently with uncertainty.

10.5   Conclusion

SCC, economic cost of climate damage resulting from the emission of an additional ton of carbon (tCO_2), is the valuation of marginal impacts in the climate change. Determining the SCC in country-base can have an impact on the common climate agreement. SCC can be estimated using range of assumptions on uncertain parameters (discount rate, climate sensitivity economic growth, etc.) risk preferences and others. There is a gap between SCCs' domestic and global values and also a conflict the distribution of the SCC by region. Although there is a significant gap between domestic and global SCC values, due to the lack of availability of country-based climate and economic inputs, limited studies are performed into country-base on developing countries, especially in Turkey to capture the marginal damage/benefit expectations to be occurred with an additional emission. This paper aims to reveal the distributional impacts of climate change and create a forum for discussion about the strategic incentives that can be applied. The discounting assumptions are used for estimate SCC, sensitively.

STPR, in which taxes are seem as source of funding, the social values of governments, is used to estimate SDR that alters the distribution of welfare. A tax-model based on the EASS principle is employed. Since different tax rates and taxable income bands affect the different wage levels for calculated marginal and average tax rates, the elasticity of marginal utility was estimated, using marginal and average rates in different wage levels and on average-level for both income tax structure and all-in tax structure, to calculate the SDR for Turkey. Due to the differences between level margins of taxable income and avoidance of biased estimates, average tax rates were calculated, using the total-tax liabilities on wages and the total-taxable wage income, to avoid biased estimates in wide income bands. Since there are no wide income bands for Turkey, the midpoint of the relevant approximations is used as average tax rates.

The relative size of the (p) is also effective in determining discount rates and social cost of carbon. The higher (p) value, under constant elasticity of marginal utility, is resulted with the higher discount rate and smaller SCC in the scenarios. Moreover, SCC increases due to the damages from climate change that occur over time at RCP 4.5 and RCP8.5 levels. Compared to other levels, the lowest SCC value was calculated for RCP 6.5 in both with and without uncertainties. The uncertainties in the climate system's response (climate sensitivity) and in the economic harm (damage function) affect the SCC estimates. Moreover, within uncertainties, especially in developing countries, SCC rises rapidly. However, it should not go unnoticed that standard deviations are high.

In future studies, determining the SCC by regions, using equity-weighting, in Turkey can be performed to map the domestic impacts, adaptation and compensation measures, and sensitivity, considering heterogeneity. Policies can be re-evaluated, and new policies can be developed. Since there is a lack of data even on a country basis, it is essential to set up data sources and complete necessary procedures.

References

Acar AŞ, Tutkun NA (2020) Use of ensemble methods for survival prediction. Muğla J Sci Technol 6(2):158–164.

Ackerman F, Stanton E (2012) Climate risks and carbon prices: revising the social cost of carbon. Econ Open-Access Open-Assess E-J 6:10

Akbulut H, Seçilmiş E (2019) Estimation of a social discount rate for Turkey. Socioecon Plann Sci 67:78–85

Anthoff D, Tol RS (2009) The impact of climate change on the balanced growth equivalent: an application of FUND. Environ Resource Econ 43(3):351–367

Anthoff D, Tol RS (2013) The uncertainty about the social cost of carbon: A decomposition analysis using fund. Clim Change 117(3):515–530.

Anthoff D, Tol RS, Yohe G (2009) Discounting for climate change. Econ Open-Access Open-Assess E-J 3

Berger L, Emmerling J, Tavoni M (2017) Managing catastrophic climate risks under model uncertainty aversion. Manage Sci 63(3):749–765

Broome, J. (1992). Counting the cost of global warming, The White Horse Press

Burke M, Hsiang SM, Miguel E (2015) Global non-linear effect of temperature on economic production. Nature 527(7577):235–239

Cai Y, Lontzek TS (2019) The social cost of carbon with economic and climate risks. J Polit Econ 127(6):2684–2734

Dell M, Jones BF, Olken BA (2012) Temperature shocks and economic growth: Evidence from the last half century. Am Econ J Macroecon 4(3):66–95

Dietz S, Stern N (2015) Endogenous growth, convexity of damage and climate risk: how Nordhaus' framework supports deep cuts in carbon emissions. Econ J 125(583):574–620

Duchateau L, Janssen P (2008) The frailty model. In: Statistics for biology and health series, Springer

Evans D (2004) A social discount rate for France. Appl Econ Lett 11(13):803–808

Evans DJ (2005) The elasticity of marginal utility of consumption: estimates for 20 OECD countries. Fisc Stud 26(2):197–224

Evans D, Sezer H (2002) A time preference measure of the social discount rate for the UK. Appl Econ 34(15):1925–1934

Evans DJ, Sezer H (2005) Social discount rates for member countries of the European Union. J Econ Stud

Falkowski P, Scholes RJ, Boyle EEA, Canadell J, Canfield D, Elser J, Steffen W (2000) The global carbon cycle: a test of our knowledge of earth as a system. science, 290(5490):291–296

Florio M, Sirtori E (2013) The social cost of capital: recent estimates for the EU countries. Available at SSRN 2723379.

Greenstone M, Kopits E, Wolverton A (2013) Developing a social cost of carbon for US regulatory analysis: a methodology and interpretation. Rev Environ Econ Policy 7(1):23–46

Grün C, Grunewald N (2010) Subjective well being and the impact of climate change, Proceedings of the German Development Economics Conference, 61

Guo J, Hepburn C, Tol RSJ, Anthoff D (2006) Discounting and the social cost of carbon: a closer look at uncertainty. Environ Sci Policy 9:205–216

Halicioglu F, Karatas C (2011) Estimation of economic discounting rate for practical project appraisal: the case of Turkey. J Developing Areas, pp 155–166

Halicioglu F, Karatas C (2013) A social discount rate for Turkey. Qual Quant 47(2):1085–1091

Hänsel MC, Quaas MF (2018) Intertemporal distribution, sufficiency, and the social cost of carbon. Ecol Econ 146:520–535

Hope C (2006) The marginal impact of CO_2 from PAGE2002: an integrated assessment model incorporating the IPCC's five reasons for concern, The Integrated Assessment Journal, 6, 19–56

Huntingford C, Lowe JA, Booth BB, Jones CD, Harris GR, Gohar LK, Meir P (2009) Contributions of carbon cycle uncertainty to future climate projection spread. Tellus B: Chemical and Physical Meteorology, 61(2):355–360

Jensen S, Traeger CP (2014) Optimal climate change mitigation under long-term growth uncertainty: stochastic integrated assessment and analytic findings. Eur Econ Rev 69:104–125

Kaplan Z (2014) The social cost-benefit analysis of investment projects and sample application. Doctoral dissertation, Master Thesis. Gazı' University Institute of Social Sciences, Ankara

Kazlauskienė V (2015) Application of social discount rate for assessment of public investment projects. Procedia Soc Behav Sci 213:461–467

Kazlauskiene V, Stundziene A (2016) Estimation of social discount rate for Lithuania. Trends Econ Manage 10(26):39–47

Kırkbeşoğlu E (2006) Construction of mortality tables for life insurance sector from the 2003 Turkey demographic and health survey. Unpublished master's thesis, Hacettepe University Institute of Population Studies, Ankara

Knutti R, Hegerl GC (2008) The equilibrium sensitivity of the Earth's temperature to radiation changes. Nat Geosci 1(11):735–743

Kula E (1984) Derivation of social time preference rates for the United States and Canada. Q J Econ 99(4):873–882

Kula E (1985) An empirical investigation on the social time-preference rate for the United Kingdom. Environ Plan A 17(2):199–212

Kula E (1987) Social interest rate for public sector appraisal in the United Kingdom, the United States and Canada. Project Appraisal 2(3):169–174

Kula E (2004) Estimation of a social rate of interest for India. J Agric Econ 55(1):91–99

Kula E (2012) Discounting: does it ensure intergenerational equity? In Weiss J, Potts D (eds) Current issues in project analysis for development, Edward Elgar Publishing: Cheltenham (UK)

Lemoine D, Rudik I (2017) Steering the climate system: using inertia to lower the cost of policy. Am Econ Rev 107(10):2947–2957

Lopez H (2008) The social discount rate: estimates for nine Latin American countries. World Bank Policy Research Working Paper, (4639)

Norberg R (2002) Basic life insurance mathematics. Lecture notes. Laboratory of Actuarial Mathematics, University of Copenhagen

Newbery D (1992) Long term Discount Rates for the Forest Enterprise. Department of Applied Economics, Cambridge University, for the UK Forestry Commission, Edinburgh

Nordhaus W (2007) The challenge of global warming: economic models and environmental policy. Yale University, New Haven, CT

Okullo SJ (2020) Determining the social cost of carbon: under damage and climate sensitivity uncertainty. Environ Resource Econ 75(1):79–103

Pearce DU, Ulph D (1999) A Social Discount Rate for the United Kingdom. GEC Working Paper, 95–01

Percoco M (2008) A social discount rate for Italy. Appl Econ Lett 15(1):73–77

Pigou AC (1932) Desires and satisfactions. In: The economics of welfare. London Macmillan & Co. ltd.

Ramsey F (1928) A mathematical theory of saving. Econ J 38:543–549

Renshaw AE (1991) Actuarial graduation practice and generalized linear and non-linear models. J Inst Actuaries 118:295–312

Ricke KL, Caldeira K (2014) Maximum warming occurs about one decade after a carbon dioxide emission. Environmental Research Letters, 9(12):124

Ricke K, Drouet L, Caldeira K, Tavoni M (2018) Country-level social cost of carbon. Nat Clim Chang 8(10):895–900

Roe GH, Baker MB (2007) Why is climate sensitivity so unpredictable? Science, 318(5850):629–632

Schad M, John J (2012) Towards a social discount rate for the economic evaluation of health technologies in Germany: an exploratory analysis. Eur J Health Econ 13(2):127–144

Sezer H (2006) Regional welfare weights for Turkey. J Econ Stud

Sharma RA, McGregor MJ, Blyth JF (1991) The social discount rate for land-use projects in India. Journal of Agricultural Economics, 42(1):86–92

Shelunstsova M (2009) Evaluation of a social discount rate for the Russian federation. In: The international conference on administration and business. Bucharest, Romania, pp 714–720

Slade ME (1982) Trends in natural-resource commodity prices: an analysis of time domain. J Environ Econ Manag 9:122–137

Stern N (1977) Welfare weights and the elasticity of the marginal valuation of income. In: Artis, M. and Nobay, R., (eds.) Proceedings of the Aute Edinburgh Meeting of April 1976, Basil Blackwell

Terzioğlu MK, Sucu M (2015) Gompertz-Makeham parameter estimations and valuation approaches: Turkish life insurance sector. Eur Actuar J 5(2):447–468

Tol RS (1997) On the optimal control of carbon dioxide emissions: an application of FUND. Environmental Modeling & Assessment, 2(3):151–163

Tol RS (1999) The marginal costs of greenhouse gas emissions. The Energy Journal, 20(1)

Tol RS (2006) Multi-gas emission reduction for climate change policy: an application of FUND. The Energy Journal, 3

HM Treasury (1997) Appraisal and evaluation in central government, Treasury guidance. Stationery Office

HM Treasury (2003) Appraisal and evaluation in central government, The Green Book, London: HMSO

Uzunkaya ZC, Uzunkaya M (2012) An estimation of the economic discount rate for Turkey. Republic of Turkey Ministry of Development

Van den Bijgaart I, Gerlagh R, Liski M (2016) A simple formula for the social cost of carbon. J Environ Econ Manag 77:75–94

Van der Ploeg F (2020) Discounting and climate policy (No. 8441). CES

Weitzman ML (2013) Tail-hedge discounting and the social cost of carbon. J Econ Lit 51:873–882

Winton M, Takahashi K, Held IM (2010) Importance of ocean heat uptake efficacy to transient climate change. Journal of Climate, 23(9):2333–2344

Zhuang J, Liang Z, Lin T, De Guzman F (2007) Theory and practice in the choice of social discount rate for cost-benefit analysis: a survey (No. 94). ERD working paper series

Chapter 11
The Role of Rating Agencies in Sustainable Economy

Nurdan Ateş and Fatma Cesur

Abstract The purpose of this study is to reveal the functioning of the Capital Markets Board rating activities and analyze their effects on our country's economy. At the same time, by taking into account the COVID-19 epidemic, which has been on the agenda all over the world obviously, it is aimed to evaluate the processes of rating activities and their effects on the world market, especially on our country. In a way, under the shadow of the pandemic, by taking the Rating Agencies are under the scrutiny, our article has been shaped within the framework of revealing the predicted economic consequences during and after the epidemic period.

Keywords Capital markets board · Rating activities · Covid-19 · Mood's · S & P · Fitch · Pandemic

11.1 Introduction

All the world countries aim to have an effective economy. The first step of this is to be financially strong and achieve growth. Economic growth is a process starts with economize and continue with raising the investments and production. In this context, increasing the saving incentives and transforming productivity into investments gain importance. Capital market is an important factor for channelizing the fund flow in economy. Rating activities considerably contribute to development and maturing

---

This chapter was produced from master thesis written by Nurdan Ateş titled "Sermaye Piyasası Kurulu Derecelendirme Faaliyetleri" (Capital Markets Board Rating Activities) under supervision of Assist. Prof. Fatma Cesur in the Master Programme on Economics, Social Graduate School, Trakya University in 2012.

N. Ateş
Economics, Trakya University, Edirne, Turkey

F. Cesur (✉)
Department of Economy, Faculty of Business Sciences and Economics, Trakya University, Edirne, Turkey
e-mail: fatmacesur@trakya.edu.tr

of capital market. The ratings of credit Rating Agencies are being qualified as an effective indicator for the credit paybacks of foreign aids and credits the developing countries received. Rating Agencies should be independent, transparent and objective. They assure the investor. These agencies which set forth the economic, political, administrative risks of a country make available the information requested about the market within a short period of time. The also substantially contribute to financial stability by means of providing foreign fund sources at an international scale.

The most important ones of these Rating Agencies are the ones called as "big three", Moody's Investors Service Inc. (Moody's), Fitch Inc. (Fitch) and Standard & Poor's Ratings Services (S&P) (Kılıçaslan and Giter 2016:66). These are the agencies accepted and authorized to their activities in Turkey as well. However, all three of them being USA-based calls to the minds that the efforts of USA to direct the world economy at the first stage. In the end, this big three has voice 90% of international capital markets (Kaya 2018 December). For so long, the reliability of their rating activities is being discussed. In the chapters of our article, a scale of reliability was made and these discussions were mentioned.

In Turkey, the activities of Rating Agencies are carried out by two different institutions. These are Capital Market Board (SPK) and Banking Regulation and Supervision Agency (BDDK). Rating activities can either be carried out by request or without and request (SPK Introductory Handbook of Rating Agencies 2020).

11.2 SPK Capital Market Board Rating

In the simplest terms, rating is a measurement tool. It provides the measurement of the willingness and ability of the debtor to pay the principal and interest obligations and whether they are fulfilled in a timely and complete manner. The international language of the rating symbols elucidates to investors as a practical and fast reference. International symbols are specified in Table 11.1 as explanatory and in comprehensive manner.

There is a higher demand from the international markets to the capital markets of countries protecting the rights of investors. While the investors are entering into capital markets, usually they do not have any general and specific information about companies of various countries. Rating Agencies gain importance herein. They provide objective information investors need. Therefore, they help their decision making. Rating Agencies provide this with the codified rates given in Table 11.1 that each of them has specific meanings (Cesur and Ateş 2012: 12, 13).

11.3 Importance of Rating Activity

Rating Agencies perform professional analyses which the investors cannot make on their own. Present accessible and meaningful information. Besides, they provide

Table 11.1 Rating scales and their definitions

	Moody's	S&P and others	Definitions of the scales of countries or companies
Suitable to invest	Aaa	AAA	High pay back capability. Principal is secure
	Aa	AA	Pay back capability is good. Very close to the highest scale
	A	A	Has got high pay back capability but responsive to economic conditions
	Baa	BBB	Pay back capability is sufficient, but economic changes may weaken the pay back of principal and interest
Speculative investment risky	Ba	BB	Irregularity may occur in payment lay out. There are uncertainties may affect the payment balance
	B	B	For the present can pay back. In the long run success rate is low Far below the investment rate
	Caa	CCC	Some economic indicators are risky. Most likely cannot make the payments
	Ca	CC	Highly risky Have difficulties in pay backs
	C	C	The lowest rate. On the verge of bankruptcy
		D	On the verge of bankruptcy and in default, cannot pay back without rescheduling of debts

Reference Cesur and Ateş (2012: 38, 40, 44)

incentive to increase the economic efficiency of publicly traded companies or a country. They assure the fund flow in exchange of goods and services with comprehensive risk analyses. They play an active role in regulating resource distribution.

Any investor company considers investing to a country or a company, the first thing they should do is to determine the solvency of that country and that company. Developing countries demand credit from the countries having strong economies. In such circumstances, credit rating activities gain importance. They inform the resource providing country about the debt demanding country. Therefore, on the decision of whether investment will be made or not, the rating will be determinative. These agencies, playing an effective role in investment market for long years, have the capacity of low cost advisor for the investors.

Companies and countries may provide their financial needs from various ways. They finance their assets by means of two main sources, borrowing and equity capital. For example, the debt instruments, in the widest sense can be listed as bills, bonds and credit. Here, the credit Rating Agencies evaluate the reliability of this investment for the fund suppliers in bill buyers' part. In conclusion while a high credit rate decreases the interest to be paid, a low credit rate increases the cost of borrowing (Cesur and Ateş 2012:13). Here the point cannot be slurred over that, low credit rates should not be considered as "bad" investments. In certain cases, the risk criteria of the investors may differ. The important matter here is the demanded yield should compensate the risks undertaken.

11.4   How Rating Affects the Market?

Many organizations in finance sector provide their fund needs by means of taking loans from international markets. Rating activities are in the quality of guidance for determining the solvency. For the international investors, the importance of credit rating of the country they lend, in general manner the credit worthiness of the market increase day by day. Fund-providing countries predicate the rating grade as a lending criterion for investors (Aydın 2018:12 March).

In this day and time, in investment demands, the companies with credit ratings have an advantage. It is necessary to strengthen their fiscal structures for the companies or countries to receive better rates. Based on this, in Turkey as of the date of 11.09.2020, BDDK imposed an obligation of receiving rate to use credit for the companies whose annual turnover is exceeding 500 million Turkish Lira, from a rating agency authorized by Banking Regulation and Supervision Agency (BDDK 2020: 10 September). As it is seen from Table 11.2, there are nine Capital Markets Board (CMB) approved Rating Agencies in business.

Table 11.2 Capital Markets Board (CMB) approved Rating Agencies in Turkey

Agency/company name	1. DRC Derecelendirme Hizmetleri Anonim Şirketi
	2. Fitch Ratings Ltd
	3. İstanbul Uluslararası Derecelendirme Hizmetleri A.Ş
	4. JCR Avrasya Derecelendirme A.Ş
	5. Kobirate Uluslararası Kredi Derecelendirme ve Kurumsal Yönetim Hizmetleri A.Ş
	6. Moody's Investor Service Inc
	7. National Investor Services Derecelendirme A.Ş
	8. Saha Kurumsal Yönetim ve Kredi Derecelendirme Hizmetleri A.Ş
	9. Standard and Poor's Credit Market Services Europe Limited

Reference https://www.spk.gov.tr/Sayfa/Index/6/10/1 (Access Date: 2020, 05 September)

Rating Agencies gained trust of financial markets from the beginning of last century. Reports they have prepared have the key position with respect to finance. Many investors in market are informed with the rates given by Rating Agencies and make their decisions in line with these rates (Birgül 1997:65). However, in very high investments, the activities and reports of Rating Agencies, whose importance we have tried to explain above, have become questionable in our age where technology and information are rapidly accessed. Trust in these agencies becomes a subject of discussion in regard to their independence, objectivity and transparency, especially in terms of their rating criteria of the countries. All humanity's cutting up in various aspects due to COVID-19, which continues its effect in the world, is also a reason for this.

The discussions about the criteria of International Rating Agencies should be updated are frequently made today. If we list the country rating criteria of the agencies presently use; we can say that stability of cash flow, growth of exports, the openness of the economy, debt ratios, current account balance, the rate of short-term capital movements to reserves, state of reserves, and their development, social savings, public sector fiscal deficits, investments and certainly inflation. Except these above-mentioned economic criteria, the following indicators which are accepted as political risks are also determinative on rating system; electoral system and times, foreign policy developments and to what extent democracy is established, political leader and changes in agenda, structure of coalition, the state of opposition, degree of independency of central bank (Cesur and Ateş 2012:32–33).

During this period of pandemic goes on, many criteria tend to lose their importance. Because of the global COVID-19 pandemic, since the worldwide recession is inevitable, criteria priorities changed. In the economies of countries, fighting against pandemics, vaccination works, sustainability of healthcare system are gaining importance. Besides, the countermeasures taken by the governments to ensure the livelihood of the people also dominate the market. In the end, we are faced with the fact that the effects of pandemics will continue to intensify in various terms. Rating Agencies which express that the global economy will contract seriously also signaled that they would set the rates of many countries' rates back and turn the directions negative.

Another issue is that Rating Agencies publicize the dates when the rates for countries will be announced before they announce the rates of countries. Many investors make their investment plans on the basis of these dates. Unfortunately, Moody's did not a rating on the date of June 5, 2020, when they have announced, instead they explained that they did not an update for Turkey, Russia and Democratic Republic of Congo on June 6, 2020 (Zengin 2020a). Three months later, on the date of September 11, 2020, they made a new statement and they announced a rate 5 grade below the investable level with a negative view. Some of the equivalent rated countries are Uganda, Tanzania, Rwanda, Papua New Guinea, Kenya, Jamaica, Benin and Cambodia (Zafer 2020). The reason in the announcement was made; it has been considered that Turkish economy will be pushed to recession due to the pandemics. Yet, this a case envisaged for whole world.

Once at this step, if we mention about the rates given to some of European countries by Rating Agencies; Moody's stated that they have kept the rates of UK and France fixed at Aa2 and turned the view from stable to negative. They also explained that they have rated Germany with AAA rate over these countries (Kurtaran 2019). The reason of Germany's receiving good rate is its success in fighting against pandemics.

Standard & Poor's announced that Italy kept its BBB rate level, while UK's rate was approved by AA, they turned the view from negative to stable. To the contrary the UK has difficulties in healthcare system; the view has been revised in positive direction by the agency. They made announcements confirming the rates of Germany and France were not changed and they kept their rates as AA (stable) (Zengin 2020b, www.aa.com.tr).

For Turkey, Standard & Poor's pointed out that they have foreseen the economy would contract, they also underlined that, there are fluctuations in foreign exchange rates and in addition, private sector will face with high risks because of the effects of pandemics. Despite this, they informed that they have confirmed the rate and view as B+ (stable) (www.paraborsa.net, 2020 24 July). Here, this approach is more understandable and favorable comparing to Moody's.

Fitch Ratings explained that they have lowered Italy's credit rate from BBB to BBB− level and they have lowered UK's rated from AA to AA−. On the other hand, they confirmed the AAA rate of USA. At the same time, they pointed out that AA rate of France not changed, but turned the view from stable to negative (www.blo omberght.com, 2020 25 August).

The rating of Fitch for Turkey was they had not made any change in the rate and declared that it stayed BB−. At the same time, they also pointed out that the recovery in economy was strong and they foresee that this would be in "V" shape recovery (www.kanalfinans.com, 2020 20 March). What Finch meant with this expression is the economy will hit the deep and then will have a rapid recovery. But, they centered upon the matter that the foreign finance needs of Turkey may generate vulnerability.

Hence, all uncertainties will continue during the time period of pandemics unless the vaccine is available. If the severity of the pandemic is not slowed down, the efficiency of production will also decrease.

Turkey get ahead of many countries called as great since the pandemics appear with its healthcare infrastructure, operations and system. Turkey even helped out medical supplies and equipment to Italy, America and UK. When considered from this point of view, this continuum named as crisis for Turkey has got the potential of turning it into an opportunity with a right administration and intelligence cooperation.

11.5   Comparative Rates of Turkey

Almost a year will pass after the emergence of COVID-19, which the whole world was caught off guard. In this sense, the effects of pandemics are huge for the evaluation of both the years 2019 and 2020. In Table 11.3, comparative rates of Turkey for the last ten years take place.

Table 11.3 Comparative rates of Turkey for the last 10 years

Year	Moody's Rate	Moody's View	S&P Rate	S&P View	Fitch Rate	Fitch View	Short Definition	Definition
2020	Baa1 / Baa2 / Baa3		BBB+ / BBB / BBB-		BBB+ / BBB / BBB-		Investible	Medium-Low Level Speculative
	Ba1 / Ba2 / Ba3		BB+ / BB / BB-		BB+ / BB / BB-	Negative	Uninvestible	Low Level Speculative
	B1 / B2 / B3	Negative	B+ / B / B-	Stable	B+ / B / B-			High Grade Speculative
2019	Baa1 / Baa2 / Baa3		BBB+ / BBB / BBB-		BBB+ / BBB / BBB-		Investible	Medium-Low Level Speculative
	Ba1 / Ba2 / Ba3		BB+ / BB / BB-		BB+ / BB / BB-	Stable	Uninvestible	Low Level Speculative
	B1 / B2 / B3	Negative	B+ / B / B-	Stable	B+ / B / B-			High Grade Speculative
2018	Baa1 / Baa2 / Baa3		BBB+ / BBB / BBB-		BBB+ / BBB / BBB-		Investible	Medium-Low Level Speculative
	Ba1 / Ba2 / Ba3	Negative	BB+ / BB / BB-	Stable	BB+ / BB / BB-	Negative	Uninvestible	Low Level Speculative
	B1 / B2 / B3		B+ / B / B-		B+ / B / B-			High Grade Speculative
2017	Baa1 / Baa2 / Baa3		BBB+ / BBB / BBB-		BBB+ / BBB / BBB-		Investible	Medium-Low Level Speculative
	Ba1 / Ba2 / Ba3	Negative	BB+ / BB / BB-	Stable	BB+ / BB / BB-	Stable	Uninvestible	Low Level Speculative
	B1 / B2 / B3		B+ / B / B-		B+ / B / B-			High Grade Speculative
2016	Baa1 / Baa2 / Baa3		BBB+ / BBB / BBB-		BBB+ / BBB / BBB-	Negative	Investible	Medium-Low Level Speculative
	Ba1 / Ba2 / Ba3	Stable	BB+ / BB / BB-	Stable	BB+ / BB / BB-		Uninvestible	Low Level Speculative
	B1 / B2 / B3		B+ / B / B-		B+ / B / B-			High Grade Speculative
2015	Baa1 / Baa2 / Baa3		BBB+ / BBB / BBB-		BBB+ / BBB / BBB-	Stable	Investible	Medium-Low Level Speculative
	Ba1 / Ba2 / Ba3	Not Evaluated	BB+ / BB / BB-	Negative	BB+ / BB / BB-		Uninvestible	Low Level Speculative
	B1 / B2 / B3		B+ / B / B-		B+ / B / B-			High Grade Speculative
2014	Baa1 / Baa2 / Baa3	Negative	BBB+ / BBB / BBB-		BBB+ / BBB / BBB-	Stable	Investible	Medium-Low Level Speculative
	Ba1 / Ba2 / Ba3		BB+ / BB / BB-	Negative	BB+ / BB / BB-		Uninvestible	Low Level Speculative
	B1 / B2 / B3		B+ / B / B-		B+ / B / B-			High Grade Speculative
2013	Baa1 / Baa2 / Baa3	Stable	BBB+ / BBB / BBB-		BBB+ / BBB / BBB-	Stable	Investible	Medium-Low Level Speculative
	Ba1 / Ba2 / Ba3		BB+ / BB / BB-	Stable	BB+ / BB / BB-		Uninvestible	Low Level Speculative
	B1 / B2 / B3		B+ / B / B-		B+ / B / B-			High Grade Speculative
2012	Baa1 / Baa2 / Baa3		BBB+ / BBB / BBB-		BBB+ / BBB / BBB-	Stable	Investible	Medium-Low Level Speculative
	Ba1 / Ba2 / Ba3	Positive	BB+ / BB / BB-	Stable	BB+ / BB / BB-		Uninvestible	Low Level Speculative
	B1 / B2 / B3		B+ / B / B-		B+ / B / B-			High Grade Speculative
2011	Baa1 / Baa2 / Baa3		BBB+ / BBB / BBB-		BBB+ / BBB / BBB-		Investible	Medium-Low Level Speculative
	Ba1 / Ba2 / Ba3	Positive	BB+ / BB / BB-	Positive	BB+ / BB / BB-	Stable	Uninvestible	Low Level Speculative
	B1 / B2 / B3		B+ / B / B-		B+ / B / B-			High Grade Speculative
2010	Baa1 / Baa2 / Baa3		BBB+ / BBB / BBB-		BBB+ / BBB / BBB-		Investible	Medium-Low Level Speculative
	Ba1 / Ba2 / Ba3	Positive	BB+ / BB / BB-	Positive	BB+ / BB / BB-	Positive	Uninvestible	Low Level Speculative
	B1 / B2 / B3		B+ / B / B-		B+ / B / B-			High Grade Speculative

Reference www.bloombergh.com (26.09.2016–12.09.2020), www.bbc.com (18.03.2017–02.05.2018), https://www.paraborsa.net/etiket/turkiyenin-kredi-notu-kac/, https://www.cnnturk.com/ekonomi/turkiye/iste-turkiyenin-kredi-notu-karnesi?page=1 [Access Date:2020,05 October].

11.6 Trustworthiness Before Covid

If we review the year 2012, Fitch increased the rate of Turkey from uninvestable BB+ to BBB−, which is the rate of investable. This situation occurred exactly 20 years after the first speculative level rate has been received (Kılıçaslan and Giter 2016: 73).

Even though the foreign debt need of Turkey is high, political stabilization with a single party government became effective on receiving this rate. But the greatest factor is, especially after the 2008 Mortgage crisis in USA, while many of the country economies have been affected deeply and negatively but Turkey's recovering from this period less vulnerable as compared with other countries.

During this crisis period, Moody's, S&P and Fitch have been criticized due to the rates they have given to some countries. They have decreased AAA rates in 2008 with sudden decision. By coming these unethical situations to the light, especially Moody's find itself in the line of fire and made a simple explanation such as their systems that are their computers were infected in that period (Kılıçaslan and Giter 2016:74).

In addition, during the same 2008 crisis period, USA Justice Department sued S&P Agency due to giving high rates by ignoring the risks (www.yapi.com.tr, 2013 12 February). Rating Agencies experiencing loss of trust also are being criticized by some segments with respect to their independencies for their high volume incomes while they are producing the solvencies of countries.

It will be remembered that, in 2011 banks in countries having high rates collapsed overnight or they close a whole raft of branch offices or discharged staff and downsized. Bank of America announced they would discharge 30 thousand person in that period (www.bloomberght.com, 2011 9 September). HSCB closed many of branch offices in Turkey. Right after the experiences, some economists started to question the priorities of the criteria of Rating Agencies. The uncertainty of which main criterion determines the rate also became a current issue. In addition, in those years, Greece became the center of the critics by European Community. They will be heard that S&P lower the rate of Greece by three levels and decreased from B to CC (www.iha.com.tr, 2011 14 June).

If we make a comparison for Turkey between 2018 and 2019, it is seen that all three big lower our rates. The explanation of Fitch in this subject is unseating the Central Bank Governor (www.haberler.com, 2019 17 July). Again in the same period, sanction decisions for Turkey have been announced by the USA.

In the first quarter of 2020, S&P announced that they confirmed their AA+ rate for USA and Fitch also announced that they confirmed their AAA rate for USA (www.ekonomist.com.tr, 2020 27 March). Yet, while the arbitrary decisions taken by the President of USA are stunned, they were not deemed as a political intervention to economy by Rating Agencies. Therefore, credit rates of USA have been confirmed without change, whereas the reason of unseating the Central Bank Governor was seen as political influence and rate of Turkey was lowered.

11.7 Trustworthiness During Covid Period

The COVID-19 pandemic, which manifested itself in Wuhan City of China in December 2019 and spread all over the world, especially in America, France and Italy in a very short time, undoubtedly affected the economies of all countries deeply. This virus is qualified as worldwide pandemics, and at the moment these lines are being written, the number of worldwide cases recorded about 34 million 590 thousand (www.bbc.com, 2020 2 October). We are passing through a very large scale, where millions of people do not participate into production. With the rightful decisions made by governments, millions of people work from homes in accordance with isolation conditions. This lays bare the extent of the impact of the pandemic on the economy.

As it is in international level, in Turkey production, tourism and services sector took major blows and also continue to take. Particularly the foreign capital outflows from the market reaches to a considerable level. Unicredit who sold their shares in Yapı Kredi Bank is an example for this (www.dunya.com, 2020 6 February). Even if we remember, Volkswagen Company has given up from the manufacturing plant they have announced after a long survey period that they would establish in Manisa province of Turkey. Even though the picture propounded looks bad, the importance of a stereotypical word comes into play right here; "Turning the crisis into an opportunity". This picture depicted as black for Turkey, for sure can be converted to white with wisdom, efforts and right guidance. It should not be forgotten that our country is a country with an open future and a very high potential in production. If we return back to International Rating Agencies, the rates they issued besides their criteria are not transparent enough as well as their methods and functions, in fact, are topics of long-standing discussions. It should not be forgotten that the big companies that went bankrupt have been given high rates right before the 2008 global crisis.

At what level the trust on the rates given by the agencies in COVID-19 period? Today there is a considerable investor group who take these rates as references. This subject is important for the companies investing money to retirement funds shining in recent years in Turkey. But, it is observed that many investors exit from our Private Pension System (BES) in this period. Continuation of foreign money outflows in PPS portfolios is a negative directional mobility. It is also a negative picture with respect to market and primary deficit financing (www.ekonomist.com.tr, 2020 12 June).

For sure, Turkey will borrow money, will have current account deficit or will go downsizing. However, this "pandemic-based economic crisis", whose arrival we can never predict worldwide, causes hard times not only for our country but also for the whole world. In such an environment, Rating Agencies should be much more sensitive and transparent.

Nevertheless, Moody's agency's lowering the rate of Turkey distinguishably and announce at the level of uninvestable but beside this leaving the rates of some European countries fixed without revising calls to mind that, these evaluations were made far from objectivity and made under the shadow of political influences. These evaluations which were made far from objectivity without based on financial data decrease the trust for related agencies.

11.8 Conclusion and Evaluation

When examining the last two years' rating notes for Turkey, due to the high foreign exchange borrowing costs and due to the existence of situations such as high inflation, credit rate decreased by Moody's. S&P did not change. Fitch, on the other hand, changed the view from stable to negative. These rates will cause resource problem in the new credit demands.

However, because of COVID-19, the global trade came to a halt or even regression point. The very basic condition for countries to overcome this continuum with the least damage in economic terms is the strength of the health system. As long as there is no health crisis, social life can continue as usual without panic atmosphere is formed. Otherwise, mandatory measures such as quarantine that we encountered in the first place become involved. People retreat from production and service sectors in a moment. Waiting for an indefinite period of time begins at homes. As a result of all these, economy stops. Due to COVID-19, the world economy has already entered a total, unprecedented recession. Even though the economic decline is inevitable, countries can overcome this period by turning to their own resources.

Turkey can use its chance to be an alternative production country in this pandemics period where both consumption and production habits came to an extraordinary state. For the investors not acting only based on the ratings of Rating Agencies, instead strictly following the market, Turkey is a land of opportunities. After all, the whole world's line of vision on China has changed due to this pandemic. For sure, new searches will come to the fore. Turkey proved itself in different times in many areas, food, textiles, tourism and most importantly the healthcare industry being in the first places.

Net foreign exchange reserves may be lowered. There may also be a need for foreign borrowing more than in any other times. But, anyhow, at a level that allows the entry of foreign capital in Turkey, an effective confidence can be given to the markets during this pandemic period. It should be taken into consideration that international financially strong companies may go diversity except the investments in China or at least they may being in search of different countries in the sense of distributing economic risk after the pandemic. In case of Turkey seize legal system trustworthy, freedom guarantee and corporate governance level will seriously be able to speak in the markets. As a matter of fact that, when the pandemic appears, even strong economies could not be self-sufficient when it comes to the health system. If it is thought about it suddenly attracted attention with healthcare equipment aids, why not Turkey becomes the new route of investors?

References

Aydın H (2018) www.tbb.org.tr. 12 03 2018. "Kredi Derecelendirme Kuruluşları", Erişim Adresi: https://www.tbb.org.tr/Content/Upload/Dokuman/7507/TBB_Bsk_ITU_120318.pdf (5 Sept 2020 tarihinde erişilmiştir)

Birgül O (1997) "Derecelendirme Kuruluşları ve Etkileri". Bankacılar Dergisi 21:65

Cesur F, Ateş N (2012) "Sermaye Piyasası Kurulu Derecelendirme Faaliyetleri". Yüksek Lisans Projesi, T.C. Trakya Üniversitesi Sosyal Bilimler Enstitüsü. Edirne

Banking Regulation and Supervison of Agency, Bankacılık Düzenleme ve Denetleme Kurulu Kararı, https://www.bddk.org.tr/Mevzuat/DokumanGetir/806 (Accessed on Jan 21st, 2021)

Kaya Y (2018) Aralık 2018. Dünyada Kredi Notu Ligi ve Türkiye. Erişim Adresi: https:// www.alnusyatirim.com/analizler/dunyada-kredi-notu-ligi-ve-turkiye-436 (22 Sept 2020 tarihinde erişilmiştir)

Kılıçaslan H, Giter MS (2016) "Kredi Derecelendirme ve Ortaya Çıkan Sorunlar". Maliye Araştırmaları Dergisi 2(1):61–81

Kurtaran G (2019) Moody's İngiltere'nin Not Görünümünü Negatife Çevirdi. Erişim Adresi: https:// www.aa.com.tr/tr/ekonomi/moodys-ingilterenin-not-gorunumunu-negatife-cevirdi/1640108 (4 Sept 2020 tarihinde erişilmiştir)

SPK Derecelendirme Kuruluşları Tanıtım Rehberi (2020) Erişim Adresi: https://www.spk.gov.tr/ Sayfa/Index/6/10/2 (7 Sept 2020 tarihinde erişilmiştir)

www.bbc.com (Between 18.03.2017 and 02.05.2018)

www.bloombergh.com (Between 26.09.2019 and 12.09.2020)

Zafer Ç (2020) Moody's Kredi Notu: Türkiye; Tanzanya ve Papua Yeni Gine Seviyesine İndi. Erişim Adresi: https://kronos34.news/tr/moodys-kredi-notu-turkiye-tanzanya-ve-papua-yeni-gine-seviyesine-indi187440-2/ (18 Sept 2020 tarihinde erişilmiştir)

Zengin D (2020a) Moody's Türkiye'nin Kredi Notu ve Görünümüne İlişkin Güncelleme Yapmadı. Erişim Adresi: https://www.aa.com.tr/tr/ekonomi/moodys-turkiyenin-kredi-notu-ve-gorunumune-iliskin-guncelleme-yapmadi/1867088 (12 Sept 2020 tarihinde erişilmiştir)

Zengin D (2020b) S&P Fransa ve Almanya'nın Kredi Notunu Teyit Etti. Erişim Adresi: https://www. aa.com.tr/tr/ekonomi/sp-fransa-ve-almanyanin-kredi-notunu-teyit-etti-/1791840 (28 Sept 2020 tarihinde erişilmiştir)

Chapter 12
Corporate Social Responsibility Disclosure: Evidence from Bahrain

Sayed Mohamed Saeed and Adel M. Sarea

Abstract The purpose of this research is to discuss the relationship between eight firms-specific characteristics (e.g., firm size, leverage, firm age, audit firm size, profitability, industry type, ownership, and liquidity), and the level of corporate social responsibility (CSR) in firms is listed in Bahrain Bourse. A checklist method is used to measure the level of CRS, which include: community involvement, employee information, product/service information, and environmental disclosure. The main results reveal that the disclosure level of community involvement is of 54.55%, employees' information is of 61.90%, product/services information is of 60.95%, and environmental information is of 16.19%. In addition, the regression analysis reports that compliance level of CSR disclosure is positively associated with audit firm size and industry type. On the other hand, the remaining characteristics, such as firm size, profitability, leverage, firm age, ownership, and liquidity are found to be statistically insignificant in their association to the level of CSR disclosure, but they have a positive direction except firm age.

Keywords Corporate social responsibility (CSR) · Firm-specific characteristics · Disclosure · Bahrain

12.1 Introduction

Corporations become is an integral part of the society and the only way to achieve sustainability and survive in the society respects the ethical values of the society (Davis 1975, p. 13). There is a widespread academic interest in the corporate social responsibility. With respect to the CSR, the type of researches which has observant growth focuses on the determinants of CSR disclosures of the firms. The relationship of CSR disclosure as determined by firm characteristics whether financial such as

S. M. Saeed · A. M. Sarea (✉)
Ahlia University, Manama, Bahrain

S. M. Saeed
e-mail: sfadhul@ahlia.edu.bh

liquidity, leverage, and profitability or not financial such as size, ownership, and audit firm size, has been exceedingly inspected and reported in the researches which investigate the CSR (Haniffa and Cooke 2005; Mahadeo et al. 2011; Alareeni 2019).

The phenomenon of CSR is attracting increasing international attention. Today, corporations are expected not only to focus and pursue profit, but also to consider the CSR. In general, CSR means that corporations take into consideration the fears and concerns of corporate stakeholders (e.g., employees, shareholders, suppliers, government, customers, and the local community). The CSR principles include the fairness of social and environmental sustainability into the business process (Alkababji 2014; Awadh and Alareeni 2018). However, as the societies' awareness about the importance of CSR disclosure increase, the researchers become more focusing on the topic of CSR, such as, (Razak 2015) examined the association between some firm characteristics and CSR disclosure in Saudi Arabia, also from Saudi Arabia, Macarulla and Talalweh (2012) examined the level of CSR disclosure of the 134 firms that were listed on the RSE, Saleh (2009) provided empirical evidence on CSR disclosure practices in Malaysia. Sufian (2012) investigated the association between firm's characteristics and corporate social responsibility disclosure (CSRD) in Bangladesh, moreover, Yao et al. (2011) studied the determinants of CSR disclosure by Chinese firms.

This research attempts to review the relationship between firms' characteristics and the level of CSR disclosure by firms listed on Bahrain Bourse. The purpose of this research is set out to examine the CSR disclosure practices in Bahrain by analyzing the annual reports of different types of firms listed on Bahrain Bourse. That is to find out whether the level of CSR disclosure is influenced by firm-specific characteristics or not?. The study, therefore, examines the association between an eight firm-specific characteristics and the level of CSR disclosure. These characteristics include: firm size, profitability, financial leverage, firm age, size of audit firm, ownership, industry type, and liquidity.

The next section discusses previous studies as well as formulating research hypotheses to answer the research question.

12.2 Literature Review and Hypothesis Development

This study attempts to review previous studies that have been published by well-known journals in the area of CSR and identify the theoretical framework which had led to the development of the hypotheses to be tested and analyzed.

Since the CSR disclosure is voluntary, there will be no power to requiring companies to disclose CSR, which might affect its flow, or make it hostage to the interests of companies with a blind eye to the interests of stakeholders. Moreover, there is a lack in researches that investigate the CSR reporting of firms in Bahrain.

CSR defined as the voluntary obligation of firms to contribute to social goals and developments. In last few decades, corporations become more aware of the fact that it is an integral part of the society and the only way to achieve sustainability (Davis 1975, p. 13).

12.2.1   Evolution of the Concept of CSR

Madrakhimova (2013, p. 36), made a study to investigate the history of the CSR's concept, he traced that the evolution of CSR started in 1950, in the 1960s, the definitions got expanded and it began expanding in the 1970s. In 1980, some fewer new definitions appeared and the empirical research became more mature. In the 1990s, CSR continued to serve as the basic design, but inferior or turns into the alternative thematic framework.

Mohamed et al. (2014, p. 56) summarizes the timeline of social accounting in two periods; the first period when the social accounting has been discovered in the 1960s, and it was charred only the areas that concern human dimension. Then, the second in the 1980s, it was extended to the protection of the environment in the name of environmental accounting. Thus, the object of a social accounting therefore encompasses environmental and social concerns.

In a related study, Maguire (2011), p. 214) link the CSR evolution with events happened during the last four decades as given in Table 12.1.

This study contributes to the corporate social responsibility literature, because it provides insight into the CSR disclosure practices of listed companies with respect to their operations.

Furthermore, such this research is useful to the stakeholders to evaluate the level of voluntary CSR disclosure and the firm's compliance with social responsibilities and making decisions. In addition, managers may realize the importance of environmental and social disclosures and learn the determinants which lead to better disclosure practices. This will result in better provision of CSR disclosure to stakeholders.

Table 12.1   CSR evolution

Year	Event
1976	Releasing the guidelines for global corporations by The Organization for Economic Co-operation and Development (OECD) to be as a voluntary principles and standards for social responsibility of business
1977	The creation of Sullivan Principles
1984	Death of more than 3000 person in India because of gas leak at a Union Carbide chemical plant
1989	The Exxon Valdez crashes into Bligh Reef off the coast of Alaska, spilling close to 11 million gallons of oil into Prince William Sound
1990s	Allegations of human rights abuses in Nigeria and its consequences
1990s	A series of labor abuses are revealed in the Nike supply chain, such as child labor
1997	The Global Reporting Initiative (GRI) is formed by Ceres and the Tellus Institute, two Boston-based nonprofit organizations. The GRI releases its Sustainability Reporting Guidelines in 2000
2000	The United Nations Global Compact (GC) is launched by UN Secretary General Kofi Annan

(continued)

Table 12.1 (continued)

Year	Event
2000	The creation of Carbon Disclosure Project
2001	The Enron scandal and its consequences
2001	Government of French mandates CSR reporting
2003	Releasing of AA1000 Assurance Standard
2004	Creation of Socially Responsible Investment (SRI) Index
2006	Begins Issuing of policy and performance standards on Environmental Sustainability by The International Finance Corporation (IFC)
2008	Announcement of legislation to mandate CSR reporting by Sweden and Denmark
2010	Spills of about 200 million gallons of oil into the Gulf of Mexico which caused by n explosion at BP's Deepwater
2010	Issue of memorandum to initiatives efforts to promote CSR by the GRI and GC
2010	Releasing of CSR standard, ISO 26000

12.2.2 Theoretical Framework

Corporate social responsibility (CSR) can be defined as the voluntary commitment of firms to contribute to social goals and developments. In last few decades, corporations become more aware of the fact that it is an integral part of the society and the only way to achieve sustainability and survive in the society is respect the ethical values of the society, Davis (1975).

There is a widespread academic interest in the corporate social responsibility, the empirical investigations of CSR practices has produced a very diverse academic literatures that engages different theoretical perspectives in support of corporate social reporting. With regard to the empirical research on CSR, Reverte (2009) divided the empirical studies into three types, the first one related to 'descriptive studies,' which report on the extent and nature of CSR with some comparisons among periods and countries, the second one is related to 'explicative studies,' which interested in investigating the determinants of CSR reporting. The third one is interested in the 'impact of CSR information' on stakeholders.

Empirical studies have shown that CSR disclosure activism varies across companies, industries, and time, Gray et al. (1995), Hackston and Milne (1996). They have also shown this behavior to be importantly and systematically determined by a variety of firm and industry characteristics that influence the relative costs and benefits of disclosing such information, Belkaoui and Karpik (1989), Cormier and Magnan (2003).

Campbell (2007) offers a comprehensive institutional theory on CSR comprising a series of propositions specifying the conditions under which corporations are likely to behave in socially responsible ways. Chih et al. (2008) focus of this section, based on (Campbell 2007), is placed on providing an explanation of the determinants of

CSR and proposing appropriate measures to proxy for these determinants in our empirical study.

This study adopts second type of empirical studies which mentioned by Reverte (2009), and it attempts to examine the association between eight firm-specific characteristics and the level of corporate social responsibility disclosure of firms listed in Bahrain Bourse in order to evaluate the practice of corporate social responsibility disclosure. These characteristics include: firm size, profitability, financial leverage, firm Age, size of audit firm, ownership, industry type, and liquidity which some of them are widely used in such researches.

12.2.3 Study Hypothesis

Firm Size

Yao et al. (2011, p. 214) identified the determinants of CSR disclosure of corporations in China, indicated that there is an affirmative relationship between the company size and the social and environmental information disclosure.

Rettab et al. (2009, p. 41) advise that the ability of large firms to communicate their social activities to stakeholders is more than small firms. On other hand, some studies showing opposite results, like Ebiringa et al. (2013, p. 61), they found that there is a negative relationship between number of corporate social disclosed and firm size in Nigerian oil and gas sector. Thus, we hypothesize that:

H1: There is a relationship between firm size and the level of CSR disclosure.

Profitability

Most of prior researches end up with similar results related to the variable of profitability. For example, Alareeni (2018), Hussainey et al. (2011, p. 41), Ismail and Chandler (2005, p. 32), and Roberts (1992, p. 124) found that profitability has positive relation with social reporting. Thus, it is hypothesized that:

H2: There is a relationship between firm's profitability and the level of CSR disclosure.

12.2.3.1 Financial Leverage

Chek et al. (2013, p. 61) found that there is no correlation between firms' leverage and the level of CSR disclosure, and their finding was agreed with the research made by Mustaffa and Tamoi (2006, p. 314). They found that leverage is not appeared as a determinant for the company to disclose their social activities. To examine the relation between leverage and the level of compliance with CSR disclosure among firms listed in the Bahrain Bourse, it is hypothesized that:

H3: There is a relationship between firm's financial leverage and the level of CSR disclosure.

Firm Age

Firm age is defined by the time span between the sample's year and when a firm was listed on stock exchange. Yao et al. (2011, p. 31) found that firm age is negatively correlated with the level of CSR disclosure in China, and justify it by the nature of China's capital market, and therefore, it is hypothesized that:

H4: There is a relationship between firm's age and the level of CSR disclosure.

Size of Audit Firm

The firm's external auditor impacts the quality and quantity of information disclosure in annual report. Big and international audit firms require more information and adopt high quality of internal procedures in which it contributes the firm's disclosure, Uwuigbe and Egbide (2012, p. 32). This leads to the fourth suggested hypothesis:

H5: Bahraini firms audited by large auditing firms disclose more social information than those audited by small auditing firms.

Ownership

Eng and Mak (2003, p. 32) argued that the government ownership will lead to high conflict between firms financial goals and society's expectations. High portion of shares held by government will lead to high expectation of society in the aspect of social activities and programs such as training programs, donations, and pension plans (Naser 2006, p. 51). The following hypothesis is suggested:

H6: Firms with Bahraini ownership disclose more social information than firms owned by foreign.

Industry Type

Industry type is another variable used to explain the level of CSR disclosure; companies belong to different sectors and operating in different activities. Hence, companies that have manufacturing operations involved in more activities than companies with services operations, which may require them to report more social information especially in the environment and product aspect.

H7: Manufacturing industries disclose more social information than non-manufacturing firms.

Liquidity

Ezat and El-Masry (2008, p. 112) found a positive relationship between levels of company Internet reporting and liquidity. In order to test this relationship for companies listed in the Bahrain Bourse, it is hypothesized that:

H8: There is a relationship between firm's liquidity and the level of CSR disclosure.

12.3   Research Methodology

The study sample divided into six sectors: (commercial banks, investment banks, insurance, services, industrial, and hotels & tourism) as given in Table 12.2. The subsequent multiple linear regression model was fitted to the data:

$$\text{CSR Dis} = \beta_0 + \beta_1 \, TA + \beta_2 \, \text{Prof} + \beta_3 \, \text{Fin Lev} + \beta_4 \, \text{age}$$
$$+ \beta_5 \, \text{Audit F siz} + \beta_6 \, \text{Own} + \beta_7 \, \text{Ind type} + \beta_8 \, \text{Liq} + e$$

where:
CSR Dis = Corporate social responsibility disclosure
TA = Total assets (firm size)
Prof = Profitabiltiy
Fin Lev = Financial leverage
Age = Firm age
Audit F Siz = Audit firm size
Own = Percentage of Bahrain ownership
Ind Type = Industry type
Liq = Liquidity
e = Error term (Fig. 12.1).

The data for measuring the dependent and independent variables investigated in this study were collected manually from the sampled companies' annual report downloaded from their official Web sites as well as the Web site of the BSE. The 35 firms' annual reports were fully covered in the study because of its small sample size and secondly, the researcher sought to determine the level of corporate social responsibility disclosure of companies listed in Bahrain Bourse. The reports of the year 2017 were selected because they were relatively more recent at the time the study was conducted and they were easier to obtain.

	Sector	Number of companies	Percentage (%)
Table 12.2 Classification of sampled companies by sector	Industrial	2	6
	Commercial banks	7	20
	Investment banks	9	26
	Services	8	23
	Insurance	5	14
	Hotels and tourism	4	11
	Total	35	100

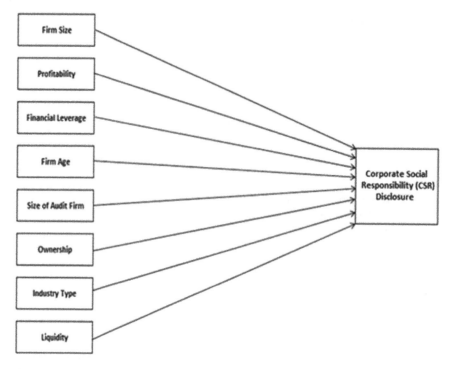

Fig. 12.1 Research model

Independent Variables:

Eight company characteristics (e.g., firm size, leverage, firm age, audit firm size, profitability, industry type, ownership, and liquidity) were examined for their association with the level CSR disclosure. The annual reports of the firms were used to obtain the data. Table 12.3 below includes independent variables of the study, their measurements, and their expected signs. It also shows prior studies that used similar measurement methods as follows.

12.4   Data Analysis and Discussion

12.4.1   Descriptive Statistics

This section discusses the descriptive statistics for the dependent and independent variables used in the study. Tables 12.4. and 12.5 report the minimum, maximum, mean, and standard deviation for the sample companies. Furthermore, it states the normality tests of the variables used in the research.

Table 12.3 Summary of the independent variables

Variable	Measurement	Exp. sign	Prior studies
Firm Size	Total assets of the firms	+	Yao et al. (2011), Moore (2001), Branco and Rodrigues (2008), Rettab et al. (2009), Ebiringa et al. (2013) and Juhmani (2014)
Profitability	Return on equity (ROE) of the firms	+	Hussainey et al. 2011), Ismail and Chandler (2005), Roberts (1992), Belkaoui and Karpik (1989) and Juhmani (2014)
Financial leverage	Ratio of total debts to total assets of the firms	+	Brammer and Pavelin 2008), Purushothaman et al. (2000), Chek et al. (2013) and Mustaffa and Tamoi (2006)
Firm age	Date of financial statements less date of foundation	+	Yao et al. (2011), (1992), Alam and Deb (2010) and Akhtaruddin (2005)
Size of audit firm	Dummy value (1 = if firm is audited by Big 4, 0 otherwise)	+	Choi 1998), (Uwuigbe and Egbide 2012) and (Juhmani 2014)
Ownership	Dummy value (1 = if Bahraini, 0 = if not)	+	Tagesson et al. (2009), Mak (2003), Naser (2006) and Ghazali (2007)
Industry type	Dummy value (1 = if manufacturing industry, 0 = if not)	+	Hackston and Milne 1996) and Tagesson et al. (2009)
Liquidity	Current ratio of the firms	+	Al-Ajmi et al. (2015) and Ezat and El-Masry (2008)

Table 12.4 Descriptive statistics for the dependent variables

	N	Minimum	Maximum	Mean	Std. deviation
CI	35	0.00	1.00	0.5455	0.30631
EI	35	0.17	1.00	0.6190	0.25105
PSI	35	0.00	1.00	0.6095	0.28567
ED	35	0.00	1.00	0.1619	0.29838
Valid N (listwise)	35				

Disclosure checklist which representing the dependent variables is divided into four categories:

i   Community involvement (CI): According to the descriptive results, the extent of first category, which is community involvement (CI) disclosure on average, is 54.54%, with a minimum of zero percent and a maximum of 100%, indicating variations in the level of (CI) disclosure in Bahrain.

Table 12.5 Descriptive statistics for the independent variables

	N	Minimum	Maximum	Mean	Std. deviation
Siz	35	5949.00	12,309,764.00	1.4163E6	2.87685E6
Prf	35	−16.23	20.90	8.2700	7.32761
Lev	35	4.15	89.69	43.8420	27.60331
Age	35	8.00	57.00	29.7714	12.58170
Aud	35	0.00	1.00	0.8286	0.38239
Own	35	0.00	1.00	0.4000	0.49705
Ind	35	0.00	1.00	0.0571	0.23550
Liq	35	0.29	12.58	2.4583	2.50534
Valid N (listwise)	35				

ii   Employee information (EI): According to the descriptive results, the extent of second category, which is employee information (EI) disclosure on average, is 61.90%, with a minimum of 17% and a maximum of 100%, indicating variations in the level of (EI) disclosure in Bahrain.

iii Product/service information (PSI): According to the descriptive results, the extent of third category, which is product/service information (PSI) disclosure on average, is 60.95%, with a minimum of zero percent and a maximum of 100%, indicating variations in the level of (PSI) disclosure in Bahrain.

iv   Environmental disclosure (ED): According to the descriptive results, the extent of Forth category, which is environmental disclosure (ED) on average, is 16.19%, with a minimum of zero percent and a maximum of 100%, indicating variations in the level of (ED) in Bahrain.

Summarizing the results of descriptive statistics for dependent variables, the amount of (EI) and (PSI) were approximately same mean, which indicating that around 61% of the tested samples disclose for them, followed by the (CI) which is disclosed by 54.55% of the tested companies, and the last category which is the (ED), got the lowest mean of 16.19%, this can be justified that the operations of most of the listed companies in Bahrain Bourse are not having a significant impact on the environment because of their nature which belong to the service field.

Eight firm-specific characteristics are representing the independent variables:

As indicated by the minimum and maximum values, there is a vast domain of variation within the independent variables.

i   The mean of liquidity was 2.46, with a minimum of 0.29 and a maximum 12.58.

ii   The mean of size was 141.6 BD millions, with a minimum of 0.6 BD millions, and a maximum 123 BD millions.

     The normality classifications of both liquidity and total assets (Size) were deviated. Subsequently, natural logarithm was used in the regression analysis to moderate skewness and to bring the distribution of the variables closer to normality.

iii The mean leverage for the firms was 43.80 with a minimum 4.15, indicating companies with somewhat high debts and a maximum of 89.69, indicating firms with very high debts.

iv The age ranges for the firm is from 8 to 57 indicating variations with a mean of 29.77.

v   With respect to auditor type, the investigator documents a mean of 0.83 and minimum (maximum) values of 0.00(1.00) proposing that around 83% of the listed firms in Bahrain are audited by a large four auditing companies.

vi Profitability ranges from −16.23 to 20.90 with a mean of 8.27, exhibitionist that 19.21 times the amount of equity of the company was consumed due to operations.

vii Bahraini ownership ranges from 0.00 to 1.00 suggesting 40% of tested samples owned locally.

viii Last but not least, industry type with and minimum (maximum) values of 0.00 (1.00) suggesting only 6% of the tested samples belong to the manufacturing field.

Table 12.6 is summarizing the Pearson correlation matrices. This will help to examine the statistical relationship among the dependent and the independent variables, and whether multicollinearity exists between the data before estimating the model. As clarified in the results, it shows that there are some moderately high correlations between variables, more specifically between firm size (Size) and financial leverage (Lev), and between social and CSR disclosures (CSR dis) and Industry (Ind). Moreover, industry (Ind) also has significant correlation with liquidity (Liq). The correlation appeared between in low degree between leverage (Lev) and two others variables which are ownership (Own) and liquidity (Liq).

Table 12.6 Correlations

	DV	Siz	Prf	Lev	Age	Aud	Own	Ind	Liq
DV-Pearson correlation	1								
Sig. (2-tailed)									
Siz-Pearson correlation	0.264	1							
Sig. (2-tailed)	0.125								
Prt-Pearson correlation	0.118	0.137	1						
Sig. (2-tailed)	0.501	0.433							

(continued)

Table 12.6 (continued)

	DV	Siz	Prf	Lev	Age	Aud	Own	Ind	Liq
Lev-Pearson correlation	−0.024	0.435**	−0.228	1					
Sig. (2-tailed)	0.891	0.009	0.188						
Age-Pearson correlation	−0.033	−0.198	0.203	−0.026	1				
Sig. (2-tailed)	0.852	0.254	0.241	0.882					
Aud-Pearson correlation	0.111	0.221	−0.169	0.287	−0.155	1			
Sig. (2-tailed)	0.525	0.201	0.331	0.094	0.374				
Own-Pearson correlation	0.187	−0.195	0.237	−0.386*	0.330	0.062	1		
Sig. (2-tailed)	0.283	0.262	0.171	0.022	0.053	0.724			
Ind-Pearson correlation	0.464**	−0.071	−0.034	−0.259	0.203	−0.215	0.302	1	
Sig. (2-tailed)	0.005	0.685	0.848	0.133	0.242	0.216	0.078		
Liq-Pearson correlation	0.365*	−0.089	0.029	−0.371*	0.057	−0.189	0.178	0.451**	1
Sig. (2-tailed)	0.031	0.613	0.868	0.028	0.745	0.276	0.306	0.007	

**Correlation is significant at the 0.01 level (2-tailed)
*Correlation is significant at the 0.05 level (2-tailed)

12.4.2 Regression Results

As illustrated in the findings (Table 12.7), F-value is 2.183 ($P < 0.01$). This outcome statistically supports the importance of the regression model. Moreover, the findings appear that R^2 is 0.402, which proposes that independent variables included in the model explain 40.20% of the variation in disclosure index (Table 12.8).

Generally, the model of CSR disclosure is accepted; two out of the eight assumptions are agreeable. Particularly, industry and audit firm size are significantly linked

Table 12.7 Model summary[b]

Model	R	R^2	Adjusted R^2	Std. error of the estimate
1	0.634[a]	0.402	0.218	0.16313

[a]Predictors: (Constant), Liq, Prf, Siz, Age, Aud, Own, Ind, Lev
[b]Dependent variable: DV

Table 12.8 ANOVA[b]

Model		Sum of squares	Df	Mean square	F	Sig.
1	Regression	0.465	8	0.058	2.183	0.063[a]
	Residual	0.692	26	0.027		
	Total	1.157	34			

[a]Predictors: (Constant), Liq, Prf, Siz, Age, Aud, Own, Ind, Lev
[b]Dependent variable: DV

Table 12.9 Coefficients[a]

Model		Unstandardized coefficients		Standardized coefficients	T	Sig.
		B	Std. error	Beta		
1	(Constant)	0.282	0.124		2.280	0.031
	Siz	1.289E−8	0.000	0.201	1.075	0.292
	Prf	0.004	0.004	0.158	0.895	0.379
	Lev	0.001	0.001	0.107	0.511	0.614
	Age	−0.002	0.003	−0.125	−0.715	0.481
	Aud	0.057	0.025	0.178	2.030	0.029
	Own	0.031	0.070	0.084	0.445	0.660
	Ind	0.343	0.144	0.438	2.384	0.025
	Liq	0.018	0.013	0.246	1.377	0.180

[a]Dependent variable: DV

to CSR disclosure. The remaining six independent variables (size, profitability, leverage, age, ownership, and liquidity), however, show statistically insignificant relationships to CSR disclosure.

Hypothesis 4 predicts a favorable relationship among company age and CSR disclosure. The findings suggest that firm age is not significant in explaining the variation in the extent of CSR disclosure. The results reported a positive association between firm size, profitability, leverage, ownership, and liquidity. However, the results are statistically insignificant.

This could be due to the actuality that older companies find it complicated to sit new procedures to take into account the social responsibility, and it takes time to acclimate with the growing awareness of societies as fast as younger firms (Table 12.9).

12.5   Conclusion, Implications, and Recommendations

A disclosure checklist was used to measure the level of CSR disclosure. Each of the 35 sampled firms' annual reports was tested. A regression analysis was used to test the relationship between the level of disclosure and (firm size, age, leverage, the size of the audit firm, profitability, industry type, ownership, and liquidity). The regression analysis indicates that the disclosure level also varies by audit firm size and industry type. Audit company size is affirmatively related to the level of CSR disclosure. This suggests that big audit firms such as the big 4 encourage their clients to have a higher level of CSR disclosure. Industry type is also positively associated with the level of CSR disclosure, mainly in the fourth category of disclosure checklist which is the environmental field, due to the nature of their operations that have a high influence on the environment, they disclose more about the environmental information. Other company merits such as size, profitability, leverage, age, liquidity, and ownership are not significant in explaining the level of CSR disclosure.

The findings of the analyses provided in this research should be particularly relevant to CSR codes. The study, therefore, recommends the regulatory bodies in Bahrain, to work on set a code of social responsibility to be guidance for the corporations in their social responsibility.

From a theoretical point of view, this study contributes to the existing literature on the association of firm characteristics and CSR disclosure, by investigating firms listed in Bahrain Bourse. Therefore, it expands on CSR compliance studies in the Gulf region, particularly in Bahrain.

References

Akhtaruddin M (2005) Corporate mandatory disclosure practices in Bangladesh. Int J Account 40(2005):399–422
Al-Ajmi M, Al-Mutairi A, Al-Duwaila N (2015) Corporate Social Disclosure Practices in Kuwait. Int J Econ Finan 7(9)
Alam I, Deb SK (2010) Human resource accounting disclosure (HRAD) in Bangladesh: multifactor regression analysis—a decisive tool of quality assessment. Cost Manage 38(3):9–13
Alkababji M (2014) Voluntary disclosure on corporate social responsibility: a study of the annual reports of Palestinian corporations. Eur J Account Audit Fin Res 59:59–82
Alareeni B (2018) The impact of firm-specific characteristics on earnings management: evidence from GCC countries. Int J Manag Financ Account 10(2):85–104
Alareeni BA (2019) The associations between audit firm attributes and audit quality-specific indicators: a meta-analysis. Manag Audit J 34(1):6–43
Awadh M, Alareeni B (2018) Measuring level of voluntary disclosures of banks listed in Bahrain Bourse. J Account Mark 7(295):2
Belkaoui A, Karpik PG (1989) Determinants of the corporate decision to disclose social information. Account Audit Account J 2(1):36–51
Brammer S, Pavelin S (2008) Factors influencing the quality of corporate environmental disclosure. Bus Strateg Environ 17(2):120–136
Branco MC, Rodrigues LL (2008) Factors influencing social responsibility disclosure by Portuguese companies. J Bus Ethics 83(4):685–701

Campbell JL (2007) Why would corporations behave in socially responsible ways? an institutional theory of corporate social responsibility. Acad Manag Rev 32:946–967

Chek IT, Mohamad ZZ, Yunus J, Norwani NM (2013) Corporate social responsibility (CSR) disclosure in consumer products and plantation industry in Malaysia. Am Int J Contemp Res 3(5):118–125

Chih H, Shen C, Kang F (2008) Corporate social responsibility, investor protection, and earnings management: some international evidence. J Bus Ethics 79:179–198

Choi J (1998) An evaluation of the voluntary corporate environmental disclosures: a Korean evidence. Soc Environ Account 18(1):2–7

Cormier D, Magnan M (2003) Environmental reporting management: a European perspective. J Account Public Policy 22:43–62

Davis K (1975) Business and society: environment and responsibility, 3rd edn. McGrawHill Book Company, NY

Ebiringa O, Yadirichukwu E, Chigbu E, Ogochukwu O (2013) Effect of firm size and profitability on coporate social disclosure: the Nigerian oil and gas sector to focus. Br J Econ Manag Trade 2013(4):563–574

Eng LL, Mak YT (2003) Corporate governance and voluntary disclosure. J Account Public Policy 22:325–345

Ezat A, Em-Masry A (2008) The impact of corporate governance on the timeliness of corporate internet reporting by Egyptian listed companies. Manag Financ 34(12):848–867

Ghazali NAM (2007) Ownership structure and corporate social responsibility disclosure: some Malaysian evidence. Corp Gov 7(3):251–266

Gray R, Kouhy R, Lavers S (1995) Corporate social and environmental reporting: a review of the literature and a longitudinal study of UK disclosure. Account Audit Account J 8(2):47–77

Hackston D, Milne MJ (1996) Some determinants of social and environmental disclosures in New Zealand companies. Account Audit Account J 9(1):77–108. https://doi.org/10.1108/095135796 10109987

Haniffa RM, Cooke TE (2005) The impact of culture and governance on corporate social reporting. J Account Public Policy 24(5):391–392

Hussainey KH, Elsayed M, Razik M (2011) Factors affecting corporate social responsibility disclosure in Egypt. Corp Ownership Control J 8(4):432–443

Ismail KN, Chandler R (2005) Disclosure in the quarterly reports of Malaysian companies, financial reporting, regulation and governance. 4(1):1–26

Juhmani O (2014) Determinants of corporate social and environmental disclosure on websites: the case of Bahrain. Univ J Account Fin 2(4):77–87

Macarulla FL, Talalweh MA (2012) Voluntary corporate social responsibility disclosure: a case study of Saudi Arabia. Jordan J Bus Adm 8(4)

Madrakhimova F (2013) History of development of corporate social responsibility, vol 4, no 6, pp 509–520. Academic Star Publishing Company

Maguire M (2011) The future of corporate social responsibility reporting, vol 40, pp 399–422. The Frederick S. Pardee Center

Mahadeo J, Hanuman V, Oogarah-Soobaroyen T (2011) A longitudinal study of corporate social disclosures in a developing economy. J Bus Ethics, pp 545–558

Mohamed T, Olfa B, Faouzi J (2014) Corporate social disclosure: explanatory theories and conceptual framework. Int J Acad Res Manage (IJARM) 3(2): 208–225. ISSN: 2296-1747

Moore G (2001) Corporate social and financial performance: an investigation in the UK supermarket industry. J Bus Ethics 34:299–315

Mustaffa MZ, Tamoi J (2006) Corporate social disclosure (CSD) Of Construction VompaniesIn Malaysia. Malaysian Accounting Review, 5(1), May, 85–114.

Naser K (2006) Determinants of corporate social disclosure in developing countries: the case of Qatar. Adv Int Account 19:1–23

Purushothaman M, Tower G, Hancock R, Taplin R (2000) Determinants of corporate social reporting practices of listed Singapore companies. Pac Account Rev 12(2):101–133

Razak RA (2015) Corporate social responsibility disclosure and its determinants in Saudi Arabia. Middle-East J Sci Res 23(10):2388–2398

Rettab B, Brik AB, Mellahi K (2009) A study of management perceptions of the impact of corporate social responsibility on organizational performance in emerging economies: the case of Dubai. J Bus Ethics 89:371–390

Reverte C (2009) Determinants of corporate social responsibility disclosure ratings by Spanish Listed Firms. J Bus Ethics 88:351–366

Roberts RW (1992) Determinants of corporate social responsibility disclosure. An application of stakeholder theory. Account Organ Soc 17(6):595–612

Saleh M (2009) Corporate social responsibility disclosure in an emerging market: a longitudinal analysis approach. Int Bus Res

Sufian M (2012) Corporate social responsibility in Bangladesh. Glob J Manage Bus Res

Tagesson T, Blank V, Broberg P, Collin SO (2009) What explains the extent and content of social and environmental disclosures on corporate websites. a study of social and environmental reporting in Swedish Listed Corporations. Corp Soc Responsib Environ Manage 16(6):352–364

Uwuigbe U, Egbide B (2012) Corporate social responsibility disclosures in Nigeria: a study of listed financial and non-financial firms. J Manag Sustain 2(1):160–169

Yao S, Wang J, Song L (2011) Determinants of Social Responsibility Disclosure By Chinese Firms. School of Contemporary Chinese Studies

Index

Lightning Source UK Ltd.
Milton Keynes UK
UKHW020605050922
408354UK00002B/29